Chilling Out

Chilling Out

The cultural politics of substance consumption, youth and drug policy

Shane Blackman

Open University Press

Open University Press
McGraw-Hill Education
McGraw-Hill House
Shoppenhangers Road
Maidenhead
Berkshire
England
SL6 2QL

email: *enquiries@openup.co.uk*
world wide web: *www.openup.co.uk*

and Two Penn Plaza, New York, NY 10121–2289, USA

First published 2004

A catalogue record of this book is available from the British Library

ISBN 0335 20072 9 (pb) 0335 20073 7 (hb)

Library of Congress Cataloging-in-Publication Data
CIP data applied for

Typeset by YHT Ltd, London
Printed in the UK by Bell & Bain Ltd, Glasgow

For Rory,
'Stay Free' The Clash.

Contents

Foreword

David Downes
Emeritus Professor of Social Policy, London
School of Economics

Four decades ago, in the late 1950s and early 1960s, Britain seemed an oasis of sanity, compared with the rest of the world, in relation to drug policy. Heroin addiction was treated as primarily a medical problem, and 'addicts', as they were then so described, could obtain their 'script' from – in principle – any general practitioner willing to take them on. The decriminalization of cannabis seemed only a matter of time, a few years at most, as the liberal elite mobilized support for some such policy. By the mid-1970s all this had changed. Those running the 'treatment centres', set up in designated hospitals to supersede general practice as the front line for meeting the demand for heroin, switched to oral methadone as a substitute. The Wootton Report of 1968, which had duly recommended the decriminalization of cannabis, was summarily dismissed as unworkable by an otherwise reform-minded Labour government. The 1971 Misuse of Drugs Act recategorized drugs in terms of their presumed dangerousness and attached increased criminal sanctions for even the smallest amount in possession.

This recriminalization of drug use now amounted to a form of prohibition. It has proved a spectacular failure. Drug use is now a hundred-fold more prevalent than it was in the late 1960s. Drug-related crime has proved a logical corollary of the criminalization of drug supply. Violence (in relation to control of territory, debt enforcement, etc.), money laundering, the corruption of officialdom and myriad offending to finance the habit – these are the inescapable forms of debasement which accompany the criminalization of drug use. Three huge misconceptions sustain this system. The first is that we can win, indeed are winning, the War on Drugs. The crime rate is going down and the prevalence of some forms of drug use have waned. Well, if we included in the crime rate the unknowable volume of illicit drug transactions, it would long ago have climbed off the scale. And fashions in drug use, as in other forms of consumer behaviour, explain at least part of the rise and fall of particular drugs. The second fallacy is that illicit drug use and its supply are in principle much the same as any other crime. Legalize drugs and you might as well legalize burglary, car theft etc. This *reductio ad absurdum*, which I have heard put forward many times in defence of our drug laws, simply ignores the most important difference between drugs and other forms of crime. The victims of burglary and car crime do not welcome burglars into their home or voluntarily hand over their car keys. The victims of pollution do not wish their lives and environment to be poisoned by noxious gases or materials. By contrast, drug users actively collude with their 'victimizers', despite the fact that – denied any alternative – they must turn to criminal networks, a recipe for the supply of costly, contaminated, cut or unpredictably strong drugs. The third big myth is that the only alternative to prohibition is outright legalization and commercialization. That is to ignore the many viable ways of *regulating* drug supplies intermediary between these two polar extremes. The 'British System' of allowing for and legitimately meeting 'unstimulated demand' was arguably much more successful than prohibition in the fields of both drugs and gambling.

How did we get into this mess? And can we get out of it? In this highly informed and stimulating book, Shane Blackman argues that, above all, we must attach far more realistic dimensions of time and space to the history and prevalence of drug consumption. In Victorian England, and long before, opium was the opium of the people: Marx might have made more of that. The interlude of minimal consumption in Britain between World War One and the 1960s, which enabled the 'British System' to flourish and to be mythologized by American advocates as an alternative to their own country's prohibitionism, was bound to fall apart once the number of addicts rose steeply and fell sharply in terms of social class. The flaw in the British system was to define the 'addict' as pathologically 'sick', rather than recognizing the possibilities of drug use being rationally and 'normally' embraced. Once pathologized, the whole history, social construction and presentation of drugs in everyday life underwent a series of distortions, denials and silences that constitute much of the subject matter of this book. There is, of course, a pathology to drug addiction, but there are also diversity and normalcy in substance consumption.

'Cultural politics' is the conceptual thread that links several themes and myriad topics in the chapters that follow. US governments learnt nothing from the disastrous experiment of prohibition, despite its forced repeal in relation to alcohol. Instead, they proceeded to apply its logic to a vast array of drugs, stereotyping and demonizing their users and suppliers in the process, deploying drugs as a strategy in foreign intervention and, via the United Nations, forcing the rest of the world to accept it as the one true road. Yet, despite prohibitionism, films, advertising and popular music are shot through with drug imagery and representations. Blackman is especially perceptive about how drugs have changed culture and society for *non*-users. He builds revealingly on the ways in which capitalist societies have traded on a major contradiction: prohibitionism coexists with, may even enhance, the commercialization of the aesthetic properties of banned substances. The capacity of subcultural theories to encompass the worlds of and trends in drug use is freshly analysed and revitalized. In the process, he mounts a devastating critique of postmodernist theories as a series of false promissory notes. The strengths and weaknesses of the 'normalization' thesis are explored and its character substantially redefined. The laudable aims of drug *education* are viewed as at odds with the core mission of drug *prevention*, which renders its methods counterproductive. Finally, in searching for a viable policy to replace the failed initiatives of the present, Blackman steers us towards the recent successes of countries as diverse as the Netherlands, Switzerland and Portugal in decriminalizing cannabis and heroin use, at least in certain contexts and within certain defined parameters. He returns to the 'responsive prohibition' strategy of John Stuart Mill as qualified freedom to consume drugs while protecting children and the mentally vulnerable.

In any text as wide ranging, trenchant and provocative as this, there is bound to be plenty of scope for questioning on occasion the force of argument and example. For instance, I do not think that the 'British System', whatever its faults, needed be abandoned so rapidly to psychiatric fashion. Better and more resourceful government, and a keener sense of social responsibility in the medical profession, could have changed the system for the better. And, given the sweep of the final chapter, I would have liked the author to offer more policy recommendations than he does from his analysis. But, one hopes, that will be a subject to which he shortly returns.

Acknowledgements

In the last ten years I have undertaken a series of research studies on young people and drug consumption for the Home Office, London health authorities, the Kent Constabulary and regional social services in Kent. I would like to thank all the different people from these organizations and the young people themselves who have given me support. This research was a key factor motivating me to write a more critical study, taking what I learnt in the field to try and advance the drug debate.

I would like to give special thanks to my partner Debbie Cox for her effort and thought in critically engaging with the text. Thanks are also due to Jonathan Wadman for his corrections and suggestions. I also thank the first-rate service provided by British Library for their interlibrary loans and the staff at Canterbury Christ Church who gave their time and help to me. Thanks to everyone at 27A where my research first started and Richard Williams for his loan of the original copies of *Oz* magazine. At the Open University Press in particular I would like to thank my original publisher Justin Vaughan and more recently Mark Barratt, plus Eleanor Hayes in production for helping me get the manuscript in shape.

I am very grateful for the help of many people at different stages of the project, including John Broad, Ken Fox, Andrew Garret, Antonio Melechi, Tim Rhodes, Tamara Makarenko, Grahan Meaghan and staff at the British Board of Film Classification, Andrew Sherratt, Damon Taylor, staff at the Advertising Standards Authority, Channel 4, Russell Newcombe, Penelope Allport, Chris Wibberley, Niall Coggans, staff at Actions Records Preston, James Mills, Louise O'Connor, David Downes, Nigel South, Alan France, Robert MacDonald, Tracy Shildrick, the Kerrang staff, Charlie Lloyd, staff at the Young Person's Kent and Canterbury Drug Addiction team, and also thanks to my students at Canterbury Christ Church University College who participated in lectures and seminars.

Introduction

Drugs are used for pleasure and may result in pain. This was the conclusion of Thomas De Quincey when he first published his writings on opium consumption in 1821. The axis of pleasure and pain represents the central paradox in both drug culture and drug prevention. Intoxication can bring forth intense feelings and visions of pure beauty for both the body and the mind. In contrast, the 'high' may also cause terrifying nightmares or push the senses into paranoia from which no return is possible. There is no escaping the fact that drug consumption can result in death. The opposites of bliss and fear attract attention by their very nature. In twenty-first century western culture these different human experiences of being in 'paradise' or in 'hell' have been appropriated for their market potential and for propaganda. The diverse possibilities of the hallucinatory experience are used in equal measure to promote commodity consumption or provide universal symbols of cultural identity and as negative resources within drug prevention to promote the fear and horror of drug doom. There is money to be made in the illicit drug trade, but also a vast amount of capital is spent on the drug prevention industry.

The French philosopher Gilles Deleuze has investigated the power of drug mediations within culture and argues that 'drugs have sufficiently changed the general conditions of space and time perception so that non-users can succeed in passing through holes in the world'.[1] His meaning is that the contemporary altered state of perception under intoxication has been disseminated by capital, through advertisements and commodification, to the extent that non-users have been initiated into hallucinatory visions. Glamorized drug-related images or drug-referenced ideas are used as marketing strategies and have become the norm in postmodern commodity production and consumption. In other words, drugs have changed the world we see, understand and believe in to the extent that it is not necessary to consume drugs to be influenced by them. Drugs have entered cultural consciousness; it is not possible to escape or be free from them. Drugs have had a significant cultural legacy from philosophy and medicine to literature and art which cannot be erased (Andrews and Vinkennoog 1967; Rudgley 1998). To try to remove drugs is to remove our human selves from history. The question we need to address is how to gain a critical understanding of drugs.

In the twenty-first century, drugs remain a major dilemma for people, nations and society, and this issue is seen in its most acute form in relation to young people. In this book I shall investigate the assumptions underlying drug prohibition and explore the contradictions of drug prevention policies. There will be an assessment of the global, political and historical context of drug prohibition policy with a detailed focus on youth, on the basis that young people are a primary target of drug prevention policies. Drug prevention and education rarely focus on young people's culture itself: the primary focus is the problem of drug prevalence, crime and antisocial behaviour, the weakness of drug models, or the failure of drug intervention programmes (Barton 2003). The book explores the uneasy relationship between drug prohibition and the popular culture industry, including film, popular music, youth culture, advertising and tourism, which has a major element within young people's lives, and a key factor in the representation of drugs. The twin perspectives of global politics and youth allow for a more holistic understanding of the implementation of drug policy and enable an investigation of the attractions of drug culture. I shall argue that drug prohibition policies rest on a number of unproven theories which remain unstated and therefore unchallenged within the main body of drug prevention discourse. For example, one of the contradictions of the anti-drug movement is that it has not been primarily concerned with ending the harm that can be caused by drugs. Prohibition has been preoccupied with using an anti-drugs discourse in pursuit of other ends (Ross 2000). John Stuart Mill realized that individual freedom to consume drugs can be manipulated and appropriated for both moral and financial gain.

Historically both the mainstream economy and governments have profited from the drug trade and in various ways they continue to profit from it. Drug prohibition is frequently assumed to be motivated purely by the desire to prevent human suffering caused by drug use, but drug control policies are also about power or may provide a means of foreign policy intervention into other nation states. Governments and entrepreneurs exploit the illegal drugs economy and its legitimate commercial cultural support system; both are highly profitable. It could be argued that drug prevention policy operates without accountability and responsibility, given that if the anti-drug movement seriously wants to end drug production in poor Third World states that are major producers, the way to do so would be by providing viable, sustainable economic alternatives. Within the current global economic order of 'free trade', those states are denied any alternative and instead are confronted by structures which increase dependency and undermine local agricultural and manufacturing production. Drug prevention operates a dual victimization of both Third World drug producers and the western drug consumer, especially young people, who are then subject to regulation and punishment.

I will investigate the contradictions between drug policy and the political and historical questions which drug education messages deny or suppress. Unless these questions and issues are addressed, drug policy is working within a flawed and partial perspective. Drug policy thrives on slogans, for example, 'drug free society' or 'give drugs a blast'. These 'soundbites' are both un- realistic and unsophisticated. My aim is to complicate the drug debate and reject the simplistic formula of current drug prevention policy. A more valid and realistic approach to the issue can only emerge once the partiality of drug prohibition has been challenged through an exploration of the full com- plexity of the 'drugs field', with the aim of contributing towards a more systematic approach to the issue.

Chapter 1 considers drug prohibition in historical perspective, looking at the legitimate colonial drug trade and the moral response by the early pro- hibition movement within nineteenth- and twentieth-century America and Britain. In particular it assesses the creation of youth as a deviant 'other' mediated through the racist term of 'assassin'. I shall examine the way gov- ernments and prohibitionists have used drugs for their own political and moral purposes to promote myths of drug madness and sexual immorality.

Chapter 2 takes as its core issue the politics of the US policy of the 'War on Drugs' from the period before the creation of the CIA to the adoption by the United Nations of the Drug-Free Society policy. I explore the historical and contemporary connections between power, politics, terror and drugs to argue that the international drug trade operates as a means of finance for secret state intelligence services, right-wing military dictatorships and death squads. The US militarization of the 'drug war' provides a means of foreign policy intervention into nation states to exert American influence and create opportunities for corporate capital.

Chapter 3 looks at drugs as cultural commodities and explores three areas: film, advertising and popular music. It builds on the argument elabo- rated by Gilles Deleuze that drugs have altered the way we view society ir- respective of actual drug use. It begins by exploring the ways that drugs are a mainstream element of contemporary society and have become a marketing device for the capitalist economy. Major corporates including Sony, Yves Saint Laurent, Fila, Virgin and Fabergé have used depictions of drugs in their advertisements to promote their products. The entertainment or culture in- dustry has consistently exploited drug representations to gain diverse audi- ences in order to accumulate capital.

Having identified the position of drugs in youth culture, Chapter 4 turns its attention to academic research which theorizes the connection between drugs and subcultures to explain deviance, abnormality and crime. I will argue that the sociological concept of subculture has a long and diverse heritage, with the added potential of being able to transform itself according to the dominant paradigm of the time. The chapter shows that each theory of subculture explains drug consumption differently.

Chapter 5 seeks to move beyond the narrow debates about contemporary drug normalization. A major failure of theorists in this area is an inability to understand that drug normalization is not only about an apparent increase in drug consumption, but also about the greater recognition and presence of drugs in culture and society. The purpose is to look at the wider picture of drug normalization starting with an assessment of drugs within ancient society. A key feature of this chapter is the argument that drug consumption has been subject to misrepresentation from nineteenth-century academic disciplines of archaeology and anthropology to the contemporary tabloid media of the twenty-first century.[2] Drug normalization is part of contemporary popular culture relayed through mass media coverage of gossip, social scandals and personal tragedies. It is also used by prohibition as a potential means to enforce greater regulation through the creation of fear.

Chapter 6 looks at the current British drugs policy and the development of drug education to influence young people to refuse drugs. It will be argued that the public policy presentation of increased tolerance towards drug issues hides within it the kernel of drug prohibition and abstinence.[3] This is demonstrated through the new managerialist approach to evaluating the impact of drug education according to targets and outcomes. Drug education in secondary schools seeks to show its flexibility through notions of choice, life skills and inclusion, but its success or failure is measured in narrow objectivist terms of behaviour change. The problem drug education faces according to Coggans et al. (2002: 8) is that 'while the theory is persuasive, there is little empirical support for it'. Thus, in order to arrive at a valid approach to the issue of drug use and young people, it is necessary to challenge the assumptions of drug prohibition in drug education.

The concluding chapter examines the context of contemporary British drug reform. Here I draw attention to the powerful prohibition lobby which has developed a new style of personalized shock tactics with the public display of images of dead young women as drug victims. I contrast these powerful media images of drug death with the growth of a more relaxed attitude towards drugs within mass culture, including the expansion of drug tourism, global club culture, the commercial production of medical cannabis and the development of the Dutch coffeeshop in the context of growing European drug normalization policies.

The book sets out to argue that intoxicants are not only used and abused by drug consumers. Drugs have been exploited by politicians, commercial entrepreneurs, medical professionals and moral campaigners to support their predetermined political, financial and ethical objectives. At its broadest level the text outlines the linkages between micro drug consumption by young people and macro drug policy formulation by western governments and the United Nations. There is a clear need to challenge the representation of drugs as bad, immoral and dangerous by critically investigating the context of drugs within past and present society, to demonstrate that drugs are a social and cultural fact of life and to show that prohibitionists who attempt to remove drugs from society are challenging the dynamic basis of our social bond and being. It is in this sense that I end with John Stuart Mill's understanding of responsive prohibition. He, more than anyone, realized that drugs are a source of power in society and that therefore we need to regulate them inside society rather than unrealistically seeking to remove them from society.

1   Drug prohibition and the 'assassin of youth'

Prohibition sees drugs as a danger to the individual and a threat to the community. Drugs are defined as 'bad' or 'evil', and therefore prohibition seeks the complete removal of illicit drugs from society. The rationale put forward by prohibition is the need for the state or global organizations, such as the United Nations, to protect society. A key theme of this chapter is that drug prohibition is about power, control and contradiction. Drug prohibition defines its objectives on the basis of rationality and scientific evidence, but it also promotes itself as visionary in terms of wanting to improve society. This total concern leads Jacques Derrida (1993: 19) to argue that prohibition puts forward claims to 'truth' and morality that demonstrate that drug prohibition is not based on science, it is a political act based on a particular moral standpoint.

This chapter examines the social and cultural politics of the drug prohibition movement. I shall start by looking at the legitimate colonial drug trade in the eighteenth and nineteenth centuries as part of capitalist development. The modern drug prohibition movement emerged during this period, when the economy and government were centrally involved in drug production and distribution as major sources of revenue. I will then assess the impact of American punitive drug legislation on the development of the 'British System' of drug controls and the supporting role played by the media through images of young people as drug victims, thus affirming the need for criminal drug control. I shall explore the way that key figures within prohibition, such as Hamilton Wright, Richmond Pearson Hobson and Harry Anslinger, have been motivated by a morality of social improvement. I will then argue that historically drug prohibition in the USA and Britain has consistently employed a racist theory of the 'other' which has promoted negative representations of drug users as Arab, Chinese, black or Mexican (Helmer 1975). At the centre of drug prohibition has been the myth of drugs as the 'assassin of youth' which propagates fearful images of degradation threatening the western way of life.

The legitimate colonial drug trade

The twentieth century can be described as the 'age of prohibition', but drugs and attempts to restrict drug production, importation and consumption began with the modern growth of European colonialism and the start of global capitalism in the sixteenth century. The modern western demand for prohibition is closely connected to a racial 'othering'. For the Church and the state drug products from the Americas or Asia were derived from non-white origins and believed to be the work of the devil which could encourage social disorder or resistance to imperial control (Inglis 1975: 51; Berkhout and Robinson 1999: 39). Divine monarchs from the Holy Roman Empire and Great Britain were quick to realize the financial benefits of drugs to the Church, colonial economy and state. At first exotic substances were limited to the merchant, political and administrative elites, but slowly the growth of new commercial substances of coffee, tea, tobacco, chocolate and opium became transformed from luxury goods into large-scale commercial commodities. Rudi Matthee (1995: 36) argues that by the early 1700s the government norm towards new products was not prohibition but taxation. For example, in England, King James I in his pamphlet, *A Counterblaste to Tobacco*, and later his son Charles I saw the product as an unhealthy and dangerous foreign import, but reluctant to ban it they preferred to elicit revenue by subjecting the drug to taxation.

Government bureaucrats and merchants quickly realized the potential for extraction of profit from people either at home or abroad from addictive substances. All European nations took a leading and developmental role in the growth of the modern drug trade. Rowntree (1905: 285) and Owen (1934: 52) argue that by 1839 opium had become the world's most valuable single commodity of trade.[1] Perhaps the highest stage of international drug trading was reached by Britain through the East India Company. According to John Newsinger (2002: 125), this provided 'massive profit for London companies and substantial revenues for the state'. Britain faced economic competition from the Dutch and Americans who were developing their vast fleets of opium ships called clippers and the use of fast slave ships (McCoy 1991: 82). British merchants with support of the British government illegally supplied opium to China, against the wishes of the Chinese emperor. During the nineteenth century Britain fought two Opium Wars with the aim of gaining access to Chinese markets by overthrowing Chinese sovereignty. The Nanking Treaty (1842) and the Treaty of Tientsin (1858) brought the British government land and the legalization of opium. As a result Johnson (1975: 306) states that 'Britain forced opium upon China'.

European colonial rulers effectively used addiction revenues to finance the construction of modern urban states, making drugs a valuable commodity in the expansion of global capital accumulation. Imperialism established new Third World economies on a dependent basis whereby the colony bought knowledge and commodities from the colonizer. This also included promotion of an ideology of international drug suppression while selling drugs back to the colonies at huge profits (Wong 1998). At the start of the twentieth century western governments were 'the biggest drug pushers in history' (Himmelstein 1978: 48). The legitimate trade in drugs such as heroin, cocaine and cannabis represented a series of major commodities that sustained global commerce among the growers, manufactures and consumers. The success of the western colonial drug trade was to generate revenues for colonial development and to provide profits for European stockholders while at the same time politically to oppress indigenous populations by subjecting millions of people to opium addiction. Western colonial control of countries in Asia led to mass addictions and strengthened the finances of colonial governments (Mill 1990).

The consequence of military victories enabled colonial rulers to promote their self-generated superiority, permitting administrators to impose their principles of beliefs and social organization on the defeated (Fanon 1959/ 1965: 122). Profits from mass consumption of drugs and even government stimulation of addiction were seen as laudable and conducive to maintenance of effective colonial rule.[2] In this sense drugs were supportive to the development of imperial capitalism and held in check demands for social reform from indigenous people. Western governments were relatively unconcerned with the emergence of drug use abroad, as the colonies were thought of as 'primitive' due to their lack of an apparent democracy or rational utilitarian principles of social progress. Encouragement of drug use amongst so-called 'foreigners' supported imperialist assumptions about their underdevelopment and served to justify colonial domination.

Emergent moral movement of prohibition

Contemporary anti-drug and anti-alcohol movements have a long ancestry. Religious groups such as the Quakers had long advocated the abolition of slavery from the 1650s and frequently criticized British colonial policy as one of revenue before righteousness. The American Temperance Society was founded in 1826. It had support from religious groups in conducting their revival style meetings and, according to Berkhout and Robinson (1999: 37), was 'similar to the new Protestant sects in trying to impose a muscular Christianity on the denial of pleasure'. Brian Inglis (1975) points out that in the nineteenth century there was a close alliance between anti-tobacco campaigners, the temperance movement and the anti-opiumists. During this period the Quakers took on a central role in drug prohibition on a global basis, often containing members who overlapped in different campaigning organizations.

The first financially viable anti-drug group was the (Anglo-Oriental) Society for the Suppression of the Opium Trade (SSOT). It was formed in 1874 in Birmingham, later moving to London, by Edward Pease, Arthur Pease, Thomas Hansbury, Arthur Albright and F. Storrs-Turner, who were affluent Quaker missionaries, merchants and bankers. The Quakers international prohibition strategy of moral persuasion took two forms: first, through their well-respected corporate identity deriving from their organizational body the Society of Friends (Harding (1998: 7); second, through the establishment of their journal in 1875, the *Friend of China*. Johnson (1975) argues:

> [SSOT] published the proceedings of annual meetings, decisions of the Executive Committee, speeches by missionaries, MPs and doctors. It listed public meetings held under SSOT auspices. It also summarized, reprinted, and analysed miscellaneous opium information: newspaper articles, articles in missionary newspapers, medical reports, government statistics and policy decisions, criticisms by pro-opiumists, and correspondence with anti-opium groups in Holland, the United States, Australia, New Zealand, Japan etc. Several informational pamphlets and/or books were published; leaflets were prepared for distribution at public meetings. In addition, SSOT members wrote letters and articles to leading newspapers, magazines and professional journals.
>
> (Johnson 1975: 309)

The prohibition work of the SSOT was international, although only in English, and presented its moral message on a highly repetitive basis. This modern organizational basis enabled the Quakers to distribute information quickly, thereby presenting itself as a body observing and responding to public feelings. However, to claim that it was a popular apparatus for the public surveillance of society's morality, according to Berridge and Edwards (1987: 180), is a fiction: 'the public opinion it sought to create was not broad based, but the opinion of the influential elites in society'. The anti-opium movement remained steadfastly elitist and this was reflected in their combination of moralistic and medical judgements which were the basis of their professional support. Morality and health were closely defined in terms of an individuals capacity for self-discipline and through the SSOT's close association with the temperance movement drug use came to be defined as a disease of moral weakness.

Within the prohibition movement, medical judgements informed moral assessments to enable drug use to be defined as a failure of personal responsibility. In public policy terms there was a symbiotic relationship between the rise of drug control and the professionalization of medicine. Reeves and Campbell (1994: 45) argue that 'the rhetoric of this orthodox medicine was a rhetoric of science and reform that succeeded in masking not only political and racial agendas, but also economic self-interest of the medical profession and the pharmaceutical industry'. Medicine quickly colonized new fields of personal, social and political spheres indirectly related to medical science, combining social regulation and medical intervention on a moral basis. For the prohibition movement, recognition of this new expertise enabled medical solutions to moral problems to be transformed into technical strategies for treatment or to form a scientific basis for the criminalization of the drug user. The success of prohibition with its apparent medical science to achieve legitimacy was a result of its professionalization but especially its social and political connections.

Modern American drug prevention

During the nineteenth century Britain and the USA introduced legislation to restrict access to the consumption of drugs, including the 1868 Pharmacy Act and the 1906 Food and Drugs Act, but these measures were largely piecemeal and dealt with the prescription system and poisons. The first anti-drug legislation introduced by the San Francisco Board of Supervisors in 1875 was a local ordinance aimed at Chinese immigrants who consumed opium within opium dens.[3] The local ordinances were also aimed at the perceived threat of black and Mexican drug consumers (Cockburn and St. Clair 1998). This early anti-drug legislation was ethnocentric and centred on the fears of sexual corruption of young women and men by 'foreigners' who were seen by politicians and the media as polluting the purity of the race. Under missionary zeal this local xenophobia was translated into a national concern and the 'protection of native races' became a foundation for the first international meeting the discuss the regulation of drugs. Global drug prohibition started with the 1909 Shanghai drug conference 'World War on Opium Traffic', which resulted in the Hague Convention of 1911. The cornerstone of global drug prohibition began with the Harrison Act in 1914, introduced by Francis Burton Harrison as a result of intensive lobbying by Dr Hamilton Wright.

The USA became a colonial power with the acquisition of the Philippines through its victory in the 1898 Spanish–America War. David Musto (1973: 26) argues that almost immediately US missionaries entered the Far East and saw their role as stopping the opium trade. Under the moral stewardship of the Right Reverend Charles Brent, Dr Hamilton Wright and Dr Charles C. Tenney, a former missionary in China, the USA began to formulate global drug control policies. These key moral reformers, particularly Brent and Wright, were also the US representatives at the International Shanghai Opium Conference in 1909.

Wright was also responsible for the failed pre-Harrison anti-narcotics Foster Bill in 1910. These drug prohibitionists launched far-reaching anti-opium campaigns on the basis that drugs brought a decline in morals through contamination with 'degenerate races' (Lusane 1991).

Dr Hamilton Wright promoted notions of 'otherness' and racial degeneracy by suggesting that young American white women were being seduced by Chinese men through use of opium and that cocaine led black men to rape white women (Musto 1973: 43–4). In a similar vein he charged drugs 'to be a creator of criminals'. In the USA racist laws were passed such as the Chinese Exclusion Act of 1882, followed by the federal government ban on opium importation and smoking among the Chinese, while white Americans were not banned from consumption. John Helmer (1975) shows that in America the media also promoted racist discrimination which differed little from comments by moralists like Wright, Brent and Hobson who were guilty of inflating statistics and spreading horror stories. This point is elaborated by David Courtwright who states that the moral crusaders had two problems:

> Smoking cocaine was uncommon in the early twentieth century and few Blacks, criminals or otherwise, injected the drug. The second problem is that there is little concrete evidence of such crimes. Those who alleged a cocaine-inspired crime-wave tended to be long on generalities and short on specifics.
>
> (Courtwright 1995: 212)

Undaunted, the moral crusaders' generation of fear was beginning to prompt legislation and their fantasized debauchery was commonly supported by a racist and xenophobic press. The press chose to promote fictitious stories in order to boost circulation such as 'New York Girls Doped and Kidnapped for White Slave Trade'. Such was the power of fiction, as Lusane (1991: 34) reveals, that the *New York Times* asserted that 'Southern sheriffs had switched from .32-caliber guns to .38-caliber pistols to protect themselves from drug-empowered Blacks'. Cocaine fiction had reached the point where drug users themselves had become bulletproof.

Bertram et al. (1996) see the anti-drug crusade movement as being rooted in the puritanical strain of American culture which demands public control to foster moral and model behaviour. Two leading drug prohibitionists who used the 'other' theory were Congressman Richmond Pearson Hobson 1870–1937, and Harry J. Anslinger, Commissioner for the Federal Bureau of Narcotics (FBN). Hobson and Anslinger were supported by the dominant elite in US society and were able successfully to promote the contemporary myth that America's drug problem stemmed from threats within society by foreign minority cultures pursuing immorality and from outside the state by hostile nations. Hobson and Anslinger were part of the anti-alcohol prohibition movement (King 1972: 70). Hobson began his career as a leader of the temperance movement through his fundraising for the Anti-Saloon League. Woodiwiss (1998: 15) argues that the crusader received a percentage of the money donated and 'decided that moral crusading was a lucrative career to pursue'. In 1911 he proposed the first national prohibition legislation, which was unsuccessful, but after the Volstead Act 1919 was passed, he moved from prohibition of alcohol to prohibition of drugs. His moral propaganda was effective and strategic and he founded a series of organizations reflecting global aims: International Narcotic Education Association 1923, World Conference on Narcotic Education 1926, World Narcotic Defense Association 1927.

The importance of Hobson's crusade is that it fused what Bewley-Taylor (1999: 36) refers to as 'a quasi-medical approach to heighten anti-drug sentiment' derived from the nineteenth-century anti-opium movement, with contemporary forms of mass propaganda to millions through publication of school textbooks, and newspaper and radio programmes aimed at young people. Hobson's personal discrimination against foreigners and dislike of the ethnic minorities and the lower class became the basis for his 'othering' strategy. As a populist moralizer his aim was to shock through exaggeration that played on people's sexual and racial fears from a position which announced that civilization and the destiny of the world was at stake due to drugs. His liberal use of negative and biblical descriptions have a contemporary resonance. He asserted that drugs were a 'contagion' and that users were 'lepers among our people', further suggesting that 'drug addiction is far more incurable than leprosy, far more tragic to its victims, and is spreading like a moral and physical scourge', warning that young 'drug addicts are the principal carriers of vice diseases'.[4] Diana Gordon (1994: 194) highlights in particular that Hobson's metaphor to describe heroin users as 'the living dead' was a means to summon moral perversion and unconscious fear of the physical deterioration of the young body.

In politics and the media discriminatory beliefs were the common order of the day. Young black men were referred to as 'crazy niggers' and the Chinese population was collectively described as the 'yellow peril'. These exaggerated racist claims were part of the misconceived ideals of social Darwinism and the eugenics movement. The prohibitionists were not alone in their espousal of extreme ideas. The opinions and values of xenophobic crusaders were widely proposed and given space within the popular press (Williams 1980). Anti-drug crusading became respectable and profitable. Newspaper editors, industrial manufacturers and business leaders saw money and political influence in moral campaigns. Bertram et al. (1996) show that high status social groups such as masonic lodges and charitable clubs[5] used their influence to promote their public relations as fighting this contagious social sickness. Leading organizations and political figures of American drug prohibition demonstrate that demands for moral reform are fundamentally political in nature because their aim is to achieve social reform from their set position. The moral campaign spearheaded by Harry J. Anslinger as the new Commissioner of the FBN claimed drugs were the true demons of 'evil', 'disgust' and 'vice'. Moral crusaders often operate with an absolute ethic or a totality view: from their perspective what they see is completely evil or wrong. This approach asserts self-righteousness and correction without qua-lification and where the crusade is validated by religion it combines super-iority with holiness. This makes bourgeois moral reformers idealist in their ambition to change people and improve social conditions, but this humani-tarianism can also be seen as a mask for their forced morality.[6] Antonio Gramsci argues that American moralists held aspirations to achieve a control culture through intervention and surveillance. He cites the

> attempts by Henry Ford, with the aid of a body of inspectors, to intervene in the private lives of his employees to control how they spent their wages and how they lived. ... Though these tendencies are still only 'private' or only latent, they could become, at a certain point, state ideologies, inserting themselves into traditional Pur-itanism and presenting themselves as a renaissance of the pioneer morality and as the 'true' America.
>
> (Gramsci 1971: 304)

Thus during the twentieth century the modern 'anti-drug consensus' created by public charity campaigns, media representations and government intervention was based on the assumption that public policy and public in-terest were one and the same.

Anslinger and the 'assassin of youth'

The leading figure of drug prohibition in the twentieth century was Harry J. Anslinger, head of the FBN from 1930 to 1962. His impact on national and global drug policy was profound and complex.[7] Kinder (1991) considers that Anslinger's racism was an everyday part of his drug prohibition strategy, which identified ethnic minority groups and foreigners as responsible for America's drug addiction problem (Kinder and Walker 1986). The power of Anslinger's discriminatory beliefs depended not merely upon repeatedly as-serting his comments, but such xenophobia was actively supported within institutional frameworks of popular culture, for example the popular press, and also at local level within moral reform groups such as temperance orga-nizations and racist groups like the Klu Klux Klan. Anslinger was regarded as a popular public figure through his radio and TV appearances and he was supported by the political elite for his extreme views. Anslinger was praised by conservative newspapers published by the Hearst empire, magazines of the temperance and prohibition movements, and the Methodist Church. He had strong admirers in Congress for his oppressive policies and received public praise. McWilliams (1990: 19) notes that this was typical of the 'adulation bestowed on Anslinger' at both national and international levels.

It would be wrong to accuse Anslinger of establishing the ideological connection between youth, race and drugs because from the nineteenth century, racial fears had played a central part in the discourse of anti-drug campaigners including Wright and Hobson. This can be seen through the coverage of the William Randolph Hearst newspaper empire, for example, in articles by Winifred Black who also wrote under the name of Annie Laurie.[8] She supported the anti-drug policies of the Italian fascist dictator Benito Mussolini, in her article of 9 March 1928: 'Mussolini Leads Way in Crushing Dope Evil'. She affirmed Mussolini's warning by adding that drugs are a 'hideous contagion like a leprosy in the community'. For over 20 years on a near daily basis she relentlessly constructed a fearful representation of the drug fiend threatening young people and American civilization. She poured forth a steady series of sentimentalized melodramas about the seduction of young white children and women by Mexican marihuana and posited that crime was a result of black people made 'crazy' by cocaine. However, beyond the popular 'adventure' stories of moral xenophobia were more serious cases of brutal racist murders, burnings and torture. Lusane (1991: 34–5) argues there was both 'harmony' and 'alliance formed between temperance groups and racist organizations such as the Klan'. The newspaper empire of William Randolph Hearst ran drug stories as racist tales where the 'evil' hemp drug was used on young people by seductive black-eyed 'senoritas' who were 'wanton women' (Silver and Aldrich 1979). Hearst's papers brought an alteration of language to hemp by renaming marihuana as 'marijuana' in order to make a stronger connection with the Mexican racial minority group (Cockburn and St.Clair 1998). In 1937 Anslinger wrote 'Marijuana: Assassin of Youth'. Murder and xenophobia have been consistently combined through fact and fiction as key ideological strategies of the prohibition and moral reform movement.

Anslinger used xenophobia and the image of young people as the victim of drugs as a means to achieve his personal goal of absolutism. The key factor which Anslinger promoted through his 'legendary hatred of people of colour'[9] was the highly disturbing message of brutal murder. Anslinger's first major piece of prohibition legislation was the Marihuana Tax Act 1937. In promoting the permanent prohibition of cannabis, Anslinger combined the cocktail of racial minorities exploiting youth, the seduction of young women into immorality and murder. Anslinger's (1937: 150) 'Assassin of Youth' paper gives a useful insight into his use of 'othering'. Anslinger was not the first drug prohibitionist to exploit the myth of the 'assassin'. For example, Dr A. E. Fossier (1931: 247) morbidly details how Arabs used hashish for 'every sensual pleasure', committed 'ruthless atrocities' and 'massacred Christians'. He argued that 'Indian Hemp' brought the 'worst addiction, the most brutal and bestial crimes'. Anslinger's paper identifies the origin of cannabis use as non-American. He argues that it was first used by 'Ancient Egyptians', Persians and the military order of the Assassins where the purpose was, according to Anslinger, to turn young men 'into swine', and 'under the influence of hashish, for them to engage in violent and bloody deeds'. Anslinger then provides a succession of case studies on the impact of cannabis in support of his claim that cannabis is the 'killer weed' which leads to rape, insanity and the murder of children, young people, parents and police officers.

These selected narratives of the young 'assassins' were repeatedly told in newspapers and magazines, on radio and the television by Anslinger and his colleagues on a wide basis as everyday stories of drugs (Becker 1963). A good example of the power of Anslinger's dogma over proof of evidence is detailed by McWilliams (1991). He argues that Anslinger's favourite case was that of 21-year-old Victor Licata, a young Mexican in Florida who hacked to death with an axe his mother, father, two brothers and sister. Licata did smoke cannabis and did murder his whole family with an axe. McWilliams (1991: 367) states:

> Anslinger's testimony was factual, but it was not complete. He did not mention that eleven days after the murder a psychiatric examination report appeared in the Tampa Times confirming that Licata was criminally insane and subject to 'hallucinations accompanied by homicidal impulses'. Authorities also concluded that his insanity was most likely inherited and was not marihuana-induced.

It is now recognized that the term 'assassins' is an ideological construction which Albert Hourani (1991: 96) states was 'brought back to Europe during the time of the Crusades'. A key figure in spreading the message was Marco Polo who in the thirteenth century described a cult organization called the Assassins, who were a sort of medieval death squad sent to kill specific leaders. Polo maintains that the leader of the Assassins was Alaodin, a greatly feared Sheikh of the Mountains in Mulehet. He details how the sheikh created an artificial paradise whereby he tricked all the strong male youths from 12 to 20 through administering a potion that makes them sleep. They were then placed in the created paradise garden at Alamut where Polo (1958: 71) states 'the ladies and damsels stayed with them all the time, singing and making music for their delight and ministering to all their desires'. After a few days of pleasurable excess the male youths would be transported out of the paradise believing that Alaodin was a prophet and were then prepared to follow any order given by the sheikh. The young Assassins eagerly enacted each act of murder according to Polo so that they would be able to return the sensual paradise fuelled by hashish.[10]

Polo's description of sexual immorality, intoxication and brutal murder carried out by non-white people has been the basis of enduring stereotypes of fear and infatuation for centuries (Jay 2000). Polo's focus on the erotic and exotic potential of intoxication was affirmed by Samuel Purchas in his 1626 tales: 'Purchas His Pilgrimage'. The modern etymological root of the word 'assassin' linked to hashish comes from Silvestre de Sacy in 1801, as a result of his contact with Napoleonic soldiers returning home from the Egyptian campaigns with cannabis (Rudgley 1993). Rosenthal (1971) is critical of Marco Polo's poetic licence and de Sacy's racial construction. He argues that Hashishiyah was a slang term for a lower class of people with a disreputable character. The derogatory nickname of hashish eaters was well established and in general use by the twelfth century. Thus he argues (1971: 43) that this implies 'doubt as to whether the name Assassin is really to be connected with the meaning "hashish" among the many possible connotations of the Arabic word'. De Sacy's theory of the origin of the word assassin is now understood to be inaccurate as it reproduces a racial othering. However, its use as a metaphor to evoke pleasurable fear rapidly entered into literary and popular culture through the writings of Fritz Hugh Ludlow, Bayard Taylor[11] and Alexandre Dumas's (1845) *The Count of Monte Cristo*. De Sacy's vision of the Orient had a significant impact within high European culture especially his 'Chrestomathie arabe' 1806 and 1826,[12] of which Edward Said (1978: 129) argues that De Sacy praises the ecstasies of cannabis in the Garden of Cafour. He constructs lurid descriptions of Arab people consumed by sex and violence. The connection between orientalism and drug intoxication was enhanced through nineteenth-century painting focusing on the pleasurable voyeuristic gaze lingering over youthful bodies visualizing drugs and decadence, for example, in paintings by Delacroix, Ingres, Gerome and Trouillebert. For Edward Said (1978: 127–130), de Sacy 'was the father of Orientalism'. In the twentieth century Anslinger used 'orientalism' through the metaphor of drugs as the 'assassin of youth', and brought a new and intentionally disturbing message to drug prohibition. But paradoxically the metaphor has been a consistent and productive image employed by both anti- and pro-drug campaigners.[13] In the twenty-first century drugs as the 'assassin of youth' are commodified into an attractive 'coffee-table book', for example, Sherman et al.'s (1999) *Highlights: An Illustrated History of Cannabis*. The text offers an alluring cocktail of youth, sex, drugs and danger while it also reproduces racist propaganda and western imperialism.

Harry Anslinger conducted a militarized propaganda campaign against cannabis which became a personal obsession. McWilliams (1991: 367–8) argues that from his appointment Harry Anslinger was the recognized authority on drug problems who withheld statistics and manipulated records to establish the US government's position that cannabis caused insanity. Anslinger's intention was to gain an emotional response to the disturbing effects of the drug. This resulted in marihuana prohibition and created a new group of criminals to serve the purpose of sustaining Anslinger's position and funding for his Bureau of Narcotics. During Anslinger's reign there were few critical voices. One of his most consistent critics was Indiana University sociology professor Alfred R. Lindesmith. He published an article in 1940 titled 'Dope Fiend Mythology' stating: 'The "dope fiend mythology" serves, in short, as a rationalization of the status quo. It is a body of superstition, half-truths and misinformation which bolsters up an indefensible repressive law' (p.208).

A key strategy of the bureau was to discredit opposition to their drug policy, for example, from individual academics such as Lindesmith or professional associations such as the American Bar Association (ABA) and the American Medical Association (AMA). In particular, the *La Guardia Report* (1945) brought an extreme response from the bureau which viewed its findings as a hindrance to law enforcement since it contradicted their negative view of marihuana. The report challenged the connection between marihuana and mental illness. Users were found to be neither violent nor erotic, nor did they progress to more dangerous drugs. As King (1972: 71) argues:

> Anslinger opposed all public discussion aimed at enlightening Americans about the drug problem or exploring alternatives to his over-bearing policies, on the ground that anything akin to education or open-mindedness would aggravate the situation and stir the curiosity of potential new victims. Those who questioned his Bureau were denounced as 'self-style experts', bleeding-hearts, ax-grinders, and 'meddling do-gooders'.

The hegemonic power of Anslinger's bureau was pervasive. Not only was it able to publicly discredit the findings of the *La Guardia Report*, but Boonie and Whitbread (1974: 201) argue that it forced the AMA to withdraw its formal approval of the report. Further, they state that the editorial of the *AMA Journal* suddenly launched a surprising and hostile condemnation of marihuana which 'was probably written by Anslinger himself'.

Anslinger's representation of marihuana as the 'killer weed', heightening intoxication leading to the sexual violation of 'white young virgin girls' by foreign men, or the 'decapitation of a young man's best friend', establishes what Julia Kristeva (1982) calls the power of horror. Hearst's newspapers, Anslinger's bureau and the US government through their repetitive use of such images can be seen as feasting on abjection through the creation of repulsive images and officially sanctioned announcements of fear.

What Kristeva usefully elaborates is the way that institutions use a dynamic combination of abomination and fascination through a sustained focus on death, sex and excess as a means of attraction and repulsion to intensify control. Evidence for the construction of horror within drug prohibition can be found from the selected atrocity tales told by the victims of drugs and also government decision-makers such as the drug czar William Bennett, who on the American television programme *The Larry King Show* affirmed that beheading was a suitable punishment for drug dealers. He said: 'Yeah. Morally, I don't have any problem with that.'[14]

Drug prohibitionists sought to use horror to demand harsh sentences and punishment which became enacted in the Boggs Act 1951 and the Narcotic Control Act of 1956. Under these measures mandatory minimum penalties were raised from 5 to 20 years for the second offence and from 10 to 40 years for the third offence. Drug use had not merely become a life sentence, under the 1956 Act it had also become a death sentence, where juries could impose the death penalty on any adult who sold heroin to a minor. Yet by the late 1950s American society began to change. This is shown especially through the modern Kennedy presidential campaign. Hemmelstein (1983) argues that the bureau faced inept stagnation through its inability to respond to new social and cultural changes. The repeated warnings concerning cannabis as leading to murder, immorality or violence asserted by the bureau failed to materialize as drug consumption slowly grew to become a recognized popular recreational activity amongst young people. The bureau's inertia was dramatically overthrown when it created a new threatening image of youth and drugs as leading to political subversion of society: the new fear was that drugs could permanently alter consciousness against traditional American values.

Drug control and the British military state

During the First World War, British drug policy arrived under a military state through DORA 40B (Defence of the Realm Act), issued on 28 June 1916. This section argues that emergent British drug policy was shaped by Sir Malcolm Delevinge, Under-Secretary at the Home Office who secured punitive drug controls in Britain. Strang and Gossop (1994: 343) state: 'The Home Office used its influence to try to push Britain towards a similar system as the US and a reliance upon an entirely penal approach with criminal sanctions against both users and prescribing doctors.' During the establishment of the British system of drug control, the media played a supporting role through their moralistic and sensational portrayal of drug use and their criminalization of the drug user. Before DORA 40B it was possible to purchase drugs from the best shops in London such as Harrods.

It is possible to identify three key establishment figures who played an influential role in making drugs a criminal matter: Sir Malcolm Delevinge, Under-Secretary at the Home Office; Sir Edward Henry, Metropolitan Police Commissioner; and Sir Francis Lloyd, General Army Officer Commanding the London District. DORA 40B was an extension of legislation to the general public which had already been introduced by the Army Council applying only to armed service personnel. Carol Smart (1984: 35) argues that it was now a criminal offence for an individual to be in possession of drugs without professional authorization: this act established British drug prohibition. Under wartime conditions the drug issue became strongly linked to national security and the media were quick to alert the public to dangers of wild drug parties, sexual immorality and secrets recklessly given to the German enemy.[15]

Sir Malcolm Delevinge and Sir Edward Henry pursued the drugs issue to consolidate their professional autonomy and to bring drugs under the jurisdiction of criminal law. As Metropolitan Police Commissioner, Henry saw drugs as a cause of crime and argued that drug users should be convicted. He stated: 'It might then be possible to deal severely with the unauthorized persons who, using as their tools burglars, thieves, prostitutes, sodomites, men living upon the earnings of women and other nefarious persons, are at present with impunity doing such infinite harm.'[16] While Henry advocated prison for the drug consumer, he was opposed to sanctions against opium because it provided important trade revenue for the British empire.[17] Henry and Delevinge may have pursued prohibition policies, but Brian Inglis (1975: 165) states that while 'the British Government was professing to be taking measures to reduce consumption of opium and hemp drugs, its agents in India were in fact busy pushing sales in order to increase the colonies revenue'. Parssinen (1983: 186) argues it was Delevinge who drafted the original DORA document which became the basis of the Dangerous Drugs Act, 'as well as the 1921 regulations, with no prior consultations with medical men or pharmacists, much against the wishes of the Ministry of Health officials'. Berridge (1984) reveals there was little evidence that a drug problem existed. She highlights the Report of the Parliamentary Committee on the Use of Cocaine in Dentistry (1917) which argued there was little need to continue the restrictions imposed by DORA. The Committee stated: 'We are unanimously of the opinion that there is no evidence of any kind to show that there is any serious, or, perhaps, even noticeable prevalence of the cocaine habit amongst the civilian or military population of Great Britain.'[18] This evidence was not publicly debated due to its unpopularity amongst elite professional groups and figures, including Delevinge, as it would undermine their institutional expansion. Delevinge tried to keep public politics out of drugs and secured the criminalization of the drug user, which although challenged by the medical profession ultimately brought forth not merely a British compromise but increased institutional regulation of social behaviour.

British media representation of drugs as the 'assassin of youth'

Berridge and Edwards (1987) suggest that it was not until literary re-presentations appeared in the writings of Charles Dickens, Edgar Allen Poe and Oscar Wilde that the opium den took on a more mysterious, sexually threatening appeal. The media showed only a minor interest in the small avant-garde cliques of the 1890s who experimented with drugs, and struggled to present this bourgeois circle of radical bohemians to the public. The British popular press preferred to direct its hostility against the Chinese male population, resulting in structural discrimination against the Chinese in the 1909 London County Council by-law which prohibited opium smoking in licensed sailors' boarding houses.

The American press had led the way and the British press soon followed and increased their readership through fantasized depiction of ethnic men seducing young white women with drugs. A preoccupation with cross-racial sexual relationships, xenophobia and fear for the purity of the white race was an everyday part of western culture in the early twentieth century. Parssinen (1983: 117–18) argues that in newspapers a 'potent symbol' was that of the 'young white virgin, drawn to her demise by rigged gambling games and opium'. Headlines told stories of 'White Girls Hypnotized by Yellow Men', 'East End Dens of Vice/Babies of Every Colour', or 'The Lure of the Yellow Man/English Girls', 'Moral Suicide'/Fatal Fascination'. Similar headlines sold newspapers after the First World War, and these themes were repeated in pulp fiction novels and films throughout the 1920s and beyond (Tracy 1978). British imperial racism and bourgeois literary culture created the myth of drug enslavement as a popular 'otherness', which became a pleasurable horror for the masses through modern film and pulp literature, for example, in the writings of Sax Rohmer. The culture industry packaged drug danger as an attractive and thrilling commodity where consumers bought into the intoxication of drugs as the new 'assassin of youth'.

During the early 1900s, drugs were not a common political issue and there were few voices in support of recreational drug use. Perhaps the most prominent advocate was Aleister Crowley. According to Marek Kohn (1992) in his study on *Dope Girls* the media's interest in arousing public anxiety through the combination of drugs and young women started during the period 1900 to 1925 where he examines the tragic deaths of four young women related to their drug use: Edith and Ida Yeoland, Billie Carleton and Freda Kempton, all of whom were actresses, models and dancers. In the 1920s photographs used in newspapers of both Billie Carleton and Freda Kempton emphasized their feminine beauty, sexual attractiveness[19] and innocence.[20]

The drug-related deaths of actress Billie Carleton in 1918 and dancer

Freda Kempton in 1922 became the first contemporary British drug scandals.[21] Both were independent young women of different social standing who were recreated within the media as innocent young victims and denied their modern female autonomy. From the 1920s onwards the British media and government saw drugs as a vehicle for wider social, cultural and medical intervention, not only to restrict modernity, reassert tradition and regulate female actions but to reinforce the criminal explanation of drug use. For Marek Kohn, Carleton and Kempton were independent young women who challenged feminine passivity and whose use of drugs was undermined and inverted. The press acted as a male conservative force against social change. Berridge (1980: 16) argues that it was always young 'emancipated women [who] were regarded as particularly at risk from drugs'. Thus these young women became negative icons, manipulated to represent emblems of society's corruption.

The dominance of the criminal explanation for drug use over the medical or disease understanding was supported by tabloid hysteria focusing on the apparent ease with which the bourgeoisie could be corrupted by drugs. The fear of drugs took a new and more dangerous imagery after the Kempton case as a result of the criminal drug trials of Edgar Manning, a West Indian man, and Brilliant Chang, a Chinese man. By 1926 drugs had firmly become associated with immoral criminals, for example, the *World's Pictorial News* serialized 'revelations' by Eddie Manning, the self-titled 'Dope King of London'. In eight instalments the ex-prisoner spoke of sexual orgies, the drug deaths of young socialites, the corruption of young upper-class women and the ruination of business men and lawyers to drugs. During the twentieth century under British law drug use was criminalized and came to be seen as a matter for the Home Office and the police.

The 'British System' of drug control, 1920 to 1968

This section explores what is known as the 'British System' of drug control from 1920 to 1968 which assumes that regulation of drug use took place through medicine as a form of treatment. Rutherford and Green (1989: 385) argue the Rolleston Committee's (1926) main recommendation that 'a prescription shall only be given by a duly qualified medical practitioner when required for purposes of medical treatment firmly established the role of the medical profession in British drugs policy for almost forty years'. For Gerry Stimson and Rachel Lart (1994: 331) there never was a system for dealing with drug problems. For them the 'British System' was created by its commentators. The term was coined by E. W. Adams, who served as the secretary to the Rolleston Committee. Furthermore, Nigel South (1999: 89–90) challenges the argument that medical autonomy was provided by the recommendations of the Rolleston Report 1926 because 'its framework was ultimately regulated by the Home Office and the police; its parameters if not its everyday practice were, at the end of the day, marked out by controls not treatment'. The British System may have been a myth but during this period the medical establishment were able to consolidate and advance disease theory as a 'scientific' approach to the social problem of drugs and this in turn legitimated their authority. The attraction of this theory was its flexible integration of medical and moral understandings which defined drugs as a criminal or medical matter not a political issue (Pearson 1991: 167).

The 'British System' was a secretive creation formed, according to Berridge (1984: 27) with 'little political or public input'.[22] The end result of the Dangerous Drugs Acts 1920 and 1923 was that the control of drugs became a matter for the police and therefore drug users became criminalized in the American manner. However, after the Rolleston Report 1926 the medical profession gained an institutional and intellectual power base by being able to control specialist understandings and treatment related to drug addiction. The struggle of institutional power relations amongst the bourgeoisie was partly responsible for the contradictory appearance of British drug policy, which is described by Philip Bean (1974) as pretending to do one thing while actually doing another; in other words to assert medical control but really to operate criminal control.

The real issue of the 'British System' was not one of contradiction, but of class distinction. As an area of social discourse the medical profession defined its specialism in pursuit of class self-interest and was able to safeguard its power to control drug users through its monopoly of knowledge on drug addiction. The new knowledge asserted its regime of truth through the science of disease theory and the emergent psychiatry profession which sympathetically allied itself towards the doctors. Berridge (1984: 28) states: 'Medical humanitarianism was maintained only so long as there was a limited middle class and respectable adult clientele.'[23] The class-based nature of British drug policy is seen by Berridge (1984: 33) to start from its origin. She argues: 'The prison doctors who gave evidence to Rolleston and who saw a different class of addict took a distinctly harsher line, generally following the old penal line of abrupt withdrawal.' Disease theory of drug use was not an emancipating truth; it served the discriminatory power of professional class privilege. Foucault (1984) argues that medical truth is produced and transmitted under forms of control and that it is possible to identify key players who have professional interests which serve one aspect of power. But at the same time the various factions within the bourgeoisie may experience professional conflicts of interest with other status groups. The medical profession armed with its disease theory of drug use was able to legitimate its intervention into the area of the social and moral by defining the drug user as a 'sick' person.

Both Berridge and Parssinen note that models of scientific progress – particularly those linked to control of people's use of drugs and alcohol – consistently contain a rigorous morality. This was demonstrated through the close links of medical specialists with moral reform groups such as the temperance movement, the SSOT and the Quakers. The dual influence of medicine and morality was explicit within the construction of theory and explanation put forward on the apparent drug disease. In this way scientific theory came to reflect not merely the concerns of the moral movement for reform but also became its causal evidence. The advancement of disease theory is key to understanding the medical profession's distinction between medical and non medical use of drugs. The drug prohibition movement could accept no conception of moderation in drug use, and in this way disease theory reflected this total concern by articulating the drug user as in a state of neurosis suffering from a disease of the will. By defining a form of social behaviour as representing a disease, doctors joined their fellow supporters as moral crusaders to fight immorality with science. At its core Rolleston's notion of the drug user as a 'sick' individual reflects the nineteenth-century understanding that an individual's pleasure or vice were a moral problem for society.

In the twentieth century, Carol Smart (1984: 35) argues that the medical profession transformed this 'individual evil into a "scientifically" identified threat to the fabric of society'. The conceptualization of social behaviour as contributing to disease naturally led to the concept of treatment. The institutional convergence between the medical establishment and government enabled the rationale and creation of treatment provisions sanctioned by legislation imposing drug controls. The success of the medical profession in establishing its legitimacy in this area also enabled the growing psychiatric movement to develop more advanced forms of control over the individual by extending the model of insanity to drug use.

Drug 'hypnotism' and insanity

In the 1950s the accusation that drug use led to mental health problems was not new; it began with De Quincey's (1821) *Confessions of an Opium Eater*. In Britain during the 1950s the link between cannabis and madness was relaunched by Dr Donald Johnson (1952, 1953) in his studies on 'insanity-producing drugs' which Antonio Melechi (1997: 21) describes as 'two deeply paranoiac booklets on the subject of hallucinogenic drugs and mental health'. Johnson's hostility towards cannabis is supported in the foreword by H. Pullar-Strecker, MD, Hon. Secretary, Society for the Study of Addiction. Johnson states:

Hashish. This outlandish drug has no medical value and is taken for its pleasurable effects only. Unlike the pain-killers, it has no duties to perform, no blessing to confer. Hashish is an antisocial drug; it is not without reason that it gave the word 'assassin' to our language.

(Johnson 1952: 5)

Pullar-Strecker and Johnson deliberately ignore the nineteenth-century studies on the therapeutic value of cannabis by Dr William Brooke O'Shaughnessy (1843), Dr J. Russell Reynolds (1890), the American medical companies Eli Lilly and Parke-Davis and medical prescriptions for cannabis prepared by the London pharmacist Peter Squire of Oxford Street. Moreover, Pullar-Strecker (1952: 6) incorrectly argues that cannabis 'is a newcomer to this country. Very little was known about it here, even amongst doctors'.[24] This level of ignorance is astounding given that accounts of the therapeutic and social use of cannabis date from the works of Herodotus and Claudius Galen.[25] Throughout the foreword, Pullar-Strecker's medical focus is on morality and a particular concern to assert that youthful drug use is associated with an apparent 'underclass' which may induce the downfall of society. The text is a moralistic monologue from a respectable high-status medical professional.

Both propaganda and ignorance are combined in Pullar-Strecker's and Johnson's assessment that cannabis use is a vice that encourages mental illness, murder and sexual malaise. Johnson, fuelled on by lascivious accounts in the *English Sunday Graphic, Daily Express* and *Evening Standard* during 1951, cites the drug prohibition work of Harry Anslinger as an example of good practice.[26] He translates Anslinger's xenophobia and moral stereotyping into Britain, arguing that drug use started 'amongst the coloured population'. Johnson predicts the downfall of civilization and society. Young people are described as drawn to the attraction of 'dancing girls' who are defined as vulnerable to 'sinister ends' connected with 'hypnotism' through 'hot jazz dancing clubs'. He affirms his vision by asserting 'there is a link' between drugs and dancing, a 'compulsive urge to move their bodies in sympathy' to the 'Devil's Weed'. These accounts were lent credibility because they were presented as scientific and objective, but it is that clear these medical professionals exploited the tabloid portrayal of cannabis as lowering morality and increasing sexual temptation across racial groups through intoxication. What is also absent in their accounts is the historical knowledge that sustained consumption of cannabis reduces sexual potency, as detailed by Dioscorides,[27] Galen,[28] and Pliny.[29] For his evidence Johnson uses the erotic and exotic imagination of French symbolists such as Baudelaire and American writer Fritz Hugh Ludlow to demonstrate his case that cannabis encourages vice amongst the young.

American idealization of the 'British System'

In the USA during the 1960s there were calls for reform of drug policies. It was argued that criminalization of the drug user had increased drug abuse and crime. The American demand for a medical approach towards the drug problem led to what Gerry Stimson and Rachel Lart (1994: 331) understand as the discovery of the 'British System' of drug control. American theorists Rufus King, Alfred Lindesmith and Edwin Schur[30] articulated the achievements of the 'British System' and commented on Britain's lack of a drug problem. This assessment amounts to a 'myth of praise'. Berridge (1984: 18) argues: 'The British System of control and its apparent success was ... looked to as a shining example of what could be achieved by a medical form of control.' American drug reformers tended to romance the 'British System' of drug control because of its apparent flexibility and compassion focusing on scientific rationality and medicine rather than enforcement and criminalization. During the early 1960s this idealization became a central element in the campaign of American drug reformists calling for more liberal drug policies. For Edwin Schur (1964: 81) the case for reform was proven: 'it is clear that American policy cannot achieve its stated aim'. American worship of the 'British System' created an atmosphere of self-congratulation and complacency within the British medical elite who were against taking panic measures.[31] In the mid-1960s Glatt et al. (1967: 105) stated: 'The British System seemed even more attractive when reports appeared of successful therapeutic methods based on it.' However, the 'British System' of drug control fully collapsed as a myth as a result of the growth in young heroin users and the large-scale emergence in the 1960s of new drugs such as LSD and purple hearts which were consumed by young people across the class structure not on the basis of 'sickness' but leisure (Yates 2002).[32]

Idealization of the 'British System' brought misinformation. It suggested that historically Britain did not develop a punitive drug policy and it failed to address the conflict and competition between elite ideologies within an institutional framework where competing groups pursued their own professional self-interest and survival. The oversimplification is to assert that the Home Office was at war with the medical profession for control over an area of practice and policy, i.e. drug control. This flawed formulation asserts a heroic battle between the forces for liberalism represented by the medical profession and conservatism represented by the Home Office. But it was not a case of win or lose for medicine or the police because both sides won in their ability to increase control over the individual, and consolidate professional self-interest and their position of legitimacy. This misconception avoids considering how knowledge is used to support existing power relations. Foucault (1984: 73) argues that capitalist societies operate on the basis of a political economy of truth, where 'truth is centred on the form of scientific discourse and the institutions which produce it; it is subject to constant economic and political incitements'. Looking closely at the 'British System', David Downes (1977: 89) argued it was not a case of reform or incarceration because 'this system has now been well and truly exposed as little more than masterly inactivity'.[33]

The myth of the successful 'British System' is a political construction which supported the interests of elite cultural groups.[34] As Foucault (1984: 74) asserts, it should not be understood in terms of science or medicine, but in terms of the pursuit of truth and power gained by the profession. Drugs as an area of discourse were subject to an 'economy of truth', in that certain types of knowledge become legitimate and self-reinforcing, irrespective of their value, because they are supportive of the bourgeois economy and its professional classes. Prohibition brought an expansion of institutional regulation where the bureaucracies of medicine and punishment defined the legitimacy of their intervention and brought forth their own procedures and protocols. Institutional regimes such as the 'British System' superficially gave the appearance of pragmatic reform, accommodating social change whilst maintaining the status quo.

Conclusion

This chapter has explored the contradictory legacy of drug prohibition, specifically looking at the metaphor of drugs as the 'assassin of youth'. The contradictions underlying drug control policy are apparent in government involvement in the colonial drug trade, leading prohibitionists' use of a racist theory of the 'other', the medical profession and their development of the disease theory of drug use which defined the drug consumer as 'socially sick' and requiring medical intervention, and finally the bureaucratic power of law enforcement institutions which sought to define the drug user as a criminal. In each of these cases, drugs were used as a discourse to legitimate professional self-interest and also as a strategy to expand power where interventions were fused with moral precepts.

I then examined the way in which the prohibition movement brought about the criminalization of drug use through their moral campaign to both change and protect society. Their anti-drug propaganda was based on an ideology of racial purity, which was driven by the construction of a dangerous 'other' in the form of sexualized 'foreigners' and intoxicating 'drugs' which corrupted young people's morality and thus made drugs a threat to the future of society. Finally, I argued that government, media and the culture industry have mutually reinforced a voyeuristic image of drugs as dangerously exotic, erotic and fearful through the metaphor of drugs as the 'assassin of youth'.

2 Pleasure doomed
A history of drug control policy

The stated purpose of America's 'drug war' policy is to eradicate drugs from society. The aim of this chapter is to present an alternative history of illicit drug politics which examines American complicity in the growth of the illicit global drug business. I shall explore the social and economic features of drugs as a source of political state repression used by mainstream corporate culture and extreme right-wing regimes. I will argue that drug production and distribution are closely associated with the brutal suppression of people's rights. There will be an assessment of America's 'drug war' policy focusing on the counter-espionage activities of the Central Intelligence Agency (CIA) in their search for the 'truth drug' and their involvement in the international drug trade as a means of finance for covert intelligence operations, to support military dictatorships and death squads (Epstein 1990). Moreover, it will be argued that American interests underlie US drug prohibition in that the United Nations 'Drug-Free Society' policy can be used as a justification for intervention into the affairs of other countries, via aid or intelligence operations. In this way US policy is presented as being liberal or benevolent when in fact the 'drug war' acts as a cover for the pursuit of economic and political interests (Gray 2002).

I will start with an introduction to Klaus Barbie because his actions demonstrate a continuity of corruption and oppression from the Second World War to the latter part of the twentieth century. A key point I wish to highlight is that state intelligence services, the military, right-wing rebels and criminal organizations have used the international drug trade as a source of revenue and as a means to impose repressive domination upon populations including both exploitation of and experimentation on people (Bullington and Block 1990: 39). During the 1940s Klaus Barbie was a leading Nazi torturer, fascist and mass murderer. Barbie spent much of his time in Lyons where he took sadistic pleasure in murdering Jewish people and communists, but his special preference was to cause torment and pain for the men and women of the French resistance. According to Linklater, Hinton and Ascherson (1984) and Bower (1984) he subjected his prisoners to endless rounds of genital mutilation, confinement with the butchered corpses of their friends, torture using hot irons and needles and beatings with spiked chains; prisoners' heads were repeatedly plunged into toilets filled with urine and excreta. Barbie also assembled prisoners before mock firing squads to prolong their agony and to extract information through methods of brutal terror.

By the 1980s Klaus Barbie was a leading figure in one of the world's largest drugs empires in South America. In the summer of 1980 Bolivia experienced what Cockburn and St. Clair (1998) call a 'Cocaine Coup'. Paramilitary soldiers led by Klaus Barbie and Stefano Delle Chiaie, an Italian neo-fascist, murdered trade union leaders and leftist groups and eradicated political party opposition. R. T. Naylor states:

> In 1945 US Army intelligence acquired Klaus Barbie, the 'Butcher of Lyon', from the Gestapo. He was put on the payroll to mold clandestine Nazi cells in eastern Europe into anti-Communist spy rings. In 1951 he was given a new name and a false passport and sent to Latin America to help the US combat 'communism', particularly in Bolivia.
>
> (Naylor 1994: 166)

During his time in Bolivia, Klaus Barbie organized national security in order to protect the billion-dollar earning drug trade. While acting as a paid agent of the CIA, Barbie received formal rewards and honorary status for his counter-insurgency operations which kept the Bolivian drug trade effective and lucrative, especially for his own private company Estrella, later Transmaritania. The key to Barbie's efficiency was to liquidate rival drug suppliers, and through his position of internal security chief, to subvert and then brutally crush popular democratic organizations. In Bolivia, the Los Novios de la Muerte [the Fiancés of Death] were a death squad composed of Nazis, international terrorists and murderers.[1] The functioning of the death squad was a continuity for Barbie from his days of torture and inhumanity in France, and was soon to become an export model for other repressive dictatorships in Argentina, Chile, Peru, Colombia, Burma and Thailand, or counter-insurgency groups such as the Contras in Nicaragua.

US Paperclip Project

Only recently has it been revealed to American citizens that their country has been extensively involved in secret government sponsorship of international terrorism and authoritarian actions. The nature of such secrecy kept American people in ignorance, believing that US foreign policy was honourable and compatible with 'traditional American values'. Kathryn Olmsted (1996: 6) states that during the 1980s and 1990s critical investigations 'brought these secret powers into the open, they forced Americans to acknowledge that their country had tried to kill foreign leaders, had spied on civil rights leaders and had tested drugs on innocent people'. These actions are far from new.

Leslie Cockburn (1989) points out that America has consistently been involved in undertaking secret wars and counter-espionage, from the inter-war period when America was not a member of the League of Nations.

The United States was initially not able to establish its prohibitionist view on drug policy and compel agreement internationally. Walker (1992) demonstrates that this ultimately led the way to coercive diplomacy to achieve global policy aims. In the 1920s during prohibition, Harry Anslinger attended international conferences on the suppression of illegal traffic in alcohol. His success in stopping the flow of bootleg alcohol across the West Indies brought him to the attention of the prohibition authorities in the Treasury. Kinder (1981: 172) also notes Anslinger led an investigation into the Bolshevik movement in cooperation with the British Intelligence Service, focusing upon the global threat of Soviet imperialism. John McWilliams (1990: 15) confirms that Federal Bureau of Narcotics (FBN) agents were on loan to both the Office of Strategic Service (OSS) and later the CIA. They performed secret duties and 'were involved for years in international activities with the full knowledge and approval of their boss'. The formation of the FBN with its international collaboration with the OSS and the reluctance of other countries to be influenced by US drug policy led to the development of political and paramilitary interventions on a covert basis.

American President Harry S. Truman oversaw two key developments in drug war politics during the post Second World War period. These were, first, in 1946 the Paperclip Project whose mission was to bring over 1500 Nazi war criminals described as 'scientists' to the United States to gain access to their research knowledge and organizational expertise, including notes and visual recordings of human subjects under experimentation (Bower 1987). Second, in 1947 the introduction of the 'loyalty oath' was designed to exclude disloyal Americans from engaging in what were referred to as 'subversive' or 'un-American' activities, in order to enhance US national security. Policies are clearly expressed by American President Herbert Hoover:

> It is now clear that we are facing an implacable enemy whose avowed objective is world domination. .... There are no rules in such a game. Hitherto accepted norms of human conduct do not apply. .... If the United States is to survive, long standing American concepts of fair play must be reconsidered. ... We must learn to subvert, sabotage and destroy our enemy by more clever, more sophisticated, more effective methods than those used against us.[2]

Initially the Paperclip Project rationale was based on the need to defeat the Japanese empire, but later justification was put forward in terms of the Cold War struggle against communism. Such was the power of propaganda that, as Kathryn Olmsted (1996: 185) argues, even 'Cold War liberals wanted the secret agencies to have complete freedom to fight communism'. One well-known American academic who took part in operation Paperclip was sociology Professor Talcott Parsons (Diamond 1992; Simpson 1998; Trumpbour 1989). On his German trip to recruit Nazi collaborators, one of his crucial contacts was Nicholas Poppe. Poppe worked for the SS think tank, the Wannsee Institute, which developed plans for the 'final solution' to the 'Jewish question'. Nicholas Poppe became professor at the University of Washington in 1949 and later conferred a degree of academic respectability on the politically neurotic show trials of McCarthyism. Talcott Parsons was founder of 'structural functionalism', a total social theory which sought to achieve the scientific status of sociology by purging itself of political values. Wiener (1991: 78) states that 'by materially assisting in this intelligence process, Talcott Parsons contributed to some of the most anti-democratic and anti-intellectual trends in postwar American political life'. The strategic basis for Paperclip operations was the rehabilitation of fascists to serve American global policy (Simpson 1988). Herman (1987: 11) argues that at the Nuremberg Trials 'large numbers of fascists were being protected and positioned for Cold War service. Most of these were not scientists with scarce skills – they were mainly bureaucrats and army intelligence personnel many of them mass murderers'. Thus the Paperclip Project brought together Klaus Barbie and the CIA to support an ideology promoting the fear of communism, and made common cause first over individual mind control and second political state control. The next section examines these aspects of control culture.

The truth drug and the CIA

The American military and police interest in a 'truth serum' to make people confess under narcosis can be traced back to the work of Robert House first published in 1897 and 1899. House claimed that under drugs 'it is impossible to lie'. The term 'truth serum' was first used by Calvin Goddard in 1932 and elaborated into 'narco-analysis' by Stefen Horsley in 1936.[3] This experimental research was undertaken largely on criminals who were captives in prison or hospital and identified by Jean Rolin (1955) as a form of torture where information is extracted under fear and abuse of power.

Prior to the CIA, the Office of Naval Intelligence (ONI) and the OSS were interested in gaining access to information about mind control. From the early 1940s, OSS chief General William Donovan became preoccupied with the development of speech-inducing drugs for use in intelligence interrogation. Both the OSS and the ONI became preoccupied with mescaline when, as Lee and Shlain (1992: 5) describe, they 'learned of mind control experiments carried out by Nazi doctors at the Dachau concentration camp during World War II'. Nazi war criminal Karl Tauboeck worked for the German company I. G. Farben.

He was an expert on sterilization and in particular on the effects of drugs on animals and humans. Hunt (1991: 164) details that the Gestapo had been working on the development of a truth serum for years and Tauboeck became a major source of information for the CIA 'especially his secret wartime work on speech-inducing drugs'. The chemical company I. G. Farben manufactured the nerve gas used in poison gas experiments at Auschwitz concentration camp. Under Paperclip the director of the company, Otto Ambros, later become a consultant for the American company Grace, Dow Chemists and he also worked for the US Army Chemical Corps where he continued his experimentation on American soldiers.

Under the National Security Act of 1947, the Central Intelligence Agency came into existence. The Act also contained a single clause allowing the new agency to perform 'other functions and duties' that the president might direct – in effect 'creating the legal authority for the CIA's covert operations to break any law in pursuit of their objectives' (McCoy 1991: 492). Initially the military's search for the truth drug was started by the navy in 1947 under Project CHATTER (1947 to 1953). The second set of experiments began with Project BLUEBIRD in 1950 which was retitled Project ARTICHOKE in 1952. The CIA programme of research into drug-enhanced techniques of interrogation and mind control for covert operations began in April 1953 under the code name MK-ULTRA. The whole programme of MK-ULTRA was headed by Dr Sidney Gottlieb, while Harry Anslinger agreed to lend a number of senior officers to the CIA, including George Hunter White, who as a field officer administered LSD to all types of unsuspecting American people (Bullington and Block 1990: 44–5).

John Marks (1979), in his study *The Search for the Manchurian Candidate*, details the way that America used Nazi scientists' experiments to conquer 'Inner Space' as defined by the CIA and 'Outer Space' through National American Space Agency (NASA). The objective of Paperclip was to advance military technology and strategic intervention to create a control culture (Simpson 1988). Linda Hunt (1991: 234) specifies that 'both the army and the CIA MK-ULTRA experiments stemmed from Nazi science'. However, the American people were neither told the full story about Nazi recruitment nor about experimentation on their own citizens. As the CIA programme of super-secret research into the power of drugs to modify human actions for purposes of espionage proceeded from mescaline, cannabis and cocaine through to LSD, it became clear that the CIA also proposed to target young Americans seen to be in need of an 'alteration of personality'. These operations were planned at the highest level of state policy and it was the Director of the CIA, Allen Dulles, who in 1953 instituted a programme for the covert use of chemical materials. Under Richard Helms, its director from 1967 to 1973, the programme of covert use of LSD increased. Helms described LSD as 'dynamite' and asked to be instructed in its use against specific state leaders (Andrews 2001).

Previously Helms was famous for having gained an interview with Adolf Hitler in 1936 while working for United Press (Marks 1979: 13).

Certain Nazi scientists who were brought to America gained government grants to continue their experiments – among them Otto Ambros and Friedrich Hoffmann. Linda Hunt (1991: 166) suggests that after Hoffmann's arrival at Edgewood Arsenal, Maryland, the chemical experiments moved on to looking at LSD application as the 'truth drug'. Hoffmann was a CIA consultant and his work was exemplary for the Bluebird Project. Hunt states: 'At least a thousand soldiers ... were given up to twenty doses of LSD to test the drug as a possible interrogation weapon.' The experiments of Nazi scientist Dr Kurt Plotner focused on the use of mescaline as a speech and truth-inducing drug under interrogation. Crucially, Plotner was advancing towards drugs as a means of behavioural modification or mind control. His research came to the attention of Boris Pash who had already supervised unsuccessful experiments into interrogation. Pash was a Russian emigré to the United States who was closely associated with other Nazi war criminals, including Dr Eugene von Haagen and Kurt Blome, who were joint heads of the Nazi biological weapons unit which infected prisoners with diseases such as TB and bubonic plague. Boris Pash went on to be the head of CIA Program Branch 7 at the time when the CIA began funding Project Bluebird in an effort to replicate and advance the Dachau research using LSD (Hunt 1991).

Robert Proctor (1988: 284) states that the results of the Nazi medical experiments were 'not the product of a tiny band of marginal or psychotic individuals'. Previously, in the Third Reich's concentration camps such as Dachau and Auschwitz, the Nazi scientists' research victims were Jews, gypsies, communists and homosexuals. Now their laboratories were transferred to America.[4] Lee and Shlain (1992: 24) note: 'The CIA victimized certain groups of people who were unable to resist: prisoners, mental patients, foreigners, the terminally ill, sexual deviants, ethnic minorities.' Proctor (1988: 286–7) argues that German scientists were influenced by the 'American eugenics' movement and viewed social and youth problems such as crime, poverty and drugs as medical and biological problems. Nazi drug experiments were promoted as medical strategies to control populations, an applied mechanism with the power of scientific rationality cleansing what others perceived as social problems.

Initially MK-ULTRA experiments took place on North Korean prisoners of war, but they soon focused on American citizens. No effort was made to gain informed or prior consent because the aim of the CIA was to experiment on uninformed human subjects to make them talk freely. During the 1950s the government tested LSD on figures who would later dominate the next decade's revolutionary youth culture, including Timothy Leary, Ken Kesey and Allen Ginsberg. John Marks (1979: 121) states that when LSD escaped the government's control and went on the street no one at the CIA 'foresaw that young Americans would voluntarily take the drug'. He maintains that due to their obsession with control culture the agency were incapable of gaining insight from their own LSD experiments because they sought to impose rather than create an altered state of consciousness for drug users. It was not LSD which the CIA were so much obsessed with as the whole notion of the truth drug which became an addiction and ultimately led the CIA to develop a haphazard programme of surprise testing of hallucinogens on security staff, politicians, military leaders, students, the poor and individuals with alternative or radical views.

Under Sidney Gottlieb, 'spike operations' were overseen by George Hunter White, a dual agent for the FBN and CIA who established a series of safehouses. In recent years, as US government files have been declassified, researchers have been able to access information showing the full range of CIA and FBN activities in the area of covert drug experimentation. Using this evidence,[5] Cockburn and St. Clair (1998: 207) state:

> [Using two-way mirrors] White would sit on the lavatory, martini in hand, watching prostitutes give CIA designer drugs to their un-suspecting clients. White called this operation *Midnight Climax*. He assembled a group of prostitutes, many of them black heroin addicts whom he paid in drugs, to lure their clients to the CIA-sponsored drug and sex sessions. The women, who were known by the San Francisco police as George's Girls, were protected from arrest.

After his retirement George Hunter White, in a private letter to Sidney Gottlieb, spoke of his days: 'It was fun, fun, fun. Where else could a red-blooded American boy lie, kill, cheat, steal, rape, and pillage with the sanction and blessing of the All-Highest?' (Lee and Shlain 1992: 35).

The CIA's drug experimentations known as behaviour modification programmes never really lost their Nazi voyeurism in the sense that human subjects were tested without consent. One example is the case of Frank Olson, a specialist in the airborne delivery of biological warfare agents. At a CIA drug experimentation meeting, Sidney Gottlieb spiked Olson's alcoholic drink with a large amount of LSD. Olson's body was found in the early hours of the morning. He had jumped through a closed window to his death ten floors below. The apparent suicide of the scientist who leapt to his death was quickly covered up by the CIA. Over 20 years later President Ford gave a public apology to the Olson family. During this whole process MK-ULTRA director and 'spiker' Dr Gottlieb was given immunity from prosecution. Through his death Olson later became one of the CIA's leading propagandist symbols behind the notion of 'a bad trip' and the drug prevention mythology that LSD makes you want to fly. The misinformation of the Frank Olson story remains a major form of anti-drug propaganda (Ignatieff 2001).

Drugs as a political and military strategy

The 'McCoy Thesis' outlined in 1972 and consolidated in 1991 was developed by Alfred McCoy in his book *The Politics of Heroin*. He documents the idea that American intelligence forces have cooperated with international criminal and drug organizations since the early 1940s. Through both covert and overt military interventions, US foreign policy and CIA operations work to maintain surveillance of or achieve regulation over different peoples and states. A key accusation is that American foreign policy has supported right-wing insurgency movements against democratically elected governments where there have been large-scale violations of human rights (Kruger 1980; Marshall 1991). Corrupt regimes are propped up by the US government with financial and material assistance to military dictatorships providing they improve investment opportunities for American corporate companies. US foreign policy turns a blind eye to drug production where the profits finance the regime it supports. Here political objectives are seen as being of more importance than suppression of drug production (Blum 1995; Gray 2002).

For McCoy, the CIA's complicity in the global drug trade had its beginning with the pre-CIA security operations of the ONI which procured the protection services of Mafia leader Charles 'Lucky' Luciano. His aggressive sex–narcotic strategy was undermined when accumulated evidence of violence against three women was sufficient to sentence him in 1936 to a 30- to 50-year custodial term (Duke and Gross 1993). McCoy (1991) describes that, deprived of its leader, the Mafia's drugs empire was about to enter decline when a sudden change restored the Mafia's position. Luciano was asked by the ONI to help supply information about sabotage and security at the New York docks and gather intelligence to prepare plans for the 1943 Allied invasion of Sicily. Using recently disclosed government information, Cockburn and St. Clair (1998: 134) state:

> US intelligence agencies arranged for the release from prison of the world's preeminent drug lord, allowed him to rebuild his narcotics empire, watched the flow of drugs into the largely black ghettos of New York and Washington D. C. escalate and then lied about what they had done. This founding saga of the relationship between American spies and gangsters set patterns that would be repeated from Laos and Burma to Marseilles and Panama.

A popularly known example of CIA collusion in the suppression of democratic values was fictionalized in the 1971 film *The French Connection*. McCoy (1991: 60) argues that the background to the movie dates back to the late 1940s in Marseilles when 'CIA operatives supplied arms and money to

Corsican gangs for assaults on Communist picket lines and the harassment of important union officials'. For the CIA, the purpose of breaking trade union solidarity was twofold: first, Marseilles was a key distribution centre for the delivery of the Marshall Plan exports to Europe; second, the port was vital to supply French imperial forces in Vietnam with arms to fight the civil war against Ho Chi Minh's communist uprising. During the first Indochina War 1946 to 1954 the CIA allied itself with the Corsican criminal syndicate run by the brothers Antoine and Barthelemy Guerini. With such support, McCoy (1991: 18) argues that 'the Corsicans overcame their rivals and for the next quarter century used their control over the Marseilles waterfront to dominate the export of heroin to the US market'. In establishing a political and repressive partnership with the Corsican underworld, the CIA's actions were complicit in advancing the drugs economy.

Benedict Anderson (1991) in his study *Imagined Communities* considers the passionate beliefs that generate individual identity through a collective sense of nation. I want to use his idea about 'imagined', but to apply it with reference to what has been described as Drug McCarthyism developed by American foreign policy and pursued by CIA counter-insurgency operations. During the post-1945 period America began to globally promote an 'imagined catastrophe' where communism and drugs were understood as evils which threatened world civilization. The primary threat promoted by US foreign policy was the fear of communism. The CIA saw European socialist governments and trade unionism to be as threatening as Soviet troops in eastern Europe and China's new communist government. For the American administration, drugs with its own already created fear linked to foreign 'others' became utilized to supplement the Cold War threat: drugs augmented communism as the imagined catastrophe.

On American drug policy, Bullington and Block (1990: 52) state that 'relations with an apparently friendly anti-Communist government will never be sacrificed for drug control'. In the 1950s Senator Hubert Humphrey announced that they 'should ... stop talking so much about democracy, and make it clear that we are quite willing to support dictatorships of the right if their policies are pro-American'.[6] In 1964 Thomas Mann, President Lyndon Johnson's czar for Latin America, stated that 'the US would no longer punish military juntas for overthrowing democratic regimes'.[7] Little had changed by the 1980s when a Drug Enforcement Administration (DEA) agent remarked: 'Drugs are a serious problem. But Communism is a greater problem.'[8] Kruger (1980) argues that the CIA used international drug connections both to finance their own covert action and also as a means to gather intelligence about insurrection movements through the strategy of selling weapons. Kruger's assertion is that US foreign policy and drug enforcement have been supportive of military coups to support right-wing and military police states, providing training in guerrilla warfare, terrorist strategies and campaigns of torture.

This financial support led to the creation of death squads in South America, Asia and other countries responsible for government assisted terrorism which destabilized states through systematic repression (Arnson 2000). Kruger sees American financial aid to corrupt regimes as supporting fascism, which has led to the overthrow of democracy or the support for rebel groups to undermine elected governments.

During the Cold War period American foreign policy promoted itself as liberal and enlightened with its claim to be fighting the global aspirations of Soviet imperialism and emergent Chinese communism. Similarly, the American military, the FBN and CIA were projected as the last line of defence against political subversion through drug culture. According to Kinder (1981: 189), Anslinger used both Russia and China as scapegoats for understanding US domestic drug addiction, warning that 'any kind of dirty work ... forwarded their communist cause'. In the context of drug McCarthyism, there was no requirement to produce substantive evidence against those accused of being communists or having drug links.[9] The Daniel Subcommittee of Senators 1956 stated: 'Subversion through drug addiction is an established aim of Communist China. Since World War II, Red China has pushed the exportation of heroin to servicemen and civilians of the US and other free nations of the world.'[10] In reality French and American intelligence services integrated their covert warfare against communism with the Golden Triangle opium trade. McCoy states:

> Operating beyond the controls of bureaucracy in Paris and Washington, a small cadre of clandestine warriors struck ad hoc alliances with tribes and warlords who inhabited the mountains of the Golden Triangle. With their support, the CIA and its French counterparts were able to penetrate China on intelligence missions, monitor its long border for signs of impeding Chinese attack, and mobilize tribal armies to battle Communist guerrillas.
>
> (McCoy 1991: 129)

The French colonial government's abolition of its monopoly opium trade meant that the French intelligence and paramilitary agencies lacked funds for covert operations to fight the First Indochina War (1946 to 1954). Thus, in order to retain their power, the intelligence service strategy was to control most of the opium trade. Cockburn and St. Clair (1998: 242) state: 'Ho Chi Minh made opposition to the opium trade a key feature of his campaign to run the French out of Vietnam. The Viet Minh leader, Ho Chi Minh argued that the French were pushing opium on the people of Vietnam as a means of social control. A drugged people, Ho said, is less likely to rise up and throw off the oppressor.' The victory in 1949 of Mao Tse-tung's Chinese People's Liberation Army over Chiang Kai-shek's Nationalist Army brought new politico-drug alliances because Chiang Kai-shek's[11] right-wing army the (Kuomintang) KMT were financed through the opium trade. The displacement of this anti-communist army into the Shan states of northern Burma on the Chinese border, where the KMT warlords traditionally controlled the Golden Triangle opium trade, became of interest to the CIA.[12] From this position of strength the CIA and the KMT would be able to block the assumed communist expansion. From within Burma and Thailand[13] the CIA-backed KMT forces undertook many minor invasions of China for military intelligence.

In 1955 the United States took over from France in the Indochina War, although there was little difference in policy which was to prevent communist leader Ho Chi Minh from becoming president of Vietnam. The United States military began to train the same hill tribes' mercenaries as the previous colonial French regime, while also exploiting the opium trade. However, the CIA were more directly involved in establishing repressive dictatorships, such as that of Ngo Dinh Diem in 1954, and then engineering the coup and murder of this leader when he no longer suited political ambitions in 1963. In effect the puppet regime in South Vietnam established by the United States became unstable through systematic corruption, from the air force, civil bureaucracy, army, and navy to members of government. The source of corruption was the expanding profitability of the young American GI market for heroin in South Vietnam and the international market for narcotics, especially in the United States. Bullington and Block (1990: 40) state that 'US Special Forces flew Golden Triangle opium and heroin to Bangkok and other centres', through Laos, already infiltrated by the CIA, and on to Saigon's international airport. Christopher Robbins, in his 1979 study *Air America*, describes how it was the norm, not an irregularity, that the airline used by the CIA's client army collected and distributed opium on CIA planes flying the American flag. It appears that although army officials were concerned about young American soldiers becoming addicted to heroin, their militaristic tunnel vision was to fight the 'evil' communists and to defend what they suggested was a democracy. The economic stability of Vietnam was fragile in that it was partly based on the sale of narcotics to an invading army who was fast becoming a mass addict. Cockburn and St. Clair (1998: 249) state: 'CIA-transported opium engendered an addiction rate among US servicemen in Vietnam of up to 30%, with soldiers spending some $800 million a year in Vietnam. In the early 1970s some of this same heroin was being smuggled back to the US in the body bags of dead servicemen.' By 1971 the White House estimated that 34 per cent of American soldiers in Vietnam had commonly used heroin. The American troop withdrawal began in 1972. Duke and Gross (1993: 100) conclude that 'America's anti-drug policies are routinely subordinated to interests and objectives that seem more pressing or more important'.

Thus McCoy's thesis is that the CIA were complicit in the drug trade through their political and military strategy to defeat an imagined evil known as communism. The CIA support for secret wars using the fanatical anti-communist and corrupt KMT army who controlled the opium trade aimed to intensify and promote covert military action in China, Laos and Vietnam. As a result of CIA alliances and interventions, the apparently anti-communist mercenary groups and factions within military dictatorships successfully gained their income from the drug trade to consolidate their rule. McCoy (1991: 192) states: 'By the early 1960s the Golden Triangle had become the largest single opium-growing region in the world – a vast reservoir able to supply America's lucrative markets.' The diverse drug dealing alliances forged by the CIA continued to receive American assistance on the basis of their loyalty to US anti-communist ideals. The end result was that enormous profits were derived from the illegal drugs as they were transformed from a cash crop to a military and strategic commodity to support repressive political regimes.

US militarization of the 'drug war'

For Presidents Kennedy, Johnson, Nixon, Reagan and Bush, US foreign policy focused on fighting the communist enemy, promoted as a fearsome monster. Crucial to this American nationalist ideology was the assertion that communism was an expansionist threat, but after the end of the Cold War communism was no longer a viable mask for counter-insurgency and therefore narco-terrorism became the new global threat. The image of an apparent narco-anarchy was used by US foreign policy to further counter-insurgency under the guise of narcotic enforcement. The American Ambassador to Columbia, Lewis Tambs, promoted the image of 'narco-trafficking' in close association with leftist 'narco-terrorists' or 'narco-guerrillas' (Gordon 1989). The original accusations against Colombian communist rebel groups were never proven, yet as Bullington and Block (1990: 49) argue, 'narco guerrillas' became 'a stock phrase in the Reagan administration'. The work of counter-insurgency has always involved 'subcontracting out' killing either formally or informally. Jonathan Marshall (1991: 62) states: 'Both the CIA and the Army now officially assert the legal authority to kill individuals designated by the president as "terrorists" who pose an immediate threat to the United States citizens or the national security of the United States.' The US military found a new role training Latin American public security personnel in counter-drug and support operations.[14]

Edward Herman (1987) argues that the American administration has been a leading exporter of military and police training to Central and Latin America, including methods and technology of torture. In 1962 President Kennedy's administration established the Office of Public Safety (OPS) to train foreign police officials in South East Asia and Latin America. The official support for the 'Green Berets' as an international intelligence force came from President Kennedy and Attorney General Robert Kennedy, and was popularly celebrated in 1966 by Staff Sergeant Barry Sadler's American number one chart hit 'The Ballad of the Green Beret'. Military training as a basis for counter-insurgency included surveillance techniques, interrogation procedures, methods of conducting raids, riots and crowd control. By the early 1970s the OPS had considerable independence in its operations and had trained police forces of military states on an international basis. Huggins (1987: 165) notes that US exports of security operations ended in 1974 'when Congress could no longer ignore evidence of systematic violation of human rights by United States trained and equipped police forces'. However, OPS was not fully dismantled. As Marshall (1991: 14) reveals, Congress prohibited foreign police assistance 'except for combating drug traffic'. On this basis narcotic programmes occupied the gap left by the demise of the OPS. US officials insist that, due to the corruption of the police in Third World countries, it is essential for the military to take the lead role in the drug war through technical and intelligence resources provided by the United States (Andreas 1998). However, Peter Zinrite (1998: 168) states that 'the United States is aiding and training troops within whose ranks are some of the worst human rights violators'.

Martha Huggins (1998: 195) argues that over the last two decades new police assistance programmes which continue to violate human rights have replaced the OPS. US covert operations and the practice of conducting secret wars has effectively hindered the development of democracy. For example, in Nicaragua the US sponsored the Contras on the basis of supporting an anti-communist group. The CIA supervised and aided the right-wing Contras who raised money by running drugs into the United States. Huggins states:

> The new police assistance initiatives had become even less account-able to Congress – as demonstrated by the US negotiations with Iran in the mid-1980s and by the covert supply of arms to Nicaraguan Contras ... such operations brought United States foreign policy full circle, back to supporting with private funds a privatized militia run privately by government officials.
>
> (Huggins 1998: 195)

Gary Webb's (1998) disclosure of the CIA alliance with the drug smuggling Contras ultimately led to counter-denial and a renewed personal promotion of the Contras' cause from the president of the United States (Schroedor 2000). Leslie Cockburn (1989) details that the American President Ronald Reagan stood on a platform alongside Contra leaders and stated 'I'm a Contra too'. The US Kerry Subcommittee found 'There was substantial evidence of drug smuggling through the war zones on the part of individual Contras,

Contra suppliers, Contra pilots, mercenaries who worked with the Contras, and Contra supporters throughout the region'.[15]

The drugs economy is an exemplar of 'free market' economics functions to support state militarized capitalism, where right-wing ideologues in collaboration with drug cartels use brutality and terror to support their oppressive hegemony. Cockburn and St. Clair (1998: 177) use the example of the company Merex, controlled by Colonel Otto Skorzeny, one of Hitler's Nazi stormtroopers, stating: 'During the height of the Contra War, Oliver North's operation would turn to Merex to consummate a $2 million weapons deal, thus underlining the essential continuity of Nazi alliances in American agencies from Army Intelligence to the Office of Strategic Services to the CIA to Reagan's National Security Council.' Thus US aid in the form of security assistance programmes effectively operate within fragile Third World democracies, allowing the president or executive to modernize the police force and equip the armed forces in return for their support for the regime. Through its foreign policy the administration is able to interfere in the sovereignty of nations; for example, under President Clinton support came from Tactical Training Teams (TATS). Peter Zinrite (1998: 167) argues: 'The teams pull together intelligence from human and technical services to select targets and plan operations to be carried out by host nation military and police forces and the United States DEA agents.' In effect these TATS design prepared plans for the host countries' military or police personnel to execute, whereby the US military direct these counter-drug operations previously carried out by the host nations police and military. In certain Latin American countries reliance on American aid becomes integrated into parts of the state apparatus or is tolerated by the state for the purpose of social control and counter-insurgency and according to Christina Johns (1992) is productive to state terror and anti-democratic forces. John Pilger (1999)[16] argues that 'Violence is a constant, with more than 2,000 trade unionists assassinated and thousands disappeared and killed by drug-trafficking paramilitaries who ... are often indistinguishable from a military trained for civil repression – many in the US.' Here it would appear that the United States is content to allow drug enforcement to be used as a pretext, given that the result is to keep in power regimes which are sympathetic to American capital (Mokhiber and Weissman 1999).

American drug hegemony

American drug hegemony is a complex programme which fuses together foreign policy with the strategy of 'drug war politics', to serve US global political ambitions and expand economic interests. The American administration repeatedly justifies its military and political support to elites in some

Third World countries as serving the needs of international drug control policy, but it consistently refuses to accept the link between repression, violence, the military and drugs. Christina Johns (1992) maintains that the combination of US drugs policy and IMF austerity measures effectively consolidates the position of what she terms 'indigenous oligarchies'[17] in Latin America who profit from the relationship with western capitalism. The debt reduction package under the New International Economic Order is far from neutral. Its strategy is to foster market-orientated economics and strikingly resembles imperialist exploitation in that it singularly benefits western capitalism. Developing countries' debts to the west are enormous. For Naylor (1994: 13–14) the central question remains the nature of these loans and aid packages which US foreign policy makes conditional through supporting the IMF. The IMF and World Trade Organization only give loans on the basis of countries pursuing free market policies acceptable to the United States. Therefore developing countries are forced to sell their state industries to European or American companies. Here the accumulation of capital fails to benefit the people because land and wealth is concentrated amongst an elite which depends on the status quo and which acts to prevent social reforms.

Naomi Klein (2000) demonstrates that western capitalism manipulates market economies politically through the debt regime and furthermore that US drug policy imposes sanctions and restrictions on the export of certain crops or commodities. On this basis poor countries become unable to repay their debt through legitimate economic means (Akiba 1997: 610). Because of low wages and high unemployment, the majority of the population remain in poverty and are unable to produce and spend an income to consume commercial and manufactured commodities; so limiting the market for domestic industry. Therefore, an orchestrated fall in prices of various raw materials and commodities prevents poor countries from taking part in capital accumulation. Western capital accumulation has historically exploited the oppressed in that the west reaps all the benefits and distributes the cost to the Third World. The end result is that Third World countries experience failed economies which become transformed into drug economies. Drug production flourishes through trafficking and corruption, and drug crops replace an entire national economy in countries which in some cases have been destroyed by oppressive international debt.

Due to the desperate need for foreign exchange to pay off debt, and the lack of alternative means of repayment, Bertram et al. (1996: 16) argue that countries 'have created mechanisms to allow their financial systems to absorb as much foreign exchange from the drug industry as possible'. Naylor (1994: 178) argues that the drug economies have become so deeply entrenched that they constitute a parallel state with a parallel economy. A Peruvian central bank official states: 'Coca is our first export product. It is illegal, but it provides us with needed reserves. It helps the country's balance of payments ...

The problem with hot money is that these funds could leave in a second and the country would be without reserves.' The drug economies of various states employ hundreds of thousands of people and are linked to the government and military. Thus intervention to achieve drug prohibition would not only threaten the immediate viability of a country's economy, but would also directly threaten political and military leaders and result in massive unemployment problems[18] and political instability.[19]

For certain economies such as Colombia, Bolivia and Peru, it is estimated that over 70 per cent of real gross national product is drug related and in Colombia the drug Mafia owns 42 per cent of the best land[20] (Durlacher 2000). Drug traffickers are able to pay entire army brigades,[21] or offer to pay off their countries' debt with cash in exchange for immunity[22] (Bowden 2001). In Latin America the austerity of IMF policies fed the coca business, as unemployment increased and the decline of capital intensive industry encouraged a shift towards the informal economy. The IMF programme of economic reform saw a massive devaluation of the currency of Bolivia and Colombia. Petrol prices rose tenfold, exchange controls and subsides were abolished, wages were frozen, and public companies were abolished or privatized. In both Bolivia and Colombia the banking system officially went bankrupt under US policy and IMF programmes. Chien et al. state:

> As part of its IMF 'reform' of 1985, the Bolivian government introduced laws facilitating the movement of coca profits into the banking system. These laws enabled the buildup of foreign exchange, which consequently boosted the local currency and checked inflation. In Peru and Colombia, as well, official policy is that no questions are asked and indeed tax amnesty is granted on repatriated revenues.
>
> (Chien et al. 2000: 303)

The United States offers aid to regimes on the basis of their stand against communism and assistance in drug control policy, although military aid is always dominant over economic aid. Military aid to Third World countries brings some economic benefits but is used by the military, police and drug Mafia to keep at bay public opposition to social and political reforms. Where countries fail to deliver on either of these policies, the strategy is to stop aid. On this basis there is a direct connection between the national debt of poor countries and their narcotics policy (Del Olmo 1998: 277). Christina Johns (1992: 136) states: 'The United States pays lip service to democracy but has consistently sided with dominant military and economic elites who openly discourage or actively repress democratic expressions of mobilization and protest.' George Monbiot (2001a) specifies that United States training of terrorists at the 'School of America' (SOA) in Georgia has consistently produced efficient killers and has been named by Human Rights Watch[23] as providing training in torture and extra-judicial killing. Noam Chomsky (1994: 55–7) quotes from UN Special Rapporteur on executions, Amos Wako:

> There are currently over 140 paramilitary groups in Colombia today trained and financed by drug traffickers and possibly a few land-owners. They operate very closely with elements in the armed forces and the police. Most of the killings and massacres carried out by the paramilitary groups occur in areas which are heavily militarized where they are able to move easily and commit murders with im-punity.[24]

In Latin American the security forces which implement US drug strategy are easily corrupted at all levels of operation within the state due to the high profits available from drug production and the high degree of poverty within these military dictatorships (Campbell and Brenner 2000). Death squads and paramilitary organizations in Third World countries are notorious for carry-ing out human rights abuses, often with the assistance of the police and military. Through its foreign policy of a militarized drug strategy, the Amer-ican administration is interfering in the sovereignty of nations, supporting corrupt regimes at the expense of democracy and failing to achieve a decline in the production of drugs. The war on drugs translates into systematic re-pression, leading Chien et al. (2000: 305) to conclude: 'The US has tolerated, assisted, or protected the drug trade as a means to achieve other policy ob-jectives. At this level the fundamental objective is the promotion of US pri-vate sector interests, for which the War on Drugs abroad has served as a vehicle.'

Alonso Salazar (1990: 37), in his ethnographic study of drug cartels in Medellin, routinely describes examples of violence perpetrated by the death squads. For example, in Colombia[25] and Mexico[26] America's Watch and Amnesty International have produced evidence of high-level army officers being involved in atrocious acts carried out by private death squads and the sanctioning of counter-insurgency under the guise of drug enforcement. America's war on drugs has brought militarization of Third World law en-forcement, and raises the question of whether the US government is morally responsible for human rights violations. Martha Huggins (2000: 222) sees a close relationship between some Third World countries' acceptance of American aid in the form of IMF loans and agreement to support American capital as part of the expansionist ideology of accepting the market economy. She argues that the market conception of control leads to privatized forms of law enforcement 'because within the dynamic of a marketized exchange sys-tem among "free" participants who define their own interests irrespective of others' rights, "internal security" and policing are things that not only can be, but should be, bought and sold within a market.' For her the logic of the market-type solution leads to death squads for hire.

The Colombian armed forces kill at will and without mercy. Bruce Campbell and Arthur Brenner, using a range of evidence from human rights organizations, state: 'The Colombian government tolerated or encouraged the formation of some death squads so that it could continue to seek foreign aid and investment, especially from the United States' (2000: 315). They suggest that some death squads operate in partnership with the armed forces and paramilitary units, at the behest of the drug cartels, while others are composed of 'off-duty' police hired by multinational corporations to 'clean up' urban streets. Colombia is not a military state but the military can act at will and arrest anyone. This leads Knoester (1998: 98) to argue that: 'Unlike a military dictatorship, the Colombia military has power with no responsibility. Perhaps, this is the example and role model for how a democratic government should function to receive funding from Washington.' He elaborates further that Colombia's gross domestic product has grown steadily in the last 40 years and now Colombia is the fastest growing market for American goods, but at the same time the United states is also the largest investor in Colombia. American drug hegemony can promote the economic opening up of the Latin American countries to private American capital and serves US investors and indigenous elites who benefit from trade.

Drug prohibition policy and fascism

The rationality of drug prohibition has been part of American modernity which has sought to shape and influence nations on a global scale. Using scientific evidence and moral arguments, American drug hegemony supports a belief in American globalization. Fredric Jameson (2000: 51) argues that self-importance lies at the core of American internationalism in that the USA wants others to consider its interests as universal ones. E. P. Thompson (1985: 39–40) argues that 'Middle America believes that United States militarism is about the export of freedom'. For him America's 'hegemonic nationalism' operates on an expansionist basis disguising itself as a mission on behalf of humanity, under the pretence that America 'is the universal Future'. American drug prohibition policy has been consistently promoted as a popular principle of modern democratic morality and drug control laws established at the United Nations are defined as synonymous with advancement of modern civilization. Dissenting nations are accused of being undemocratic, morally undeveloped, socially devious and encouraging terrorism.[27] Leo Panitch (2000: 13–14) argues that the twenty-first century has ushered in a new imperial state where America seeks dominance through the twin operation of policies to bring about globalization, and increased intervention into rival states to affirm or intensify US imperialist interests. He sees the result as 'American capacity to manage the radical restructuring of global capitalism in forms that reproduced their imperial dominance'.

Thus it would be wrong to understand the American debacle in Vietnam, a series of presidential scandals and corruption, or the American inability to control Middle East countries as representing a decline in US global influence. Nicos Poulantzas (1975: 87) argued that 'American capital has no need to re-establish its hegemony for it has never lost it'. For Poulantzas, globalization has not brought the disappearance of national states, but has enabled American monopoly capitalism to expand inside nations. America's war on drugs needs to be seen as a continuation of neo-colonialism where America pursues its capital interests conducive to the free market and private investment. The drug war is an effective mask to subvert the sustained economic regeneration of Third World countries corrupted by debt and unable to co-ordinate economic nationalism because American aid has, according to Chien et al. (2000: 303), 'served above all as a tool for the pursuit of elite interests'. Latin American dictatorships are dependent on international capital, but at the same time neutralize threats to their power base through what Martha Huggins (1998: 118) identifies as 'an ideology linking national security to economic development'. For her the elites who run these bureaucratic authoritarian dictatorships 'are in part the product of the internationalizing of United States security through foreign policy assistance, with a particular mode of centralizing internal security characterized by authoritarianizing the state and social control'.

In *Fascism and Dictatorship* Poulantzas (1974) identifies the bourgeoisie as crucial to the rise and consolidation of fascism. In Latin America and some Asian countries[28] the US foreign policy of the 'drug war' and the consequent policies pursued by Third World governing elites conform to Poulantzas's argument that fascism involves the destruction of peasant land reform, the smashing of organizations belonging to the labour movement, and the privatization of public resources and security systems. Furthermore, American aid and US influenced organizations such as the World Bank, World Trade Organization and IMF contribute to the reorganization of hegemony within unstable Third World states through the sale of military resources to support the interests of American corporate capital (MacCoun and Reuter 2001). Poulantzas's assertion is that the growth of fascism is linked to the support of monopoly capital. For Gramsci (1971: 310), 'Americanism' is an intensifying form of economic exploitation and authoritarian cultural repression 'ingeniously combined with persuasion and consent'.

In the Third World where the military take power as a result of instability, the elites pursue policies favourable to corporate capital which may involve forms of protection for drug production and military action against opposition movements (Giraldo 1996; Monbiot 2001b). Drug cartels, the military and governing elites are preoccupied with what Poulantzas calls 'power fe-tishism' in their desire for public idolatry, pursuit of corporatism, obsession with the 'cult of the leader', anti-parliamentarianism and ruthless aggression through use of death squads. The drug lords are part of a successful petty bourgeoisie who enter into effective alliance with corporate capital, to the extent that drug lords have been positively willing to pay their country's international debt in return for amnesty (Bowden 2001). The creation of both a dual economy and the eventual integration of the formal economy with the informal economy sees drug cartels and governing elites functioning as equal partners, where the military and the police force are in collision within the state apparatus consolidating the fascist conquest of power.

This section has suggested that governing elites, drug lords and the military combine the duties of administration, police, judiciary and national security. Aijaz Ahmad (2000: 293) argues that the frequency and intensity of violence under fascist regimes is consolidated through the ruling elite's creation of 'a culture of cruelties'. The drug trade provides income for the state and employment for the people, but its corruption and reliance on American aid or 'hot money' creates an undemocratic basis for society where human rights have little value. Poulantzas's insight into the growth of fascism as a form of bureaucratic authoritarianism under repressive international debt, alongside intrusive American aid bolstering corporate interests, allows us to see the 'drug war' as a strategic US foreign policy which seeks to advance American hegemony, but also results in the diminution of democracy. The cover for US intervention into nation-states occurs through American reg-ulation of an international crisis which in turn promotes the United States as the last upholder of democracy (Huntingdon 1999).

Global prohibition

The United Nations 'Drug-Free Society'

The United Nations (UN) is concerned with resolution of international con-flict, enforcement of international accords and upholding human rights on a global basis. It also plays an important part in the development and im-plementation of international drug controls. David Bewley-Taylor (1999: 185) argues that the 'United States has effectively used the UN in an effort to create a prohibitive norm for international drug control and promote its own moral value system towards drug use in other nations'. The UN and World Health Organization (WHO) are two major institutions that have responsibility for international drug control and policy. These global organizations are assumed to be rational and efficient, to support the implementation of international laws judged to be scientific and based on consensus. The position of the UN and WHO is to enact prohibition to uphold international agreements and fight what is described as the 'war on drugs'. These two leading bureaucracies use their legitimacy to define the consumption of certain drugs as both illegal and harmful. For Bewley-Taylor (1999: 213), the key to understanding global drug prohibition is the powerful influence of America on the UN International Drug Control Programme. While the United States is often reluctant to keep up its payments to the UN, successive American presidents have given high priority to the UN's drug control functions. For example, in 1995 President Clinton warned that the United States would punish any state that declined to cooperate in drug prohibition.[29] As Elizabeth Joyce (1998: 183) states, the United States 'believes its methods of policing drug consumption and trafficking should serve as the models for the rest of the world'.

The UN and the WHO affirm the hegemony of American drug prevention. Where compliance is not achieved, US military General Rosenberger (1996: 29) states that 'militarization of the drug war is consistent with America's determination ... to eradicate the drug abuse menace'. Where domination of American drug policy has not been accomplished through agreement, it moves to coercion. Walker (1996: xxii) argues that the US government deployment of hegemonic drug control strategies contains 'many aspects of repression, coercion, and incorporation'. During the post-1945 period the UN and the WHO did not deviate from American drug control policy. According to Bewley-Taylor (1999: 85), the WHO and UN were heavily influenced by Harry Anslinger and 'fully endorsed the commissioner's ideas linking cannabis with crime and insanity'. Bewley-Taylor suggests that the WHO staunchly supported US prohibition and the American dominated UN drug control apparatus. The UN prohibition policy successfully labelled drugs, including cannabis, cocaine and opium, as not only dangerous for individuals but also morally harmful for the whole society. The power of American drug hegemony can be seen in the way that Anslinger's successful removal of cannabis from the America Pharmacopoeia was carried over into WHO policy. Aitken and Mikuriya state:

> The World Health Organization had committed itself in 1952 to the flat statement that 'there is no justification for the medical use of cannabis preparations'. In 1956 they recommended 'extension of the effort towards the abolition of cannabis from all legitimate medical practice' and in the same year were 'pleased to note the decision ... to place cannabis drugs ... together with heroin.
>
> (Aitken and Mikuriya 1980: 273)

Focusing on a series of policy interventions and high profile professional relationships, Bewley-Taylor (1999) argues that US drug policy was adopted at the WHO and UN and that these organizations routinely accepted pronouncements from the FBN and the CIA on drug prohibition. Rufus King (1972: 88) demonstrates the way that the US administration consolidated its anti-cannabis position at the UN in the late 1940s by 'vigorous US sponsorship'. The power, authority and legitimacy of such organizations in their apparent fight for democracy in the Cold War period remained unquestioned. The US domination of drug policy was achieved at the UN through the 1953 Opium Protocol, the 1961 Single Convention on Narcotics and the 1988 UN Convention against Illicit Traffic in Narcotic Drugs and Psychotropic Substances. Ann Dally (1995) argues that the WHO has been used as a scientific supplicant to confirm the UN position which is already predefined by American policy. Her argument is that these global organizations have not been impartial. Under the influence of American drug hegemony, the UN adopted anti-drug policies on an international basis which failed to recognize cultural difference and diversity within major areas of the world including South America, Asia and Africa. International drug control treaties depend on the existence of national legislation and sufficient resources to ensure enforcement. The United States is able to use its economic and political power as a lever on other nations by combining matters of drug control with financial assistance and military aid.[30] This allows the US military to have access to host nations or intervene in their affairs (McAllister 2000).

Drug prohibition, according to the United Nations and World Health Organization, rests on scientific evidence about the chemical nature of the drugs being regulated.[31] Jacques Derrida (1993: 2) challenges this scientific logic of prohibition, stating 'the concept of drugs is not scientific, but is rather instituted on the basis of moral and political evaluations'. Although Derrida agrees that, in general, institutions protect the law, society and citizens, this is achieved through a political intervention that obscures the real history of drugs and fallaciously brands drugs as a moral stigma.[32] Under the United Nations the prohibition message of a 'Drug-Free Society' has become a global approach to drug prevention. UN Drug Control Policy (1992) states that: 'Today, it is widely believed that a "Drug-Free Society", although far off, is nevertheless possible'. On 8 June 1998 the Secretary-General of the UN called on all nations to say yes to the challenge of working towards a drug-free world. The UNDCP and UNICEF update in December 2001 was entitled 'A Drug-Free Environment – A Child's Right'. The UN 'Drug-Free Society' policy forms the rationale to a range of organizations across different nations, such as 'Partnership for a Drug-Free America' and 'Kids in a Drug-Free Society' which advocates the notion of 'Drug-Free Zones' or promote 'Against Drugs' activities. In America, the Church of Scientology is a leading sponsor of efforts to create a 'Drug-Free USA', with its 'Drug-Free Marshals' who deliver drug education. The 'Drug-Free Society' can be described as a quasi-religious movement which seeks to convey the message that drugs will never be permitted to become an integral part of society. A key aim of the 'Drug-Free Society' movement is not merely to protect society, but to 'improve' society, often described in terms of a 'vision' (Barton 2003).

The UN 'Drug-Free Society' policy as a global approach to prohibition enables the USA to criticize other countries for their lack of commitment to drug free goals (Hartnoll 1998). Any nation which is seen as rejecting such a clear and apparently straightforward policy against drugs is condemned and publicly presented as immoral, criminal and a threat to the 'free world'. This criticism quickly turns to enforcement as nations are required to accept international drug policies. Countries which are reluctant to agree to American policy wholesale experience withdrawal of financial support from the World Bank, IMF and WHO (Green 1998). In the Third World binding agreements, threats or offers of support then become forms of leverage for the United States to intervene in nation-states under the guise of national security, military support and financial protection (McCoy 1991; Blum 1995; Gray 2002).

In countries where there is an unstable democracy or rule by the military, acceptance of the 'Drug-Free Society' policy is complex. Acceptance of the policy may be undertaken as a strategy to end internal conflict between warring factions who use drugs to fund their particular struggle. Here ordinary people actively support such developments as they see a 'Drug-Free Society' policy as a positive strategy towards freedom and increased safety. The 'Drug-Free Society' is then seen as a practical resolution to reduce the military involvement in guerrilla struggles and war. The 'Drug-Free Society' policy is about removing the centrality of the drug presence in unstable states. The intention is to control the military, to remove the heroin and cocaine drug barons. It is a macro drug policy primarily concerned with drug trafficking rather than individual drug use. In Third World countries which have a close integration of drugs with the formal economy and where leaders do not require support from the people, the 'Drug-Free Society' policy is merely a cosmetic exercise undertaken by leaders to ensure the continued flow of external revenue and to guarantee their own security. In the west the 'Drug-Free Society' policy is seen in different terms. It is identified as a threat to individual liberty, personal expression, freedom of action and choice, or, as libertarian Thomas Szasz (1996) argues, it opposes 'our right to drugs'. The 'Drug-Free Society' policy within the west is equally complex because here drug consumption is associated with the diverse meanings related to styles of youth and cultural consumption. This policy then becomes a means for the state to undertake surveillance of the individual and impose custodial sentences.

Conclusion

This chapter has looked at the relationship between drugs and democracy, focusing on the development and expansion of American 'drug war' policy. Historically, evidence suggests that America's anti-drug policies have been flexible to the administration's global political aspirations to fight the perceived threats of communist expansion and 'narco terrorism'. I have argued that drug war policy is not motivated purely by the desire to prevent human suffering caused by drug use, but that drug control policies are also about power and provide a means of finance for secret state intelligence services, right-wing military dictatorships and death squads. The chapter sheds light on the connections between the CIA, US militarization of the 'drug war', American foreign policy interventions and the UN 'Drug-Free Society' policy which serves as a proxy for entry into other states on the basis of providing financial aid for security, subject to allowing American corporate industry to operate.

3 Drugs as cultural commodities

An analysis of drugs in film, advertisements and popular music

This chapter looks at the way in which drugs are a regular part of commodity consumption. Drugs routinely appear in Hollywood films and are the subject of popular songs in the charts. At the same time drug imagery and drug symbolism is used to sell ordinary products from soft drinks and soft fruit to cars, trainers and computer hardware. Within consumer capitalism diverse drug references play a dynamic part in the marketing of commodities for profit. Major corporate and small private companies exploit these drug connotations as part of their marketing strategy to attract customers, especially when promoting these products as part of young people's leisure and lifestyle. The use of drug images by legitimate business as part of their global advertising creates a contradiction because at the same time these substances are prohibited by law, and their possession is an offence deemed serious enough to draw a custodial sentence. Government, as one branch of the state, gives out a singular message of drug prohibition, but in free market capitalism we find a range of drug representations employed by entrepreneurs to capture a market. The drugs economy remains illegal but its commercial cultural support systems are highly profitable and legitimate. Representations of drugs are not restricted to exploitation films, minority music interests or marginal quirky commodities: drugs are mainstream. This chapter examines the extent to which drugs have become an everyday aspect of consumer culture and choice. I shall look first at the position of drugs within the medium of the cinema, and second at the use of drug imagery by the advertising industry. Finally I shall explore the representation of drugs within popular music.

Drugs in cinema

Drug scandals and the age of the silent film

Drugs were a familiar factor in the early days of cinema, in the development of the silent movie. The portrayal of drugs in these silent films was diverse and exploitative as the film makers struggled with the new medium to capture the public imagination and the public's money. During the 1890s the first silent pictures were viewed on kinetoscopes, most often in amusement arcades, and were about half a minute in length. The first drug film, *The Chinese Opium Den*, was made by W. K. Laurie Dickson for the famous Thomas Edison company in 1894. Most early drug movies focused on non-white people using drugs (De Grazia and Newman 1982).

From the 1900s to the late 1920s silent films progressed from depicting opium smoking to heroin and cocaine injection. During this time the modern stereotypical narrative of drug use was framed, and it proved popular amongst audiences who demanded excitement from the new screen. The drug narratives were simple and outcomes predictable. The storyline reflected the discriminatory cultural values dominant at the time. The portrayal was highly racist; addiction led to moral and sexual corruption for young women, financial poverty and ruination for young men. The drug plots defined young people as 'drug victims', where drug use leads to hallucinations, violence, heroin use and then murder. By the 1920s there were set character types such as the drug fiend and drug addict who used intoxicants to control people's minds or achieve personality transformation. Subsequently prostitution, suicide, crime, Satanism and murder became long-running drug themes for the film industry.[1]

In America and across Europe such drug narratives were endlessly repeated in the multifarious films featuring Dr Fu Manchu, Sherlock Holmes and Dr Jekyll and Mr Hyde. Early silent film actors who performed the role of drug users were often highly acclaimed; for example, Lon Chaney,[2] who is known for his characterization and specialist make-up in such famous Hollywood epics as *The Hunchback of Notre Dame* and *The Phantom of the Opera*. He devised imaginative make-up, portraying himself as an opium-smoking Chinese man in the drug films *Bits of a Life* (1921), *Outside the Law* (1921) and *Shadows* (1922). The silver screen held people in a trance before the powerful evil of drugs, where the ultimate narrative of terror was realized: a deranged man could kill a child, force his wife into a brothel and mastermind a heinous criminal empire. The storyline of drug terror was a circular narrative; it captured the imagination of customers and seductively 'forced' them to pay for the limitless fantasy of cinematic drug horror. The end result was that cinemas were full and Hollywood's reputation for exciting entertainment soared as drug representations became a strategic capital investment in the film industry. Punters regularly returned to the safety of their cinema seat for more trepidation.

Drug use in films during the 1920s was not restricted to the melodrama, thriller or horror genres. Both opium and cocaine were also the subject of comedy in American and British films.[3] One of the first cocaine comedies to set the scene was *The Mystery of the Leaping Fish* (1916), featuring the detective Coke Ennyday, who uses cocaine and opium to fight a gang of drug-dealing foreigners. Douglas Fairbanks Senior plays Coke Ennyday, who is always completely high or in need of a high in order to capture villains in his outrageous chequerboard suit and his chequerboard painted car. The following year *Easy Street* provided Charlie Chaplin with the opportunity to momentarily explore drug comedy when he is pushed onto a needle and the surrounding gang of criminal addicts are then subject to his reincarnation as a super boxing champion. In 1922 the magazine *Vanity Fair* published an article called 'Happy Days in Hollywood' stating:

> Last week little Lulu Lenore of the Cuckoo Comedy Co. gave a small house dance for the younger addicts. 'Will you come to my "Snow"-ball?' read the clever invitations. In one corner of the living room was a miniature 'Drug-store', where Otho Everard kept the company in a roar as he dispensed packages of cocaine, morphine and heroin. The guests at their departure received exquisite hypodermic needles in vanity boxes which have caused many heart-burnings among those who were not invited.
>
> (Starks 1982: 46)

Michael Starks (1982) in his study of drugs in the movies describes how during the early 1920s drug consumption in films began to reflect drug usage amongst the Hollywood film stars. Drug consumption in Hollywood remained secret behind studios' or stars' doors until a series of scandals occurred. Rumours and stories of 'snow' or cocaine parties were a common feature amongst the Hollywood elite and extras who took a 'sleigh ride'.

During the 1920s three drug scandals occurred which resulted in pressure for increased censorship as a result of sustained coverage from the US tabloid newspapers. The first disgrace occurred in 1921 with Roscoe 'Fatty' Arbuckle, one of the Keystone Kops,[4] who was involved in the death of a young woman called Virginia Rappe after a sex and alcohol party during prohibition. Arbuckle was charged with manslaughter but after three trials was acquitted. The second scandal was the unresolved murder of the film director William Desmond Taylor in 1922. The director's lust for drugs and sexual pleasure is noted by Kenneth Anger (1975: 39–40), who speaks of Taylor's life in 'L.A. and Hollywood dens where strange effeminate men and peculiarly masculine women dressed in kimonos sat in circles, where guests were served marijuana, opium and morphine, the drugs were wheeled in on tea carts'. The third scandal for Hollywood was the drug-related death of the silent film idol Wallace Reid, a Paramount Pictures star, who appeared in a series of classic Hollywood silent films.[5] The American public was shocked at the death of their 'clean' true American hero who had everything but lost it all. The tabloid press exploited the potential of Reid's drug death, reporting 'Wally Reid's Mother Begs Mr Hearst to Declare War on Drug Menace' (Silver and Aldrich [1923] 1979: 152). His mother launched her moral crusade with an illustrated book on his life, while his wife now called herself Mrs Wallace Reid[6] and set up her anti-narcotic campaign across America with the film *Human Wreckage* (1923). Made by the Ince Corporation, this was the first in a series of anti-drug exploitation films. The financial purpose of these Hollywood productions was to capitalize on people's fear through their sympathy and their bewilderment at losing a loved icon. These anti-drug films were promoted as educational, but were little more than propaganda and fantasy which lingered on voyeuristic salaciousness.

Fast living continued amongst the Hollywood elite and drug deaths began to increase. Olive Thomas, who took part in the 'Ziegfeld Follies', and starred in the film *The Flapper* (1920), died of heroin aged 21 in 1922. Dixie Dixon died in the same year and Barbara La Marr overdosed in 1926. Mabel Normand, previously known for her love of 'cokey', died in 1930. By the mid-1920s a range of actresses such as Alma Reubens, Mary Nolan, Birdie Green, Paulette La Fargue, May Hoffman, Minnie Leder and Lilian Miller had been arrested for possession of cocaine or heroin (Anger 1975; Starks 1982). The newspaper empire of William Randolph Hearst used these drug scandals and deaths alongside coverage of sexual decadence within Hollywood to sell papers. The 'yellow' tabloid papers suggested that surveillance of Hollywood stars was a moral cause, but this was a thin disguise to increase circulation rather than to clean up the film industry. In reality there was no deep-seated morality to Hearst or his newspaper empire; newspaper editors found that voyeuristic coverage of stars and their exploits commanded huge public interest and thus profit. With over 40 million Americans attending cinemas during the 1920s, Hearst identified Hollywood stars as a direct source of income. The tabloid papers printed special supplements and doctored photographs. Hearst had close connections with Hollywood – his mistress was the actress Marion Davies – but he seemed oblivious to his own hypocrisy.

Censorship and the anti-drug movie

Hollywood introduced its own moral overseer in the person of Will Hays, a republican politician and Presbyterian elder who was the head of the Motion Picture Producers and Distributors of America from 1922 to 1945. He introduced the Motion Picture Production Code (MPPC) in 1930, although it was not enforced until 1934. In essence, Hays's role was a modern public relations exercise and as a national figure he presented the public image of censorship and encouraged the film industry towards self-regulation. Although he was a member of moral pressure groups including the Masons, the Knights of Pythias, the Kiwanians, the Rotarians, the Loyal Order of the Moose and the Elks, Kenneth Anger (1975: 43–6) states that 'Shifty' Hays had been called to a Senate committee on three occasions for charges of political corruption.

In collaboration with studio moguls, Hays compiled Hollywood's 'Doom

Book', which contained the names of 117 Hollywood figures connected with decadence: he was also known as 'czar of all the rushes'. In the 1930s the MPPC lacked enforcement, but this changed under the influence of the Legion of Decency, a Catholic pressure group, which called for censorship. From 1934 to 1967 this conservative group of American Catholic bishops was backed by the Pope. The director of the Production Code Administration (PCA) was Joe Breen in Hollywood, while Will Hays's office was in New York. Breen was a major figure of authority who implemented the code, and who later took over Hays's office as the MPPC's enforcer until 1968. Breen's long tenure in charge of censorship can be described as allowing a religious minority to impose a cultural straitjacket on film (Miller 1994, Shapiro 2003).

Hays and Harry J. Anslinger were two key institutional figures of drug censorship within the American film industry. They did not create the anti-drug film genre, because anti-narcotic films had been made at the very start of the motion picture industry. Their authority to impose censorship was gradual and drug themes remained a minor feature of some important silent films such as Rudolph Valentino's *Son of the Sheik* (1926), where we see cannabis being used by hookah smokers. Cannabis use was also the dominant theme of other films such as *Notch Number One* (1924) and *High on the Range* (1929); both these silent westerns focus on betrayal and murder linked to marijuana use. A powerful anti-drug propaganda film was *The Pace That Kills* (1928). It followed in the footsteps of *Human Wreckage*, where drugs are shown as leading young people into corruption, prostitution, sexual immorality and death. The real impact of Hays and Anslinger on drug censorship is not only in their support for anti-drug propaganda films but also their regulatory influence, which brought a periodic decline in the focus on drug consumption within the film industry. The two important early anti-drug propaganda films were *Marijuana – Weed with Roots in Hell* and *Reefer Madness* (both 1936). They were inspired by Anslinger, who provided the title for a third anti-marijuana film, *Assassin of Youth* (1935). In all three films sexual inhibitions are shown to be lost as a result of drug consumption, where young people are driven wild and commit murder.

The 1930s saw Hollywood's successful transition from silent to sound movies. This was accompanied by an increase in censorship and regulation, although the horror genre retained strong elements of drug use as a means to induce fear. The horror king Boris Karloff played in a series of films portraying the effects of drug consumption including *The Mad Genius* (1931), where a 'dope fiend' steals the insane ballet master's drug stash. Karloff also stars as the monster in the classic version of *Frankenstein* in 1931, where he craves and requires sedation through drug injection. *The Mask of Fu Manchu* (1932) shows him as the evil doctor, located in the headquarters of his drug empire. Meanwhile, *Dracula* star Bela Lugosi not only played drug addicts on screen but consumed large amounts of drugs himself and was admitted to Los Angeles

General Hospital to cure his morphine addiction. In *White Zombie* (1932) and *Night of Terror* (1933), and also in the later *Ape Man* (1943), we see dramatic plots where drug injections are conducted to achieve power and authority over others.

Two leading anti-drug propaganda films more directly supported by Hays and Anslinger were *Cocaine Fiends* (1939) and *To the Ends of the Earth* (1948). The former was a sound film remake of the silent film *The Pace That Kills* (1928). The latter, with its focus on an evil foreign drugs empire, was the first Hollywood film permitted to tackle heroin since the establishment of censorship and the Federal Bureau of Narcotics' (FBN) interest in the entertainment business. A further three melodramatic drug films were permitted by the bureau the following year: *Slattery's Hurricane*, starring Richard Widmark, *Johnny Stool Pigeon*, and *Port of New York*, which starred Yul Brynner in his film debut as the head of a drug-smuggling gang. During the 1950s respected directors and actors began to portray drugs, including Orson Welles's *Mr Arkadin* (retitled *Confidential Report*) (1955) and *Touch of Evil* (1958), and Otto Preminger's *The Man with the Golden Arm* (1955) and *Sweet Bird of Youth* (1962), the latter starring Paul Newman. The impact of the MPPC and the Federal Bureau of Narcotics (FBN) was considerable. Cocaine received little attention from the film industry from 1939 until the early 1970s with the groundbreaking *Superfly* (1972), which portrayed the cocaine dealer as hero, although the soundtrack by Curtis Mayfield is replete with anti-drug songs.

The late 1940s and early 1950s were changing times for Hollywood and censorship. Hays resigned in 1945, although he remained an associate advisor when the MPPC in 1952 was granted free speech under the First Amendment (Miller 1994).[7] Three major developments in the relationship between drugs and films took place during this period. First, there was the imprisonment of Robert Mitchum for cannabis possession along with actress Lila Leeds in 1948. The only film role available for her after imprisonment was *Wild Weed* (1949), also known as *The Devil's Weed* and *She Shoulda Said No*. The film portrays the negative side of cannabis and represents her public redemption against the intoxicant. Mitchum received a 60-day custodial sentence and two years' probation. He used cannabis for the first time in 1936 and had been an occasional user since 1945 (Starks 1982: 129). At the time Mitchum told the press with characteristic wit and cynicism that his Hollywood career was at an end, he was a 'former actor'. The drug scandal did not end his career, however; it enhanced his rebel status, consolidating his image as subversive and his popularity soared with film producers, directors and audiences for his reputation of being cool.[8] His strong presence and critical persona were a dramatic contrast to Anslinger's drug propaganda of marijuana as the 'murderous evil weed' which led to insanity and death.

Second, in 1955 Preminger made the film *The Man with the Golden Arm*, starring Frank Sinatra as the card-playing heroin user Frankie Machine.

The film did not receive the MPPC seal of approval and certain states in the USA, such as Maryland, tried to ban or censor it. Edward de Grazia and Roger Newman (1982: 91) note that Preminger critically attacked the PCA system, referring to it as the 'private club of the major studios'. Richard Randall (1968: 209) says that *The Man with the Golden Arm* had a highly profitable run and 'shattered the then prevailing belief that a costly major production was financially doomed without the seal'. The code was subsequently revised in the same year. Hollywood's cartel and the PCA stranglehold on the film industry were also challenged by the 'Road Show Movie' system, which showed to millions non-seal approved films including anti-drug propaganda films with 'guaranteed' shock realism (Miller 1994; Jaworzyn 1996).

Third, unlike Mitchum, his fellow international Hollywood superstar Errol Flynn was never convicted for drug use or faced the crisis of having to deal with a drug reputation. Flynn's autobiography *My Wicked, Wicked Ways* (1960) was published a year after his death. In it Flynn describes his drug experiences with cannabis and opium. Ever the hero on screen or in print, he suggests he conquered his drug habits and addictions and returned more powerfully to the stage. Flynn had a dangerous reputation even amongst the highest studio moguls such as Jack Warner. No aspect of his drug experience while a working studio actor was revealed to the public, but by including these drug adventures he knew his image would fit the changing 1960s.

Drugs, sex and morality

From the birth of the film industry the portrayal of sex and drugs captured people's attention and considerable profit was made by Hollywood from screening visions of vice and immorality. Before censorship the film industry did little to control movie content; the only criterion to guide the regulation of material shown was popularity. Sex and drugs were brought together through two simple narratives. There were 'bad' females shown as prostitutes, who were 'wicked women' enslaved by drugs, and there were young innocent 'good girls', who were always white and virginal, seduced by the allure of drugs. For film makers drug taking was used as a means to create and sustain more profound social anxieties. The pairing of sex and drugs enabled the press and the film industry to feed masculine insecurity while promoting male voyeurism as a basis to make capital. The newspapers set the pace and Hollywood was quick to follow, creating epics with titles drawn from sensational news reporting, for example *The White Slave Trade* (1910), *White Slave Traffic* (1913) and *The Girl Who Didn't Care* (1916). There were many 'white slave trade' films made depicting white men's sexual fear of males from different ethnic groups, who were portrayed as debilitating the purity of the white race (Kohn 1992: 31).

Michael Starks (1982: 155) argues that after the introduction of censorship in the 1920s and 1930s, nudity first became common in anti-drug propaganda films such as *Marijuana – Weed with Roots in Hell, The Pace That Kills* and *Devil's Harvest*. These exploitation movies used provocative posters with warnings and enticements, sexualized language and pictures of partly dressed women (Jaworzyn 1996). On the route to this drug fantasy of sex, madness and murder, degrees of naked female flesh were presented. Here drugs were the lead narrative and sex had only a bit part. In contrast, by the late 1960s drugs had become a central and predictable element in the making of cheap pornographic films, which showed considerable similarity with the pre-censorship Hollywood films, for example *White Slaves of Chinatown* (1964) or *The Cycle Savages* (1969), where the plot showed women being drugged, raped and forced into prostitution either by violence or by being sedated. Historically the drug–sex narrative is primarily a masculinist device for the voyeuristic consumption of women as sexual objects, where a group of men are shown to exercise total power and control over women who are presented as 'being serviced'. Initially these powerful males were portrayed as the evil Oriental master, then the gangster or drug smuggler. Later they were represented as members of motorcycle gangs and more recently they have been rock bands and hip hop artists (Cashmore 2003).[9]

Pornographic films of the late 1960s and early 1970s such as *Spiked Heels and Black Nylons* (1967), *I Feel It Coming* (1969), *Groupie Girl* (1970) and *Chain Gang Women* (1972) were largely dependent upon drugs as a predictable narrative device which transformed the woman's personality as a prelude to exploitation and manipulation. Drugs were the tool which made the female body sexually available for male heterosexual consumption. Even *Emmanuelle* (1974), the highly successful pornographic film which crossed over into the mainstream, retains a strong drug and sexual reference because the lead character was raped in an opium den. But with the development of the modern pornographic film from the 1970s onwards, for example, *Deep Throat* (1972) and *The Devil in Miss Jones* (1973), drugs were no longer required as a plot or theme because the contemporary pornographic industry focused solely on sex. Pornography of the 1970s broke the link between sex and drugs, leaving intoxicants as featuring only incidentally in films. By the 1980s drugs were irrelevant to the storyline in pornographic films, except for specialist film makers such as Hisayusu Sato with *The Bedroom* (1992) and *Naked Blood* (1996).

Drugs and comedy

The decline in importance of drug intoxication in pornography can be contrasted with the expansion of drug experiences as an element of comedy within the mainstream film industry. Throughout the movie industry drugs have been used as a device or technique in the production of humour.

Under different regimes of censorship, drugs and comedy have taken different forms. In the pre-censorship days of the early 'cocaine comedies' of Douglas Fairbanks, Mabel Normand and Alma Reubens, drug taking and drug experiences are used as a rather blunt device to cause hilarity. In other silent films such as Charlie Chaplin's *Modern Times* (1936) we have a more sophisticated presentation of drug humour, where drugs are employed to create laughter through characterization and imagination. In *Modern Times* we see Chaplin play a convict in the scene called 'The Search for the Nose Powder': he sniffs it, sprinkles it on his food and puts it on his moustache. Notably humorous, it shows him under the spell of cocaine, light hearted, buoyant, offering us a tiny twirl dance with immaculate timing (Shapiro 2002). Another comedy classic was *International House* (1933), which included opium smoking set in a Chinese hotel and Cab Calloway's performance of the marijuana song 'Reefer Man'.

Each illicit drug has been used in the contextual development of comedy. With the arrival of LSD another style of drug humour emerged. The first LSD film was predictably within the horror genre, *The Tingler* (1959), starring Vincent Price, which replicated the CIA's anti-LSD propaganda where monsters are created within the nervous system of human beings. In contrast, an early comedy thriller was *Caprice* (1967), starring Doris Day and Richard Harris. Michael Starks (1982: 155) points out that although LSD is not mentioned in the film it is clearly a humorous take on the Sandoz pharmaceutical company in Basle, where Dr Albert Hofmann synthesized LSD-25 in 1938. There followed a series of LSD comedies which brought critical depth to the genre, including Otto Preminger's *Skidoo* (1968) and Hy Averback's *I Love You, Alice B. Toklas* (also 1968), starring Peter Sellers, which contrasted the lifestyles of hippies and 'straights'. In both comedies it would be possible to suggest that drug consumption is represented more sympathetically. In contrast to Preminger's and Averback's humorous films which also posed critical questions about the dominant values in society, Russ Meyer reasserted the power of the exploitation film with *Beyond the Valley of the Dolls* (1970) conforming to the deterministic drug narrative of a sex and drugs orgy resulting in murder.

LSD plays a key part in the narrative of *The Heist* (1972), starring Warren Beatty and Goldie Hawn: after a chase the villains catch up with the couple and their escape is achieved only when their captor celebrates with a drink from a bottle of champagne filled with LSD. Afterwards we see Hawn holding the champagne bottle and wearing a fantastically ridiculous grin. Woody Allen has also used drug humour effectively to support his films: for example in *Play It Again Sam* (1972) he delivers the stoned experience whilst in *Annie Hall* (1975) he inappropriately sneezes after snorting cocaine and blows the powder all over the room and guests. Allen is dealing with irony and his drug buffoonery is clearly related back to the early cocaine comedies with Douglas Fairbanks, where absurdity is in abundance.

The comedy genre brings a different understanding of drug experiences to the film audience. Whilst drugs and sex have been a core ingredient for the 'exploitation' movie, drug humour also features in children's films, cartoons and Oscar-winning films. Drugs have now become a major resource within the film industry and could be identified as part of the norm in narrative. Drugs humour within movies takes a number of forms; for example, the casual or everyday consumption of drugs is presented at a ridiculous level in Cheech and Chong's *Up in Smoke* (1978). This film is recognized as their classic marijuana comedy. Here the presentation of reality is the drugs reality, where consciousness is determined through cannabis consumption, but as a comedy it conforms to the traditional markers of the genre where fun takes priority over storyline. Another form of drug humour is perceptual, where the viewer becomes a participant in the drug experience and is placed in the position of seeing what the drug user sees. This technique is not only associated with humour, but is also used to invoke fear and horror to unsettle the viewer. This is a common creative element in many films which use either 'spacey' visuals or surrealistic imaginings. Two contrasting examples are *The Bear* (1990) and *Trainspotting* (1995). In Jean-Jacques Annaud's superb film *The Bear*, the bear cub eats hallucinogenic mushrooms and the consequence is that we see the fuzzy and distorted world of an acid trip. The other example derives from *Trainspotting*, where the character Renton climbs into a toilet and surrealistically enters a hidden watery world. He swims majestically in his search for dope and returns to the surface of the worst toilet in Scotland. The scene is remarkable, comic and strange, but it conforms with Hayter's (1988) thesis on opiate consciousness and underwater visions.

By the 1970s Hollywood began successfully to exploit the potential of drug humour with the consequence that laughter overturned the drug fiend. The use of different comedy genres to present drug experiences has resulted in an increased visibility of drug representations in films which do not necessarily have a negative outcome. The use of humour in drug portrayals brings absurdity into ordinary and everyday reality. We laugh at or with the character as we view their situation, which can be ridiculously dangerous or outrageously funny. In these circumstances drug representations have moved from narrow anti-drug propaganda portrayals to a wider field of connotations.

Drugs in children's films

Children's films often contain comedy and drama which reveal a creative range of drug representations; classic examples might be the Mickey Mouse films, *Peter Pan, Alice in Wonderland* and *The Wizard of Oz*. In the film *Mickey's Garden* (1935) a bug spray enables Mickey to achieve a remarkable psychedelic journey. In his effort to control the insects in his garden he accidentally sprays himself as a result of Pluto bumping into him. Mickey is transcended into an altered state where in this different reality there are now giant bugs and plants in his garden. In a near De Quincey opium nightmare the cartoon hero awakes to find himself wrestling with a wriggling hose pipe. In the late 1930s Judy Garland[10] starred in *The Wizard of Oz* (1939), in which Dorothy and her companions pass out in a field of poppies; when they wake up they behold a beautiful emerald city. In *Alice in Wonderland* (1972), a musical fantasy, we see the humorous and strange movements of the caterpillar who smokes a hookah and Alice's own experience of weird psychedelic dreams as a result of eating mushrooms. In the film *Hook* (1991) by Steven Spielberg, a sequel to *Peter Pan*, we see a world ruled by imagination; where fairy dust is used by Peter Pan to fly due to the happiness of his thoughts.

The film director George Lucas changed children's films overnight with his first *Star Wars* trilogy in the late 1970s and early 1980s. Lucas developed some of his sounds, ideas and voices in his first film *THX 1138* (1970), which even provided the title of his special effects system. It starred Robert Duvall and Donald Pleasence in a futuristic drug-oriented society where there is continuous mandatory use of psychochemicals for compulsory happiness.

Two films which investigated the borderline between childhood and youth are *Christiane F.* (1981) and *Kids* (1995). Both were regarded as controversial, with their documentary style emphasizing the dangerous realism of urban life. The narrative of *Christiane F.* is an autobiographical account of a 13-year-old girl in Berlin who drifts into heroin addiction and prostitution. A major selling point in the film is the music of David Bowie, the connection being that Christiane is a fan and therefore speaking to millions of similar young people. Stephanie Watson (2000: 166) argues that '*Christiane F.* wants its youthful audience to identify with Christiane's suffering and take a lesson from it, not view drug addiction as a cool and colourful lifestyle'. There is some degree of glamorization in that Christiane is a beautiful young woman who is seen naked and lives her lifestyle to the personal accompaniment of a David Bowie soundtrack. This representation was later taken up by the fashion industry through the style of 'heroin chic' during the 1990s. With her first-person narrative set in a cold and bleak tomblike Berlin, Christiane's decline is personal and dark, yet it succeeds without being too voyeuristic.

In contrast, *Kids*, Larry Clark's film about teenage 'cool culture', is heavily stylized in its luring preoccupation of male minors engaging in sexual exploitation of girls against a backdrop of taking soft drugs. Although not quite child pornography, *Kids* has a disturbing fascination with the powerful over the weak, for superficiality rather than with substance. Ben Felsenburg (2000: 253) states that with *Kids*: 'The sense of vérité may be intended to give the audience a feel of what it is to inhabit the characters' lives, but there is a danger that in the end we learn more about our own voyeurism.' Each film aims to 'tell it like it really is' and uses the genre of realism as a form of legitimacy but both films conform to the 'exploitation' genre in their pre-occupation with nudity, sexual activity, drug use and violence. Conservatism is a powerful thread throughout the films as we see young teenagers who engage in underage sex fall into a disturbing and violent low-life culture where they consume drugs, which intensifies their personal self-destruction. From *Reefer Madness* (1936) to *Traffic* (2001) the drugs–sex exploitation movie has hidden under the banner of education and information as a means to offer taboo subjects but deliver a simple message: 'Don't do it or you'll end up like this.'

Although not necessarily designated as a children's film, the Beatles' animated musical fantasy *Yellow Submarine* (1968) contains a range of Beatles songs with drug references. Michael Starks (1982: 153) claims: 'It seems reasonable to regard this film as the first really enduring cinematic monument to LSD.' The Beatles are drafted in to save Pepperland, a musical paradise, from territorial invasion by the Blue Meanies, who dislike music. In the film you enter a magical world via the submarine, which takes you on a journey or in drug language takes you on a trip. The film consists of the trip itself and the many varied experiences undertaken on the journey. The film also coincides with The Beatles' experiences of LSD, which emerged in some of their psychedelic influenced songs, for example, 'Tomorrow Never Knows', 'Lucy in the Sky with Diamonds', 'A Day in the Life' and 'It's All Too Much'. *Yellow Submarine* has been emulated explicitly and implicitly by a whole range of contemporary cartoons, such as *South Park*[11] and *The Simpsons*. The Hollywood film production of *Scooby-Doo* (2002) from the 1970s Hanna-Barbera cartoon series, whilst not containing drugs, has defining drug features. The film follows the same format with the four teenagers, including Shaggy with goatee beard and hippie-grunge appearance, their old-style van the 'Mystery Machine', and the dog, Scooby-Doo, who eats 'Scooby Snacks' and permanently has 'the munchies'. The film shows a new conservative Hollywood morality, but still retains some marijuana jokes and the reggae song 'Pass the Dutchie' on the soundtrack. Whilst *Scooby-Doo* seeks to be clean, it is unable to cut itself free from the stereotypical drug context from which it emerged without losing its originality and sense of fun.

These representations of drug experiences within children's films have centred on humour. They do not show the process, paraphernalia or preparation for taking drugs – children's films concentrate on the consequence of intoxication through the use of spacey visuals, wit, slapstick and imaginative visions. From the examples discussed it is possible to argue that drug representations have consistently been a presence within children's cinema. The appearance of these diverse drug images is important to consider because they put forward a positive and visually expressive form of imagination integrally related to drug consumption. Drug representations in children's films primarily follow a comedy narrative. They do not promote encouragement of actual drug use. Drugs engage with children's fantasies and are experienced within the context of dreams and visions.

'New Hollywood': assessing the new casualization of drug use

'New Hollywood' first emerged in the film *Bonnie and Clyde* (1967), but it was only fully explored and exploded in *Easy Rider* (1969) due to its contemporary drug iconography and rock music soundtrack, which were integral to the narrative. New Hollywood claimed its legitimacy from what is known as auteur theory: directors transcend traditional artistic barriers to assert their own cultural significance as artists to produce not popular movies but art products (Salt 1992). Biskind (1998) argues that the sex, drugs and rock 'n' roll generation saved Hollywood and placed intoxicants at the centre of contemporary film production from the late 1960s onwards.[12] The new film makers and actors wanted to challenge not just the audience but the Hollywood old guard.[13] Two film makers who made an important contribution to the authentic aspects of auteur theory and to the status of drug representations in films are Jean Cocteau, with *Blood of a Poet* (1930) and *The Testament of Orpheus* (1959) and Andy Warhol, with *Poor Little Rich Girl* (1965), *Chelsea Girl* (1966) and *Trash* (1970). Cocteau saw drugs as an inspiration although secondary to the creative mind, whereas drug portrayals in Warhol's films are an integral part of his belief that excitement is sustained by lack of realization. Drug use causes events to be not realized and time stands still.

Easy Rider is located in the wider context of a youth counterculture. It reflects on the bigotry and corruption of American culture, where freedom can only be found temporarily in drugs and ultimately through death. Three drugs are central to the narrative of *Easy Rider*: cocaine, LSD and cannabis. Written, directed and acted by Peter Fonda and Dennis Hopper and also starring Jack Nicholson, all three were heavily connected with drugs. Furthermore, drug representations are presented on the soundtrack, for example, Steppenwolf's 'The Pusher' and Fraternity of Man's 'Don't Bogart Me'. In the recent anniversary release of the film on DVD there are interviews with the cast demonstrating that some of the dialogue and interactions in the film were improvised and derived from casual use of drugs (Colley 2000). *Easy Rider* was an international box office success, winning a series of awards,[14] and is closely linked to the previous work of Fonda and Hopper such as *The Wild Angels* (1966) and *The Trip* (1967). These films brought forward a challenging array of visual, aural and emotional forms of drug representations which have strongly influenced film directors including Oliver Stone (*Midnight Express, The Doors, Natural Born Killers*), George Lucas (*American Graffiti, Star Wars*) and Francis Ford Coppola (*The Godfather, Apocalypse Now*). *Easy Rider* has been criticized for encouraging drug use, yet in the film the characters go through a whole range of negative experiences as a result of taking cannabis, LSD and cocaine. The representations of youth culture and drug use in the film are its strongest legacy for subsequent films. *Easy Rider* represents a symbol of a generation betrayed, which accounts for its popularity with successive generations of young people.

Drugs as serious social and comedic representation

The real impact of New Hollywood's drug casualization and drug humour was that it became possible to employ drug use and drug representation in a multitude of forms and complex narratives and no longer be dependent on predictability. Dennis Grady (1993: 52) identifies certain films of the 1980s as promoting a more positive representation of drugs; these include *Nine to Five* (1980), *Romancing the Stone* (1984), *Desperately Seeking Susan* (1985) and *The Breakfast Club* (1985). He maintains that the films employ humorous marijuana scenes which result in sensitive personal disclosure, creating and reinforcing bonds of solidarity amongst different groups of people. While drug consumption in these films may be conventionally employed to generate absurdity and light-hearted moments, it also acts as a form of agency whereby characters undergo liberating experiences. Grady's argument is that drug use advances the narrative in each film through positive developments in people's lives. Characters improve their awareness and are able to break down personal barriers through showing greater sensitivity, which allows for more personal confidence to emerge. Importantly, it is the use of comedy within the context of drug consumption that allows the narrative to advance the characters beyond stereotypes and enter the everyday world of human experience.

American Vietnam War films such as *Apocalypse Now* (1979) and *Platoon* (1986) show drug use as camaraderie or for humorous moments, but their real disturbing impact is the manner in which drugs are laced into the wider political narrative of the American government losing control of its military campaign. The macro story of the White House's failure to win the war is played out at the micro level where we see soldiers abandoned in bleak contexts who are themselves lost with only drugs to feed their isolated existence. In these Vietnam War films we see explicit portrayal of cannabis, heroin and LSD use; Dennis Grady (1993: 58) argues that these movies are 'granted what may be called a "license to sin"'. Such films are permitted to explore patterns of drug use because they are set in the past and show the bad consequences of drug use. The impact of New Hollywood's stylistic drug realism, a 'licence to sin' and the use of drug comedy meant that by the 1990s the dominant message of anti-drugs was undermined by allowing other levels of interpretation to be made available to the spectator.

With new contemporary drug narratives anything becomes possible, and film makers begin to collapse genre boundaries, perhaps most clearly seen with *Pulp Fiction* (1994). The fusion of naturalistic realism and exaggerated black humour enables drug narratives to escape a mono formula and become part of the matrix of modern life. Through contemporary black comedy, narcotics can tackle serious social and moral issues, as in for example *Scarface* (1983), *Drugstore Cowboy* (1989), *Goodfellas* (1990), *Bringing Out the Dead* (1999), *American Beauty* (1999) and *Traffic* (2001). These films have powerful albeit different drug narratives but none of them fit into the convention of glamorizing substance consumption. Both *American Beauty* and *Traffic* won Oscars, although each tackles drugs with considerable difference. *American Beauty* possesses considerable depth and sensitivity in terms of drug use, humour, personal identity and nostalgia. In contrast, *Traffic* attempts ethnographic realism to provide substance, but this search for authenticity becomes lost when the film starts to resemble *Reefer Madness* and becomes a parody with its affluent innocent young white people fooling around with drugs. The film slips into stereotypical voyeurism when heroin is presented as an erotic drug bearing sexual excitement and female moral corruption.

These recent films contain varying degrees of violence and brutality and are referential to *The Godfather* (1972) and *The French Connection* (1971). These 1970s mob films established the template of gangsters, power and drugs which in turn has become a necessary convention in the representation of gangs and drugs in subsequent American and British films. However, once established, the tendency is for drug representation to become more conventional in its promotion of a drug mythology; for example, drug plots merely become an allegory for affluence. In contrast, *Drugstore Cowboy* (1989) and to a lesser extent *Gridlock'd* (1997) have an uncomfortable brutality because of the more personal focus combined with sensitive comedy, which makes us sympathize with the drug-using characters and their difficult predicament.

The conventional representation of drug users as either hoodlums or social outsiders was challenged by Quentin Tarantino's film *Pulp Fiction* (1994). Tarantino delivered the shocking authenticity of the gangster movie alongside the realism of drug-fuelled paranoia. *Pulp Fiction* has been idolized as a celebration of postmodernism due to its borrowings and parodies, but such an understanding fails to detail the film's insights and challenges. It is not reality that Tarantino offers but the imaginary. Criticized on both sides of the Atlantic for its casual and exciting portrayal of drug use and chastized for its realism associated with heroin preparation (Carroll 1998), the film has a powerful adolescent spirit and undertone of naivety which makes it attractive to young people and therefore an influence. However, moral critics of the film seem to be unfamiliar with Tarantino's aesthetic of playfulness. The film is not to be viewed as reality, with its murder, rape, violence and drug use, which ironically are presented with satirical humour. The horrifying yet funny sequence of drug consumption gone wrong is part of Tarantino's 'graffiti imagination';[15] it is a playful passionate parody which violates conventional representation of drugs. The film wants the audience to be absorbed in the pleasures and pasquinade of popular culture and also to be critically aware of the imaginary through the title itself, which cautions against realism (Polan 2000). For Roland Barthes (1977: 76) drugs in film are a fetishist subject which conform to representational order in society. For him there are few films where drugs are the 'real subject'. In most cases they are employed as a 'false articulation' to convey predetermined meaning about power, corruption or pleasure; drugs are seen as a vehicle for propaganda.

Modern drug and youth culture films

The subcultural films *Easy Rider* (1969) and *Saturday Night Fever* (1977), with their focus on youth leisure and drug pleasure, were twin influences on the British film *Quadrophenia* (1979) that in turn became the standard by which contemporary youth culture movies have been measured. This is due to its forceful realism, romantic alienation of teenage disillusionment and the position of drugs within the youth culture of the mods. A key to understanding the legacy of *Quadrophenia* is its focus on hedonistic insecurity and identity formation in the lives of young people who are part of a group. This subcultural format has been successfully followed in British cinema by *Trainspotting* (1995) and *Human Traffic* (1999). We empathize with the characters who experience moments of struggle and exhilaration: they speak to us and we recognize ourselves in a multitude of differing moments. This is achieved ethnographically in *Quadrophenia, Trainspotting* and *Human Traffic* by the defining presence of group membership, locality and language. There is little compromise to authority or respectable interests. The detailed and personal micro focus allows an opportunity to voice wider social and cultural themes, so that the narrative insists on emotional identification and the films speak for a generation. These three youth culture films have often been criticized for their positive or glamorous portrayal of drugs. Such a conclusion would be misleading because in each film there is a diversity of drug representations. It is not a case of simple drug hedonism or abuse. We see individuals getting on with their everyday lives, showing off, eating, having a drink, desiring sex, being bored, interacting with their parents, having fun and laughing. Furthermore, we see individuals in agony and distress with their drug use and their attempts to reduce or stop using. In short, we see what is special and what is ordinary in their lives and recreational drug consumption is just one of these young persons' activities. An important theme running throughout these films is the desire of the characters to curtail their substance use.

Whilst *Quadrophenia* and *Trainspotting* are concerned with established subcultural patterns, the focus of *Human Traffic* is on contemporary dance youth culture. *Human Traffic* is the most challenging of the new genre of ecstasy-related films which include *Go* (1999), *Sorted* (2000) and *24 Hour Party People* (2002). Even though *Human Traffic* is ultimately conservative in its narrative of love story and desire to abandon drug use, it is nevertheless radical in its sense of irony and surrealism. Where other films, including *Fear and Loathing in Las Vegas* (1997) and *Another Day in Paradise* (1998), put forward chemically boosted narratives, they lack the cohesive and critical sense of a youth culture conveyed by *Quadrophenia* and *Human Traffic*. A referential point is that above Jip's bed is the poster for *Quadrophenia*.

Conclusion

This first section of the chapter has explored the drug representation in children's films focusing on fantasy, dreams and magic, whilst for young people and adults drug images are consonant with excitement and risk but also fear, eroticism and laughter. Governmental and state institutions have consistently taken a political and moral interest in the control of film on the basis that film is a total influence on people's behaviour.[16] This approach towards movies is called 'classic film theory', where the cinema and its spectators are seen as conforming to a mechanistic reproduction of reality. Realizing the potential power of this medium, 'exploitation' movie makers and state-directed anti-drug films sought through shock or sensation to counterbalance other representations which were seen as pro-drug. For drug preventionists film delivers the power of drug realism by imposing on an audience a single message: that drug consumption is bad. In other words, to reverse an apparently positive glamorization of drugs[17] you promote the opposite – an aggressive anti-drug image. Drug representations in this format are propaganda, what Louis Althusser would describe as an attempt to position the audience through interpellation, to actively indoctrinate spectators to accept a particular messages (Easthope 1993: 10). However, a weakness of Althusser's theory is that the individual does not unthinkingly accept cinematic 'reel life' as a direct imitation of real life. Therefore the state's approach to drug representations in films as a means to counter the apparent positive influence of drugs through presentation of negativity is essentially a static understanding of people's subjectivity: an audience is thus made passive. The problem with this view of film is that the audience are denied their own interpretation, resulting in a loss of individual consciousness. In contrast, Stuart Hall (1980b) has argued that an audience will view a film and perform the action of decoding, whereby movies are engaged with at the level of agency rather than passivity. On this alternative basis it is possible to suggest that there is a range of meanings within drug representations in films and that messages are not fixed; they remain unstable and available for a myriad of interpretations. Individuals are undoubtedly interpellated but spectators can read different and diverse messages in films as a result of their social and cultural backgrounds, ideologies and personal desires (Stam 2000: 231).

Advertisements and drugs

This section will initially consider the historical context of advertisements for drug products before they were made illegal. I shall look at the contemporary hemp industry and its style of advertisements. There will be an examination of the commercial exploitation of youth and drug culture images undertaken by companies to market their products; in particular I shall interpret some recent advertisements for brands including Fila, Sony, Coca-Cola, Sega, Fabergé and Yves Saint Laurent. I will also look at the diverse drug images promoted by the modern poster and finally focus on the alcohol industry's use of drug references to sell products. I will suggest that the use of drug imagery within advertisements may sanction the legitimacy of intoxication. Advertising explores and exploits the potential of drug culture to offer consumers a seductive alternative form of satisfaction. Here the individual consumer may engage in a form of oppositional consumption due to the illicit status of the substance. John Storey (1999: 55) argues that consumer resistance occurs against passive commercial tastes. Drug advertisements can be seen as offering a momentary challenge or counterhegemonic pleasure, but the main aim for the company is consumption of the product itself. The consumer absorbs the slogans and logos of drug imagery without fear of arrest or prosecution.

Historically, the study of the media, advertisements and youth consumption has been saturated with the language of drug intoxication. An early formulation of this understanding is known as the 'hypodermic-needle model', where the medium's message is 'injected' into the audience. The idea of the media's hypnotic power to control and shape people's minds was introduced by members of the Frankfurt school such as Theodor Adorno, Max Horkheimer and Herbert Marcuse in their interpretation of Nazi propaganda during the 1930s. In *The Consumer Society* Jean Baudrillard (1998: 27–9) uses a narcotic metaphor to describe shopping malls as 'the drugstore', full of profusion and calculation to achieve 'happiness' and to 'sublimate all of real life'. Theories of consumption which employ the metaphor of drugs to describe the relationship between the media and the audience have a tendency to render consumers passive. The power of the metaphor equals the theorized unrepentant force of advertising with its omnipotent sign to hold people in a trance: advertisers want consumers to be under their hypnotic control (Morley 1995: 313).

Drug advertisements before drugs were illegal

The advertising of drugs and the use of drug representations to market products has a long history. For Raymond Williams (1980: 184) the advertisement is the 'official art of modern capitalist society'. Advertising is a professional system which he says 'came to power at the centre of the economy' (1980: 185). Consumption is an active part of the celebration of capitalism; it is accepted, legal and authorized. The promise of consumption is recognition of legitimacy in culture as a pleasure ideal for the individual and a manifesto for society. A advertisement for the popular Vin Mariani drink in 1899 displayed a photograph of His Holiness Pope Leo XIII smiling and an extract of a letter sent by his secretary states:

> Rome, January 2 1898. His holiness has deigned to commission me to thank the distinguished donor in His holy name, and to demonstrates His gratitude in a material way as well. His Holiness [sic] does me the honour of presenting Mr. Mariani with a gold medal containing His venerable coat-of-arms.

The advertisement claims that the product 'fortifies, strengthens, stimulates and refreshes the body and brain'. Angelo Mariani was one the world's first cocaine millionaires. He launched his concoction in 1863, made from selected coca leaves steeped in wine. Mariani was not short of praise for his cocaine wine – writers such as H.G. Wells, Jules Verne, Henrik Ibsen and Émile Zola spoke of its virtues. Monarchs and presidents offered accolades and endorsements, including Queen Victoria, the Prince of Wales (later King Edward VII), the tsar of Russia, Prince Albert I of Monaco, King Peter of Serbia, King George I of Greece and US Presidents Grant and McKinley (Rudgley 1998). Cocaine wine was clearly a popular drink amongst the aristocracy and the bourgeoisie. At the same time Harrods advertised its neat product of needle, syringe and heroin, Coca-Cola proudly spoke of cocaine in its soft drink ('There's Nothing Like Coke'), the Lloyd Manufacturing Company pronounced its Cocaine Toothache Drops an instantaneous cure, especially for children, and in the 1890s Bayer embarked on a massive marketing campaign for Heroin, a sedative for coughs, as a highly effective cure, and it was enormously popular.[18] During the nineteenth century Peter Squire's pharmacy in Oxford Street, London, produced cannabis extract. It was also available from the pharmacies of Smith in Edinburgh, De Courtive et Personne in Paris and Gastinel in Cairo (Abel 1980). In 1887 advertisements for marijuana cigarettes marketed by Grimault and Company featured in the *Illustrated London News*, price 1s 9d a packet: 'Indian Cigarettes of Cannabis Indica have been used in the hospitals and found to give immediate relief in all cases of asthma, nervous coughs, hoarseness, loss of voice, facial neuralgia and sleeplessness.'[19]

In America companies which marketed cannabis medicine include Abbott Laboratories, Eli Lilly, Parke-Davis, Smith Brothers, Squibb, Tildens and Williams. The websites of the Medical Cannabis Picture Gallery and the Schaffer Library of Drug Policy provide a range of colour and black and white photographs of bottles and jars with the labels specifying the types of medical cannabis produced from the late 1880s to the 1930s. Many of the these companies which sold cannabis remain major corporate entities. The photographs in old manufacturers' sales brochures and advertisements promoting medical cannabis specify the prescribed use, potency and ingredients of the cannabis medicine (Mack and Joy 2001). Also in their physicians' catalogues company advertisements assert that the cannabis medicine has had 'extensive pharmacological and clinical tests'; for example, Parke-Davis and Company's Cannabis USP declares that the product has been made 'to conform to a standard that has been found to be in practice, reliable'.[20]

At the start of the 1900s the range of commercial products containing drugs was broad and popular amongst the rich and the poor. Heroin, cocaine and marijuana were taken as forms of self-medication or through prescription. Dooley Worth (1991: 3) points out that drugs were promoted as improving health and vitality and recommended 'by celebrity endorsements, books, posters, music and plays'. The advertisements for these products were presented in the standard language of commercials: the products can resolve pain or offer pleasure.

The hemp industry: Marx and the 'magic' of the drug commodity

Currently consumers can purchase thousands of products made of hemp in person or online which centrally employ the cannabis leaf as its symbol. The hemp industry fundamentally exploits the visual representation of the drug derived from its imagery of defiance to offer credibility to the diverse range of available products. It is now possible to buy hemp casual clothing, sportswear and fashion for women, men and babies. Hemp products also include food and oils for health and cooking, footwear, bags, jewellery, candles, hats, hair accessories and bed linen. Hemp apparel has taken its place alongside other fabrics and foods as a regular feature. From hemp soap and hemp crunchy bars to cannabis lemonade, the product advertisements utilize drug imagery and symbolism.[21]

An additional source of legitimacy for cannabis products is guaranteed by the cultural politics of ethical consumerism. Advertisements proclaim the hemp products to be free from artificial additives, preservatives, added salt or sugar, animal fats, caffeine, GM ingredients, etc. The advertisers' dream is that cannabis products can be promoted as healthy: hemp products are easily promoted as part of an alternative choice different from the mainstream and advertised as nutritious. Advertisements consistently utilize the dual framework of legal and illegal at a subterranean level to promote hemp products for their transgressive pleasure potential.

The use of hemp as an ingredient in products is not merely a result of its flexibility, reliability and strength; it can be used in an ambiguous way in language to promote different messages.[22] For example, the word 'secret' and the idea of an 'extra boost to get you through the day' are used to market Shepherdboy's snack bar Hempower, while the Schweizer Lemonade Company's Swiss Cannabis Drink offers us the chance to 'get the magic power of hemp seeds'. Hemp commodities speak of their potential for 'relaxation', 'fun' and 'magic'. Each of these words is a standard label applied to commodities to promote excitement and imagination, but these three words are given an additional meaning when used in association with cannabis as part of the language of drug culture.

In the nineteenth century Karl Marx (1887: 76–81) examined products in terms of the 'secret' of commodities which have a 'mystical character' and a 'fantastic form' through what he termed 'commodity fetishism'. Advertisers exploit the power of drug culture to enhance the attraction of the commodity; although Marx argued that commodities have no power themselves, it is clear that advertisements want to alter this through association with terms such as 'hit', 'high', 'boost', 'trip', 'sniff', 'dream', 'addiction', 'junkie', 'buzz', 'inject', 'smack', 'toke-on', 'score some speed', and so on.[23] The aim of the advertising company conforms to what Marx initially argued, that 'magic' surrounds the product. Drug references give products a hidden source of power which engages with the consumer at an individual and active level between them and the object of their desire. Consumers of these drug products enjoy what Walter Benjamin sees as the spectacle of consumption, confirming the mystery of the drug product and preventing it from being seen as an ordinary commodity of novelty value only.

What advertisers of hemp products have been able to achieve is humour and irony in consumption. The product will not give you an experience of intoxication but when you drink the Britannia or Apres soft drink made with hemp seeds you are consuming cannabis as an 'imaginative hit'. Hemp products are cultural commodities which draw on existing understandings and attempt to establish connections with an alternative meaning. The Body Shop's use of thick paper surrounding the block of hemp soap closely resembles the cloth in which a slab of cannabis is covered. Anita Roddick launched her hemp cosmetics in 1998 on the holistic value of the cannabis plant. Here drug-related brand names are part of cultural consumption and the main aim of the advertisement is the experience of something special. Hemp went further into the mainstream when Adidas produced their Hemp sports shoe, later renamed the Gazelle Natural, made from cannabis.

During this period the corporate logo of the company became a popular symbol on shirts with the use of the cannabis leaf as a replacement for the sport logo of Adidas. The American drug tsar Lee P. Brown accused the company of an attempt to 'capitalize on the drug culture', and added that it implies 'that drugs are cool' as they are associated with the 'magic' of sporting achievement. In 2003 Virgin Mobile used a picture of a joint and the words 'the devil makes work for idle thumbs' with an additional pun stating 'no marijuana was wasted during the making of this advertisement'.

Commercial exploitation of youth culture's drug history

Drugs are part of the mainstream economy: they provide a reservoir of images and ideas with historical depth which can be exploited by advertisers to sell products. The Design Council Awards for the best advertisements often challenge orthodox representations which disrupt conservative ideas. Jobling and Crowley (1995) argue that images used by Benson and Hedges, Silk Cut, Sony, Benetton and Nike have deliberately sought to fracture conventional and even law-abiding wisdom, through the use of surrealism, illusionary art, shock tactics, irony and drug hallucination. A relevant example would be Nike's marketing slogan 'Just Do It'; here the hedonistic appeal to young people places priority on pleasure and simultaneously satirizes the drug prevention slogan 'Just Say No'. Jobling and Crowley maintain that professionals in advertising agencies are fully aware of theory, especially the process of spectators decoding advertisements. Advertisements, they argue, set out to promote visual and linguistic puzzles and meanings which are sometimes not easily accessible. This means that advertisements are packed with different levels of meaning and intention which can reinforce exclusivity or be directed at insider knowledge (Miles 1998).

The cultural values and symbols of youth culture and drug culture since the 1960s have been used explicitly within more traditionally conformist settings (Nava et al. 1997). For example, Timothy Leary's drug slogan of the 1960s was reworded in 2001 in an advertisement for *Industry Standard Europe*, a magazine for the internet economy, as 'Tune In, Turn On and Get Promoted'. The same year the Amazon internet company used the phrase 'No Need to Take a Trip Just Click' and in 2002 the internet service provider Freeserve adopted the slogan 'Mind-Blowing Offer', using 1960s references to psychedelia. Whilst the take-up of phrases does not suggest encouragement of drug use, it is valuable to consider that Timothy Leary was a drug evangelist, who in *The Politics of Ecstasy* outlined his vision of the purpose and power of drugs to change society.[24] The business magazine clearly aims to get noticed, but its rewording cannot dissolve the transgressive power of the original argument derived from its position in drug culture.

Two examples of advertisements which use references from the 1960s drug culture occurred in 1993 and 1996, first in an advertisement for Sapporo beer and also in an advertisement for the training shoe company Fila. The advertisement for Sapporo beer features a caricature of a man's face from the 1960s wearing big round sunglasses, long hair and a moustache on a swirling psychedelic background. The large headline asked: 'Had an Overdose of Pils?' The Fila advertisement said 'The Ultimate Head Trip' in large wobbly writing, and featured the trainers against a spiral background, with at the bottom of the picture the words 'Mind Blower'. The use of such phrases and graphics derives from drug representations of the 1960s. The advertisement for *Industry Standard Europe* and the Sapporo and Fila advertisements can be seen as primarily promoting a positive view of drug consumption. However, in each case the product bears no relationship to drugs; it could be suggested that they possibly condone drug taking but this presupposes awareness of the phrases and original context that generated the drug-related meanings. The advertisements clearly use drug language because it speaks of power and strangeness. In this sense the advertisers were fully aware of the attraction they would gain for their product, but could ultimately claim they were not promoting drug use, merely engaging in the practice of 'licence to sin', referring to drug use in the past, not the present.

Magazines directed at the contemporary youth culture market consistently cover drug issues and stories and regularly present articles about drugs as the main feature of an edition; for example, the front cover of *Mixmag* for October 2002 featured a large ecstasy tablet with the headline 'The £1 Pill', while the February 2001 issue of Q magazine's main headline was 'On Drugs'. Two magazines, *Later* in 1999 and *Ministry* in 2000, had complaints upheld against them by the Advertising Standards Authority for encouraging 'apathy towards drug taking'. The *Later* advertisement featured two different posters for its launch. The first poster was headed 'Get Some Coke for Jamie's Party' and featured two tick boxes giving a choice of '1 gram' or '2 litres'. The second poster was headed 'Grass' and had two tick boxes giving the choice of 'Mow it' and 'Smoke it'. In both cases the bottom of the poster read: 'Later – a magazine for men who are growing up. The *Ministry* cover feature[25] was headlined 'Free Drugs' in orange letters, under which was written 'The nation's favourite! Now available everywhere!' In addition the magazine depicted large white tablets that resembled the drug ecstasy. The headline 'Free Drugs' was clearly a successful pun on mainstream magazines which attempt to increase circulation through offering free gifts. The advertisement gave the impression that people would get free drugs, and the innuendo according to the Advertising Standards Authority was 'socially irresponsible and likely to cause serious offence'. During 2001 the television advertisement for Coca-Cola mentioned the global corporate dance company Ministry of Sound and significantly continues the drug connotation with reference to experiencing the 'rush of Coke'. Although the complaints against the advertisements were upheld, in each case the magazine put forward the notion that drugs were becoming more available. In essence their excuse, which failed, was that drug normalization has occurred.

Four advertisements' use of drug imagery

What follows is an assessment of four advertisements that employ direct drug culture imagery and have a close relationship with young adult leisure: Sega in 1995, Sony and Elida Fabergé in 1998 and Yves Saint Laurent in 2000–01. The Sega advertisement, seen in computer magazines, was for Mega Drive II with Virtua Racing and had the headline 'Score Some Speed' in large letters, with the phrase 'from a dealer near you' appearing elsewhere. Although the advertisement is obviously a pun on being able to drive fast, it is a rather brutal example derived from drug culture which attempts little irony. The word 'score' is related to attaining a record or result, but its use in this connection with the term 'speed' for amphetamine can be seen as nothing other than to purchase speed from a 'dealer', thus gaining another result. The combination of the words 'score', 'speed' and 'dealer' make this an advertisement centrally related to drug culture and only peripherally related to the product.

In 1998 Sony Computer Entertainment Europe produced a nationwide poster which also featured in its official UK PlayStation magazine for a console game. The advertisement featured a picture of a snowboarder next to a piece of rough notepad paper. The handwritten message states:

> Powder I need powder my body aches yells screams for powder. When I'm on it I get a rush a buzz the blood coursing through my veins I get really *high*. I'm floating gliding through air away from reality and then I begin to come down with a bump and I need to do it again straight away. I need to get higher than the last time **UP UP UP** WITH THE CLOUDS THE SKY. I come down with a bang. I crash out . . . no PAIN

The left-hand corner of the advertisement states: 'With 2 players, half a pipe and a bag of air competition it's the coolest game not on earth.' As with the Sega poster, the advertisement shows a careful selection of words which deliberately possess a double meaning. For example, the words used such as 'powder', 'rush', 'buzz', and so on describe drug images, but also there are the additional phrases which reinforce this ambiguous meaning. Although some of this vocabulary is used in wider culture, taken together within one short piece of text it confirms the dominance of the drug meaning. This message is reinforced by the drug wording at the bottom of the advertisement. There is a deliberate attempt to introduce ambiguities into this commercial, but its context and visual imagery, a torn piece of rough paper with doodles and ink splotches, are meant to give an impression of an aspect of alternative youth culture.

Elida Fabergé's advertisement for Fusion perfume in 1998 appeared in music and style magazines. The advertisement said: 'Oi! Where's My Fusion Wrap?' The picture showed a disc jockey holding out a piece of folded paper. The paper itself, when opened, stated: 'Fusion. The only thing worth sniffing in a club'. Also it showed a sticky label with a picture of a bottle of Fusion and the instruction 'peel here'. When peeled back, a small amount of white powder was revealed. In common with the Sega advertisement, the Fabergé commercial suggests a degree of irony and humour directly geared to its target audience, young people who go clubbing. The power of the advertisement rests with its level of agency: it engages with the consumer, asking them to 'unwrap' the folded paper, making it a conscious action to participate in the desire and sensation. In each of these advertisements drug iconography is used selectively and intentionally. Damon Taylor (2000: 340) states it is clear that such advertisements 'have obviously been very carefully placed in certain publications, they have begun to tap directly into the usage of the drug culture'. The graphics and setting are recognized by young people, they speak of their identity and reinforce their local cultural practice. On a wider scale Fabergé were one of the sponsors of the film *Human Traffic*. Here the symbols of dance culture fused with drug culture move to an international stage as the film is distributed on a global basis. It is clear that Fabergé are exploiting the contemporary mythology of youth culture to market their products to a specific audience. This demonstrates that capital is utilizing representations surrounding recreational drug use for the purpose of gaining increased profit from the free market.

Further criticism against Elida Fabergé occurred in 1999 from the Advertising Standards Authority for the perfume Addiction. The commercial featured an eyeball with the reflection of a man on it and the statement 'First signs of addiction: high temperature, mood swings, loss of appetite, dilated pupils, trembling hands and dreamlike state'. In their defence of this advertisement Fabergé claimed that the physical symptoms were of sexual arousal, not drug addiction. This is possible but the employment of ambiguous language serves the purpose of gaining attention for the product because these words have close connotations with drug culture images.

It is common for perfume companies to employ images of desire and erotic fantasy but Fabergé and Yves Saint Laurent are also using drug representations. This combination is demonstrated in the Yves Saint Laurent nationwide poster advertisement produced in 2000 and 2001 for their perfume Opium. The poster for Opium features the model Sophie Dahl, who is naked, ginger haired, very pale with some make-up on her lips and eyelids, set against a dark blue and black background. She is lying on her back with knees raised, head reclined and lips parted; her left hand cups her left breast while the right breast is exposed. In 2001 this advertisement received considerable attention from the tabloid press in terms of whether it was sexually offensive. The attention focused on the representation in terms of it being degrading for women, or a 'raunchy'[26] role model for women in contrast to thin waif-like female models on the catwalk. A key difference between the Yves Saint Laurent commercial and the 'Hello Boys' Wonderbra advertisement is that Dahl is unnaturally pale, her body is a kind of death mask. Mary Kenny argued 'you could quite easily call it heroin.'[27] Her eyes are closed, her body is pallid, she could be dead from opium consumption, the whiteness of her skin is exaggerated against the dark background. Without the concrete object, namely a bottle of perfume, the spectator is being addressed to interpret and decode the range of possible messages. The picture evokes the symbolism of Thomas De Quincey's *Confessions of an Opium Eater*, where he speaks of the death of young white women.

A key practice of commercials is to feed on other genres such as film or art and also other advertisements (Stam 2000: 303). Referentiality is a central part of the advertisement industry and the Yves Saint Laurent advertisement borrows from the era of American pulp fiction. The novel by Claude Farrere entitled *Black Opium: The Shocking Ecstasy of the Forbidden*[28] featured a naked woman lying back against a dark background, exposing her breast in the throes of sexual pleasure. In the Yves Saint Laurent advertisement for Opium it is possible to see a glorification of death through sexual ecstasy and drug intoxication; in a state of pleasure we see auto-eroticism combined with auto-stimulation. The advertisement can also be linked with the return of the British film *A Clockwork Orange*, directed by Stanley Kubrick, who had withdrawn the film from public performance. Sophie Dahl's sexual pose resembles the voyeuristic furniture in the Korova Milk Bar, where plastic naked women present their orifices and can dispense a substance called 'milk plus' from their breasts. Sexual ecstasy, intoxication and violation are brought together through the character of Alex, the narrative's lead 'droog', who uses milk plus as a mind-altering drug in preparation for committing an act of 'ultra-violence'. The Yves Saint Laurent poster is based on two styles of advertising in the fashion industry from the 1990s referred to as 'heroin chic' and 'porn chic'. These fashion styles focus on narcissistic and pleasurable loss of control and have regularly featured in *The Face* magazine. Rebecca Arnold (1999: 280) details that the models are presented in unconventional postures and bleak claustrophobic settings, dressed in scant underwear and showing shiny female skin.[29] As with the Opium advertisement, 'heroin chic' representations of young women can be seen as erotic yet disturbing because the body appears strong, healthy and sexual but the hint of drug excess unbalances the conscious consumption of pleasure.[30]

'Pictures on my wall': youth and drug culture posters

Historically, the drug poster derives from the psychedelic era of the early 1960s although this style was influenced by the Belgian Belle Époque (1880–1920) and Art Nouveau, which used images and words in a sensual and blurring naturalistic fashion emphasizing fun and pleasure (Owen 1999). During the twenty-first century the T-shirt has developed into a micro poster, used on the same basis as earlier posters to present a powerful means of direct communication. The range of drug-related T-shirts is extensive and they are available in any small town, from the standard 'I like the Pope, the Pope smokes dope' and 'Enjoy cocaine' through smiling ecstasy logos or 'illegal'/'E-legal' word play to the more specialist drug T-shirts which became a central feature of 1990s ecstasy dance culture, for example, 'Vicks: the number one dance floor drug' and 'Klubber's Nice Tripses'. The first is a pun on the homely and domestic vapour rub that helps you breathe more easily and the second a play on words on Kellogg's Rice Krispies.

Furthermore, the internet is a vast resource for drug-related designs. Poster and T-shirt catalogues are regular features in youth magazines and contain great variation and creativity in their drug-related products; examples include Push Poster, Shock Horror International, Stickitonyourwall, Blast and Olympus Designs. Certain publishers have become sensitive to the drug images they produce and have incorporated a disclaimer. For example, Pyramid Publishers states: 'Pyramid does not advocate, support or encourage the use of illegal or recreational drugs'. In addition, drug prohibition posters may themselves not have their desired outcome. In the late 1980s the government drug prevention anti-heroin poster campaign failed because the young teenage male proved too attractive for some girls, who wrote in asking for the poster (O'Sullivan et al. 1998: 129).

The contemporary style of drug posters conforms broadly to a range of fashion types. First, famous musical artists are depicted using drugs or placed within an image which highlights their consumption of or connection with drugs. The list of artists covered is endless but usually includes the Beatles, Jimi Hendrix, the Doors, Pink Floyd, Sid Vicious, Bob Marley and also more recent heroes such as Nirvana, the Stone Roses, Primal Scream, Wu-Tang Clan, and Jamiroquai. Second, there are posters which celebrate a particular film closely associated with drug consumption, for example, *Easy Rider, Quadrophenia, Trainspotting, Pulp Fiction* ('Pot Fiction'!) and *Human Traffic*. Third, there is a range of posters focusing on cannabis, skunkweed, magic mushrooms or ecstasy, through the use of very bright contrasting colours, with complex interconnected shapes such as spirals creating perceptual illusions to signify a hallucinogenic experience. Finally, there are posters that focus on irony and humour, which can be divided into four types: science fiction, joke, high culture and anti-establishment. The science fiction poster usually presents aliens employing a double meaning of language, saying 'Lost in space!' or 'Take me to your dealer!' The joke or pun poster is most often found depicting drug confusion: 'The drugs don't work', 'Being stoned', 'Magic bus', 'Flying', 'E=XTC', 'The Institute of Higher Learning', 'The Grim Reefer', 'Free the weed', 'Weeding the garden', etc. The high-culture poster shows a famous character from a painting involved in smoking a spliff; for example, Raphael's angels or the figure from Edvard Munch's painting *The Scream* puffing out marijuana smoke rings. The anti-establishment poster concerns famous figures consuming drugs such as HRH Dope, the postage stamp picture of the Queen smoking a joint with the slogan 'By appointment to Her Royal Highness'. Other top drug consumers have included Albert Einstein, the Elephant Man, Buddha, the Pope, the Statue of Liberty and the US presidents carved in stone(d) on Mount Rushmore. Drug humour has also been directed at newspapers; for example, the *Sun*, ironically portrayed as the *Someday*, with a headline 'It's legal' showing a cannabis leaf. Another target has been monetary currency, for example, the Bank of Ganja, whose bank-note is an imitation of an American dollar bill. This analysis represents only a small sample of the vast array of posters that present a range of drug-related communications and meanings. Overall, the dominant message in these posters is to signify a positive meaning for intoxicants and this is most clearly achieved through humour, where reality is subject to mockery and authority is made to appear a parody though meanings derived from drug culture.

An example of a drug picture which became both a poster and an advertisement was the photograph of Robbie Fowler, the England football player, mimicking a person snorting cocaine. On 3 April 1999 at the Premier League game between Liverpool and Everton he scored a goal, fell to his knees, lowered his face to the pitch, held a finger over his left nostril and pretended to snort the touchline. Fowler was fined £32,000 and apologized unequivocally for his action. The drug image of Robbie Fowler has since been used by advertisers. First, the image was placed in *Max Power* magazine to sell the *News of the World* newspaper. It featured a footballer snorting from a white line on a football pitch and the slogan 'If It Goes On It Goes In'. The second example was a national advertisement which featured in daily newspapers such as the *Daily Mirror* for Channel 5 television. It featured the Robbie Fowler drug image, claiming 'Chelsea on 5: Not to Be Sniffed at'. In both cases complaints against the companies were upheld by the Advertising Standards Authority. Fowler's actions were intentional and light-hearted, but subsequent replication of the drug representation removed the action from its context. Originally, what we saw was an image of drug mimicry; it was then used to sell a mainstream product. The Fowler photograph shows a dual meaning: it can be used as a sign for drug normalization or can be used as a marketing strategy for commodity consumption.

Alcoholic visions of drug imagery

During the 1990s many producers of alcoholic drinks complained about an apparent decline in business which led them to diversify from the traditional public house in order to attract 'lost custom'. However, a study by Miller and Plant (1996) suggests that consumption of alcoholic drinks by young people had risen rather than declined. Rather than accept the industry's claim about 'lost custom', it might be more constructive to argue that the alcohol industry introduced intelligence-led and niche marketing strategies to consolidate its existing consumers and also responded with innovative entertainment complexes to attract new and different drinkers. Part of this strategy was to revitalize the youth drinks market through targetting a new cultural location and its consumers, namely the rave and club culture.

During the late 1980s and throughout the 1990s the alcohol industry was under direct competition from a diversity of illegal commodities, including ecstasy, amphetamines, LSD and cannabis (Collin 1997). It is possible to suggest that the alcohol industry responded with a calculated strategy which utilized aspects of the dance culture at a general level through marketing and advertisements but at a particular level has also used specific images and brand names directly related to illegal drugs. The names included those for high-strength bottled lager, 'alcopops', ciders and fortified wines such as Diamond White, K, Ice and others. One drug-related representation on television and at the cinema has been that of the Metz drink, where the advertisement introduces consumers to the out-of-mind-and-body experience called the 'judder'. Taylor (2000: 343) argues that the alcohol industry is 'using the glamour of the drugs and popularity of dance culture to legitimize [its] product in the minds of the consumer'. The use of hallucinogenic experiences or 'spaced out' visions suggests that the key outcome of alcopops, or even Smirnoff vodka with its juxtaposition of contrasting images, is the drug trip. It could be argued that the soft drink industry in turn has responded with a series of advertisements which are linked back to the credibility of drug imagery, such as those for Dr Pepper which portray young people being talked into trying something by their peers on the pretext that it won't hurt and they might like it.

Drug culture, much like youth culture, is subject to fashions and change. Therefore, it was only a matter of time before dance culture altered from a drugs and soft drink/water-based event to one where alcohol began to reestablish itself (Garratt 1998). For the alcohol industry the financial challenge was to reintroduce the dominance of alcohol consumption into the different dance culture scenes. The return of the new diversified alcohol can be seen through photographic representation in the dance culture magazines. Over a period of ten years, there has been a dramatic increase in the number of people photographed at dance events holding not a bottle of water but a bottle of designer alcohol. The current transformation of pleasure back to alcohol in dance culture is continuing and may lead to the hegemony of alcohol within wider youth culture. In contrast, during the early 1990s Coffield and Gofton (1994: 19) found that young people associated drink culture with more negative images of older adults described as 'beer monsters'.

The alcohol industry has successfully used its research base to exploit the commercial potential within an illegal market, to achieve acceptance within youth culture via adaptation of drug references and drug mythology. To return its product to a position of dominance within the youth drinks market, the alcohol industry has manipulated features of drug normalization within youth culture in terms of their attraction and power as selling points of pleasure. Take-up of drug-related imagery by the alcohol industry aims to maximize profit. It is not that the alcohol industry wishes to promote the consumption of illegal drugs, although this could be a consequence. This type of advertising is a means to promote consumption using images that currently appeal to many young people. Drug representations are not illegal; they have become a marketing strategy to sell mainstream commercial products. Within the capitalist market advertisements appear to accept no boundaries in the pursuit of capital.

Popular music and drugs

Drug references and drug use are part of the mainstream of popular music. High-profile examples of drug use by musicians include Keith Richard's and Kurt Cobain's use of heroin, John Lennon's and Julian Cope's use of LSD, Lemmy's use of speed, David Bowie's, Elton John's and Freddie Mercury's use of cocaine, David Crosby's and Shaun Ryder's use of crack, Bob Marley's and Paul McCartney's use of cannabis, and Bez's and Brian Harvey's use of ecstasy. The primary symbolism linking drugs and music is that of the cultural outlaw, and this in turn becomes a means for commercial ends for promotion by the record company. Drugs are used by artists both to create musical experiments and to provide physical and mental stimulation when touring or producing material. Through lyrics, sound and visual representations drugs have been a hidden and explicit cultural reference point for successive generations of young people. Drug references in songs may be personal and political; they can describe ordinary experiences ranging from enjoyment to paranoia, or offer intimate information and visionary adventures. Lyrics can also provide powerful warnings about the dangers of intoxication or, through humour, drug songs can criticize and ridicule authority.

Initially I shall explore the argument that drugs within popular music are a force of subversive meaning. I will consider the historical origins of black popular music, drugs and racial discrimination and then move on to an analysis of selected pop artists who have paid homage to drugs in their songs. This section will also consider the role of the anti-drug song and assess the connection between musicians who become drugs 'heroes' and those who experience drug deaths. It will also examine the way that intoxication is used by the record industry as a public relations exercise. It concludes by looking at the relationship between drugs and musical structure.

Subversive meaning in music and drugs

During the 1940s and 1950s the sociological study of popular music artists and their relationship to drug consumption became a significant area of investigation. The leading theorist was H. S. Becker, whose early papers in 1951 and 1953 focused on jazz as a deviant subculture, where he argued that musicians' use of drugs could be interpreted as a form of resistance against the dominant culture. The pre- and post-Second World War development of jazz within the nocturnal world of dance halls, dancing girls, prostitution, drug use and illegal consumption of alcohol alongside its 'immoral' reputation served to affirm the 'deviant outsider' and self-focused image of jazz (Peretti 1994). Sociologists such as Becker were attempting to challenge deterministic theories of deviance. But at the same time that Becker and David Matza were, critically, revealing that deviant values were commonly shared throughout society, the writings of Jack Kerouac, according to Peter Townsend (2000: 117), fused jazz with drugs, sex and youth in an imagined 1950s America which promoted the celebration of transgression, thereby reaffirming the subversive myth of jazz, youth and deviance.

Popular music has a critical and subversive potential to deliver a range of messages about drug experiences and drug consumption through lyrics and related imagery which escape censorship and state control. As a cultural form popular music is closely related to street culture and also intertwined with critical artistic strategies to disrupt conventional meaning. Whether as an art-based form through jazz or commercially successful top ten hits, the subject of drugs has been delivered to audiences by focusing on personal drug experiences and the celebration or advocacy of drug use. Popular music's democratic force allows for critical intervention in people's lives, but as a form of mass entertainment it is also subject to principles of regulation. For Theodor Adorno ([1941]1990: 306) popular music does your thinking for you: 'The composition hears for the listener.' Adorno suggests that in its standardized format popular music especially for the young creates individuals who are 'rhythmically obedient'. The power of popular music for Adorno embodies the contradictions of capitalism, in that it achieves mass conformity while at the same time convincing people that they are free. For Adorno individuals suffer from regression: we are not engaged but become emotionally distracted through the excitement of the musical fetish.

From these comments it is clear that Adorno saw popular music as a degenerative form, but both Max Paddison (1996) and Robert Witkin (1998) also consider that Adorno saw the potential of popular music to be subversive rather than submissive.

For popular music to take this form Adorno specifies (1999: 12) that it must be 'critical' in order to enter into opposition and disturb dominant forms of social communication. Jeff Nuttall in *Bomb Culture* wrote: 'Drugs are an excellent strategy against society ... since 1963 [drugs] have accelerated the onslaught that artists had been levelling at the established culture since de Sade' (1968: 238). More recently, the New York DJ and dance music artist Moby has stated: 'I've always liked drug music, subversive music' (Derogatis 1996: 209). The use of drug references within songs or visual representations which deliberately obscure or hide drug meaning is an intentional form of resistance. Drug songs are transgressive because they are taken up and incorporated by the culture industry, thereby confirming the power of capital, but at the same time the music tests and challenges consensus. Edward Said (1991: 64) investigated the ideological force of music to sustain the status quo, and argues for the powerful transgressive potential of music to break from 'the ideas of authority and social hierarchy directly connected to a dominant establishment'. For him the critical force of music derives from what he calls its 'nomadic ability' to travel and occupy social space so as to 'produce an alternative discourse' (1991: 70). This creative challenge can take the form of secret codes, but can also be statements of belief in drugs as a subversive contribution towards cultural production.

Jazz, racial discrimination and drugs

At the start of the twentieth century American newspapers defined F. Scott Fitzgerald's *Jazz Age* in terms of insanity and drugs. Morroe Berger's analysis (1947: 463–6) of newspaper representations of jazz from the period 1919 to 1944 specifies that the predominant view was opposition and hostility towards the musical form. In essence, he found that jazz was defined as vulgar and needing to be kept in its place. Racial discrimination and general antipathy towards black culture meant that jazz became associated with an outlaw status and represented a positive badge of defiance for black youth in a white state. Harry Shapiro (1999: 46) details how the jazz musician became a new form of social menace. 'Jazz was blamed for endangering the morals of young people by encouraging the release of animal passions through sensual dancing, boy-girl contact, the sexual content of jazz lyrics and of course the link with drug taking.'

Harry J. Anslinger, Head of the Federal Bureau of Narcotics (FBN), devoted a substantial amount of time to hunting down black musicians because of their drug use. Shapiro (1999) notes that the names on Anslinger's 'star bust' drug policy list included Louis Armstrong, Count Basie, Cab Calloway, Duke Ellington, Dizzy Gillespie, Lionel Hampton, Milton 'Mezz' Mezzrow, Thelonious Monk, Jelly Roll Morton, Charlie Parker and Lester Young. Later the list would include Ray Charles, John Coltrane, Miles Davis, Billie Holiday, Art Pepper and others. Each of these jazz artists used drugs on a recreational basis but some also suffered major health problems. Anslinger saw these musicians as 'public enemies' and went to great length to fabricate the evils of marijuana use.

Jazz jargon, according to Charles Winick (1959: 250), affirmed its outsider status by taking over narcotic slang, which reinforced the marginality of the musician. He asserts that the drug language used by jazz artists helped 'create an environment in which it was relatively easy to regard drug use as an acceptable kind of behaviour'. Ned Polsky (1961: 149) points out that the term 'hipster' derives from a much older phrase 'to be on the hip, to be a devotee of opium smoking – during which activity one lies on one's hip'. The term 'hip' was popular during the 1920s and 1930s among young black musicians. The phrase signified drug connotations but, as David Maurer (1938) points out, the term was loosely transferred from opium to other types of drug consumption such as marijuana. Charlie Hore (1993: 93) argues that in America during this period blues and jazz songs which contained drug references were never intended for white ears. Much of the argot associated with drug taking occurs within a subcultural setting, and the musicians who used recreational drugs wrote about them, reinforcing their association with localized practice and language. Shapiro (1999: 39) estimates that by the late 1930s there were probably over a hundred popular music songs about drugs. Early terms in songs[31] to describe drugs include 'tea', 'weed', 'reefer', 'viper' and perhaps most famously Louis Armstrong's 'Muggles', recorded on 7 December 1928; 'muggles' is now obsolete slang for marijuana.

'Mary Warner' loves 'Ebeneezer Goode': drug homage in popular music

Louis Armstrong spoke of his love for Mary Jane and 'Mary Warner, honey, you sure was good' (Shapiro 1999: 25). During the early jazz age cannabis was not illegal although it was common to use argot as a cover to sing about substances. Whether the code word in the song was tea, reefer, gage, viper, weed or rosa maria, by 1937, when cannabis was banned in America, the code words began to alter and become more obscure with less explicit song titles. There remained during the 1930s a range of blues guitarists who sang about the perils and dangers of cocaine, often with a direct reference to the drug such as 'Cocaine Blues', but where the song had a more positive and upbeat message the meaning goes underground as with Chick Webb's 1938 song 'Wacky Dust' sung by Ella Fitzgerald (Ultimate 30s & 40s Reefer Songs 2004). During the 1940s and 1950s many leading jazz instrumentalists, including Red Rodney, Miles Davis, Chet Baker and Lester Young, were arrested for drug possession while others served prison sentences. Heroin was tailor-made for inducing a sense of emotional distance. Anatole Broyard (1948: 724) argues that 'the solo instrument became the narcotic . . . it entered at an unexpected altitude'. Heroin use did not deliver song lyrics which reflected the subversive content of music. Rather, the impact of the drug had its greatest force on experimental musicianship; for example, in the music of Dexter Gordon, John Coltrane and Miles Davis, who, according to Ian Carr (1982), brought the heroin experience into their musical production for artistic purposes (Wallace 1990: 123).

In the early years of rock 'n' roll Jerry Lee Lewis, Little Richard and the Everly Brothers suffered from amphetamine addiction and both Johnny Cash and Elvis Presley took speed for the purposes of touring. Shapiro (1999: 85) states: 'Speed stood at the crossroads of early rock 'n' roll and country music, consumed by performers, roadies and audiences alike.' During the 1950s the Beatles learnt their musical apprenticeship in Hamburg playing late sets night after night using amphetamines. The early drug adventures of the Beatles are captured in Iain Softley's film *Backbeat* (1993) about the life of the 'fifth Beatle' Stuart Sutcliffe. Frith and Horne (1987: 85) describe how both Lennon and Sutcliffe were part of the Liverpool art scene and through the Beatles' chance meeting with German existentialists they sought to retain elements of this bohemian lifestyle (Savage 1996). The Beatles' songs moved on to new subjects with closer links to recreational drug use after their American tours. Later, when filming *Help* (1965), they had the opportunity to experiment with LSD. During this period Lennon created some drawings and ideas which developed into the song and subsequent film *Yellow Submarine*, as an LSD experience itself. Certain songs from *Rubber Soul* (1965) and *Revolver* (1966) distinctly reveal the impact of drug consumption. On 'Tomorrow Never Knows' Lennon offers a pastoral and lyrical description of hallucinogenic intoxication. Not only is he preparing the ground for the psychedelic 1967 LP *Sgt Pepper's Lonely Hearts Club Band*, but Lennon offers drug advice, even a gentle warning to young people, about the feelings brought on by drug consumption. With songs such as 'Lucy in the Sky with Diamonds', an anthem for LSD, and 'A Day in the Life', banned by the BBC because of its positive reference to an LSD trip (Cloonan 1996), the Beatles brought a subversive contribution to the meaning of drug use. This became public when in an interview for *Queen and Life* magazine in 1967 McCartney stated that LSD had 'opened my eyes. It made me a better, more honest, more tolerant member of society' (Shapiro 1999: 117).

The Beatles spoke of recreational drug use and we find it in their material as a source of fun, absurdity and social criticism, as in 'Revolution', 'Strawberry Fields Forever', 'It's All Too Much' and 'I Am the Walrus'. The hallucinatory experience forms a backdrop to their creative cultural practice, but as a source of humour it reflects their early comments and spontaneous wit. Merriment can also be subtly combined with solidarity as in *Sgt Pepper's Lonely Hearts Club Band* on 'A Little Help From My Friends'.[32] The personalized chorus and sardonic tone of Ringo Starr's delivery oozes comradeship and irony.[33] The jocular singalong factor of drug-related music enabled listeners to participate and feel part of a generation engaged in refusal. In this sense the Beatles' use of drugs became part of their ability to be a pop group and deliver entertainment. Towards the end of the 1960s we find the Beatles, in particular Lennon, moving away from recreational drug use. By the time they recorded 'Happiness is a Warm Gun' for the 1968 'White Album' it is clear that Lennon had reached personal problems with heroin use, which intensified after the Beatles broke up (Taqi 1969). Lennon's descent into LSD obsession and heroin is also connected with the loss of the Beatles' manager Brian Epstein through his own chaotic drug consumption (Melly 1972). Awareness of Lennon's own problems and sacrifice brought empathy when he publicly acknowledged his drug addiction with the 1969 hit single 'Cold Turkey'. This song is a powerful assertion against heroin and the problems faced when trying to recover from addiction.

Beatles songs which have a drug reference engage with the listener, offering a momentary fantasy or imaginative voyage. The material is descriptive of encounters with intoxicants and relies on the images and insider knowledge associated with the meanings put forward by the artist. Drugs became an important creative facilitator for the Beatles and similarly for the Doors drug references enabled them to move beyond an adoring audience towards listeners who wanted to change the world. Both sets of artists share a desire for revolution with expressions of utopian idealism tinged with occasional hostility. For the Doors drug references start with the name, which derives from Aldous Huxley's book *The Doors of Perception* (1954), which describes his drug experimentation. This representation is reinforced and condensed in Oliver Stone's film *The Doors* (1990) where Jim Morrison is typecast as an elusive Blakeian figure whose drug consumption is portrayed as pivotal to the musical and lyrical directions explored by the band. Drug citations in the Doors' material are innumerable, from 'The Crystal Ship' to 'Five to One', where references to being 'stoned', 'tripping' and hallucination are integral themes and can be read as signposts within psychedelic culture.

Implicit knowledge is the key to understanding drug subversion within popular music. When the Byrds reached the top twenty with 'Eight Miles High' in 1966, it was not merely a beautiful poetic song; it was, as Jon Savage (1997: 190) notes, 'the first aural reproduction of the LSD rush'. A year later the Beatles' hit song 'Strawberry Fields Forever' required some inside knowledge of LSD, according to George Melly (1972: 80–1). In 1967 the Small Faces had a top twenty hit with 'Here Comes the Nice' and appeared on *Top of the Pops* singing it. The song fits into the mod culture of the 1960s but it was by no means the first song to celebrate the drug dealer as hero; for example, Charlie Parker's song 'Moose the Mooche' was about Emry Byrd, his polio-stricken drug dealer. Perhaps the most famous drug dealer as cult hero song is Lou Reed's 'I'm Waiting for the Man', on the Velvet Underground's debut LP *The Velvet Underground and Nico* (1966).

The different focus on drugs within the emergent hip hop culture reflected the contradictory experiences of young black Americans. Drugs became a topic to sing about not in terms of subverting meaning through use of hidden codes, but as part of everyday life. Drugs for some individuals were an economic strategy out from poverty – they were not linked to imagination but to an enterprise culture. For Schooly D, Eazy-E, Tupac Shakur, Biggie Smalls, Coolio and Snoop Doggy Dogg drug dealing became intimately linked to their recording careers as rappers (Ogg 1999). The potential subversive power of rap music is that it seeks to offer social realism to its audience. Therefore songs about drugs represent a lived experience of people's responses towards criminality, social aspiration and their materialistic struggles (Decker 1994: 102). Within rap the glamorization of drugs and the stories of personal and social problems caused by drugs act as a form of subversion in response to American drug prevention policies, policing strategies and economic deindustrialization, which are understood to have marginalized the black community. For Tricia Rose (1994: 106) rap music is critically responding to white American state policies which use anti-drug war metaphors as a means to intensify racial divisions that 'portray young black males as criminals'. Or as NWA describe in 'Fuck tha Police' (1988) the police brutalize black teenagers who use electronic gadgets and assume they are all drug dealers. Thus drugs became one of a series of key issues around which their material focused.

Drugs were given a more subversive representation in rap through the use of psychedelia by artists such as De La Soul, PM Dawn and Cypress Hill.[34] This style of rap is linked with the tradition of black musical artists, including Sly Stone, the Temptations, Jimi Hendrix and George Clinton, being influenced by marijuana and LSD. Ogg (1999: 102) notes that the visual imagery of De La Soul's *Three Feet High and Rising* LP brought them attention as the 'hippies of hip hop'. Their combination of intellectualism and psychedelia, according to Jim Derogatis (1996: 196), brought 'criticism from hardcore rappers', forcing them to renounce the Daisy Age concept. De La Soul's psychedelic drug reference brought different themes into hip hop, changing the rap musical genre. The breakthrough of De La Soul's hippie chic paved the way for their siblings A Tribe Called Quest's song 'Can I Kick It', where Lou Reed's 'Walk on the Wild Side' was the main sample, bringing the drug references of the Velvet Underground into hip hop. In 2001 the top ten rap single 'Purple Pills' by D12, which includes Eminem, was censored for the singles and video market. For chart success it was retitled 'Purple Hills' and was edited for its drug and sexual content. 'Purple Pills' is a drug song that seeks to be shocking and fun, but its true aim is selling units rather than offering a meaningful critique. Afroman's number one hit 'Because I Got High' (2001) is similar to D12's song in that it is broadly against drugs within the genre of humour and wit.[35] This contrasts with established reggae icons, such as Bob Marley, Augustus Pablo or Dr Almantado, who surrounded themselves with representations of 'the herb'. Afroman sings amusingly about drugs but he is pictured on his record holding a can of lager! In Britain a more realistic portrayal of drugs and everyday culture was offered by the 'rude boy' garage outfit So Solid Crew, who, like US hip hop artists before them, merge real life and projected images of drugs and violence while being stereotyped by the media. In contrast, The Streets debut album in 2002 *Original Pirate Material* is peppered with everyday drug reference, not for sensation but as descriptions of 'leisurescape' pleasures and risks.

Drugs and corruption in the music industry are detailed in Fredric Dannen's study *Hit Men*. He describes one of the most serious cases of drug excess in the record industry: that of Neil Bogart's Casablanca Records of the late 1970s and 1980s, which featured Donna Summer, Village People, Kiss and Parliament. Dannen says (1990: 177) that by late 1979 'Casablanca began to lose tens of millions a year. It had two hundred employees on salary, and a large drug budget'. Dannen interviewed Russ Regan, a Casablanca employee, who said about the use of controlled substances at the company: 'If you were into drugs, man, you were in Camelot' (1990: 161). Bogart lived the life of excess and became an infamous record industry legend. He died in 1982 and the parent company of Casablanca, the multinational PolyGram, nearly collapsed as a result of his drug adventures. Dannen maintains that the precise deficit created by Bogart's Casablanca Records has never been disclosed but the corporate label did not return to profitability until 1985, having lost more than $200 million (1990: 181). Barney Hoskyns (1996: 279) states that Bogart's 'way of allaying the fears of PolyGram executives was to put them in Mercedes convertibles and spoon-feed them cocaine'. Bogart was a maverick entrepreneur who saw music as promotion and payola. He wanted to make money and enjoy excess as a virtue. He did not see drugs as a subject matter for artists to cover in their songs although for certain acts, such as Parliament, the drug imagination became an integral feature of their narrative and journey.

Homage to drug consumption and drug representations is an important subversive element within popular music and artists from different musical genres promote reverence for certain drugs. Hip hop's most consistent psychedelic creative force has been the Los Angeles black and Hispanic group called Cypress Hill. A central feature of their drug references based on marijuana is not merely the jokes and puns to the herb, but their universal exploitation of the typeface used by Rizla cigarette papers and worship of Peter Tosh's *Legalize It* LP. Dr Dre took up marijuana with his LP *The Chronic* and single 'The Next Episode' featuring visual images of a cannabis leaf and the reintroduction of samples from the drug 'space cadet' George Clinton (Ogg 1999: 153). Long before Cypress Hill's homage to cannabis, however, the Rooftop Singers had a number one American hit and a top ten British success in 1963 with 'Walk Right In'. They were an urban folk music trio who offered a subversive message. Sajjad Taqi (1969: 30) argues that the veiled reference to drugs in 'Walk Right In', which sold in millions, 'is not only revealing an aspect of popular culture, it has the capacity of becoming propaganda of the highest order'. In Britain the closest form of contemporary homage to cannabis[36] is the dance act Nightmares on Wax, especially the 1995 LP *Smokers Delight* with its dope scales and a spliff on the back of the record cover and the gatefold sleeve with drawings in the style of Robert Crumb.[37] The second Nightmares on Wax LP *Carboot Soul* (1999) gave away a free packet of designer Rizlas featuring the LP cover in miniature. Nightmares on Wax also made a contribution to the series of compilation LPs called *Beats by Dope Demand Too!*,[38] advertised as 'quality smokin' gear'.[39]

During the early 1970s an example of cannabis worship was the band Gong, led initially by Daevid Allen, who were one of the first bands to sign to the Virgin record label. The group members had pseudonyms such as 'Bad De Grasse' and enjoyed a high level of popularity in Britain and continental Europe, undertaking extensive tours and releasing a series of successful LPs which included *Camembert Electrique, Radio Gnome Invisible Part 1 (Flying Teapot), Angel's Egg* and *You*. Gong were a leading psychedelic band who created a complex journey, inviting listeners into a strange hippie world of humorous visions and creatures such as the 'Pot Head Pixies' (Whiteley 1997: 139). The LP covers and lyrics represent a combination of stoned humour and LSD hallucinations which Donald Clarke (1998: 501) says produced challenging music within a hippie mythology. Individualism and freedom were at the core of the Gong project, offering wit and subversion for young people in the post-Woodstock era. One of their key ironies was to focus on 'tea' as a code for a hallucinogenic experience, long before Noel Gallagher offered his 1997 comment 'drugs is like getting up and having a cup of tea in the morning'. The humour of Gong's equation of tea with dope served as a parody of British society. There is nothing more normal, more British than tea, thus Gong's 'flying teapot' in the 1970s and Noel Gallagher's 'cup of tea' in the 1990s strike at the heart of conventional sensibilities to reveal that humour remains one of the most productive ways to critique the dominant culture (Macan 1997: 134).

Steve Hillage from Gong became a successful rock music producer in the 1980s and in the 1990s re-emerged as a part of dance culture with the Orb (Toop 1995: 59).[40] Sheila Whiteley (1997: 139) states: 'Hillage was to influence much of the Orb's output, disseminated their commitment to LSD and Gong mythology.' The Orb grasped Pink Floyd's psychedelic heritage and transformed it with humour, alongside Gong's subversive homage to marijuana and hallucinogens, into dance culture and chart success. These artists have produced music which is meant to be listened to in a state of intoxication, whereby the listener can engage with the narrative which focuses on a journey or trip.

During the 1990s a rock band that metamorphosed into a dance act was the Shamen, who concentrated on 'exploring the areas of altered states with mind-expanding psychedelics' (Larkin 1998: 305). Between 1991 and 1992 the Shamen had five top ten singles, the most famous being 'Ebeneezer Goode', which was number one for four weeks in September 1992 and remained in the chart for ten weeks. The record is hardly ever heard on Radio 1 today, unlike other number one records. The chorus to the song is repeated a minimum of nine times on each delivery. It is not merely that the chorus sounds like Es [ecstasy] are good, but the lyrics within the rap are a parody of the drug culture. Initially the band denied any link with drugs, inventing stories which accounted for Ebeneezer Goode as a Dickensian character. Sheryl Garratt (1998: 256) explains that the band had problems with the *Top of the Pops* producer because Mr. C, the lead singer, kept singing 'Es are good' as in the song and in one of the final takes he also added 'Anybody got an underlay?' This was a drug reference to speed, from Speedy Gonzales, 'Riba riba, underlay, underlay'. The Shamen singer later appeared on Mark Goodier's Radio 1 show, where, according to Jane Bussmann (1998: 96), the DJ questioned him about the underlay reference and Mr. C said: 'It was a rug reference. I always swore blind it wasn't about drugs.' Garratt asks, was he lying? The answer is yes. The Shamen always had a reputation as pranksters.

Drug heroes of popular music

During 2002 and 2004 new guitar bands such as the Strokes, the White Stripes, Black Rebel Motorcycle Club, the Vines, the Coral, the Datsuns, the Libertines and the Kings of Leon have been described in the music press by the term 'stoner',[41] as an integral factor behind their drug coolness and referential place in contemporary music. In 1966 Bob Dylan's *Rainy Day Women No. 12 and 35* became a leading drug hero. Drug heroes in popular music are musicians who are acknowledged drug users, speak out in favour of drug consumption or produce music that has drug reference points. Drug heroes are not necessarily drug evangelists who want everyone to consume drugs and certain drug heroes may also speak out against 'hard drugs'. In the 1960s and 1970s the Beatles and the Rolling Stones were cast as drug heroes and martyrs. Both groups faced court cases with regard to drugs and also experienced drug-related deaths of close colleagues such as Brian Epstein and Brian Jones. The Beatles paid for a full-page advertisement in *The Times* of 24 July 1967, under the heading 'The law against marijuana is immoral in principle and unworkable in practice' (Shapiro 1999: 194). The public announcement was signed by 65 individuals from the worlds of literature, pop music, politics and other parts of the establishment. Later, Paul McCartney experienced a series of cannabis arrests: he was charged for drug possession in Sweden and later in Scotland, deported from Japan in 1980 and caught for possessing marijuana in Barbados in 1984.

In contrast to the Beatles, the Rolling Stones experienced greater police surveillance. Mick Jagger and Keith Richards were arrested along with others at a party in Richards's house, Redlands, on 12 February 1967 and kept in police custody. Defending the Rolling Stones was Michael Havers, later to become Sir Michael Havers, the Attorney General. On 29 June 1967 they were found guilty and Judge Leslie Block sentenced Richards to a year in prison with £500 costs and Jagger to three months and £200 costs. They were released pending an appeal. On 1 July William Rees-Mogg (later chairman of the BBC) wrote the *Times* editorial 'Who breaks a butterfly on a wheel?', where he argued that the sentence did not fit the crime and considered tabloid journalism to be setting them up as scapegoats.

On 31 July 1967 Lord Chief Justice Parker quashed Richards's conviction and substituted a one-year conditional discharge for Jagger's prison sentence. Hanif Kureishi and Jon Savage (1995: 268) state: 'Jagger was flown by helicopter to one of the more surreal media events of the decade: a televized summit meeting with four embodiments of the establishment – former Home Secretary Lord Stow Hill, the Bishop of Woolwich, leading British Jesuit Father Corbishly and Rees-Mogg himself. The *World in Action* special for Granada TV was produced by John Birt [later director general of the BBC].' Marianne Faithfull (1995: 166) points out that the case 'transformed them from pop stars into cultural legends'. The case of Jagger and Richards's arrest and the subsequent television programme needs to be seen in terms of its close association with key figures from the political elite and media establishment. The dominant class had taken an interest in the band not merely due to their influence with young people, but because they were a capital asset with future financial power.

From the 1960s onwards certain reggae artists have consistently put forward a positive celebration of cannabis through a combination of visual representations on record covers and songs. Bob Marley regarded himself as an ambassador for ganja and his international stardom meant that he became an global drug hero and figurehead for millions of young people (Bradley 2000: 397). During the 1960s Rastafarians[42] were a scapegoat for the Jamaican press, who targetted them as dangerous and violent; soon they became identified as social outcasts and as a result were gradually seen as popular figures of resistance for Jamaican youth (Hebdige 1987). A range of successful cannabis reggae songs includes U-Roy's 'Chalice in the Palace' (1976) and in Britain Musical Youth had a number one hit in 1982 with 'Pass the Dutchie', a dutchie being a cooking pot: the song was a reworking of the Mighty Diamonds' 'Pass the Kouchie' (1981), referring to marijuana. Although Rastafarians had no official leader, by the early 1970s Marley's position as an international musical artist on a corporate record company touring the globe gave him the opportunity to disseminate Rastafarian ideas and celebrate 'the herb'. As a songwriter and black icon Marley consistently promoted cannabis as a sacred herb in songs including 'African Herbsman' and 'Redder than Red'.[43] This can also be seen on the back cover of the 1973 Wailers LP *Burnin'*, which has a large profile of Marley smoking a spliff, while inside the gatefold sleeve we see individuals going about their everyday business alongside a colour photograph of Bob smoking. The 1976 LP *Rastaman Vibration* was made to feel like hessian, and the inside of the gatefold sleeve states: 'This album jacket is great for cleaning herb.' The back cover of the 1978 Bob Marley and the Wailers LP *Kaya* shows a marijuana plant surrounding a burning spliff. Fellow Wailer Peter Tosh on his 1976 LP *Legalize It* took on the role of advocate. The front cover shows Tosh smoking a pipe in a field of marijuana while on the inside of the gatefold sleeve we see the other musicians smoking the herb superimposed on another field of marijuana. Lloyd Bradley (2000: 86) says: 'Peter Tosh was only ever summing up popular opinion of the herb's superb properties with his "Legalize It" lyrics.' Other visual examples of dope LP covers include: Dr Alimantado's *Kings Bread* (1979), where he is walking through a huge field of marijuana dressed as a doctor, stethoscope in hand, checking the health of the crop; Augustus Pablo's *Africa Must Be Free By ... 1983 Dub* (1978), on the back cover of which there are five Rastamen[44] smoking a prepared bong; Pablo's *Original Rockers* (1979), where we see the musician smoking a large wooden pipe; and *The Best of Gregory Isaacs*, which features the man himself in profile smoking a large spliff. The Rastafarian tradition in reggae has significantly contributed to drug heroism in popular music from its place as part of the religious sacrament to the everyday context of cannabis use, and the style has continued into the new century with artists including Sizzla, Bushman Yami Bolo, Luciano, Anthony B and Finley Quaye.

Dance culture as drug hero

The different musical genres of popular music have brought forward many varied drug heroes from Andy Williams's use of LSD in the 1960s to the Aphex Twin's *Drukqs* (2002), but a significant difference with the dance culture of the 1990s was that the drug hero was the scene itself. Speaking about the influence of ecstasy in popular music, the group Shut Up and Dance[45] (2001) said: 'You should be interviewing the drugs, they've got a lot to answer for, I'm telling you.' Heroic martyrdom was conferred upon dance culture by John Major's Conservative government when the Criminal Justice and Public

Order Act 1994 defined dance music in legislation as 'sounds wholly or predominantly characterized by emission of a succession of repetitive beats'.[46] Although the sound system had previously been a symbol of resistance, it had now been transformed into an actual force of resistance. Within dance culture the pivotal role of the DJ as drug hero became a major factor in their ability to read the intoxicated audience on an interactive basis to predict the mass desire for conscious bodily movement.

The contradictory effect of the legislative repression[47] was that dance culture's diverse links spread into new age politics and the anti-capitalist globalization movement (McKay 1998). The penetration of ecstasy into mainstream culture was so successful that the long reign of Conservative governments was brought to a halt by a relaunched Labour Party, which had as its election campaign music the E-anthem 'Things Can Only Get Better' by D:ream (1993). Further, during the election of the first London mayor in 2000 the victor Ken Livingstone was hailed by DJ Fatboy Slim and shared decks with the turntable hero in support of his political campaign. Fatboy Slim has consistently invoked the mythology of 'canning it' or to 'get on one matey',[48] further described in Turner (1999) by the original dance DJs such as Paul Oakenfold, Danny Rampling, Johnny Walker and Nicky Holloway, who conform to traditional rock music icons as drug heroes.[49] In dance culture DJ drug heroes construct their own romantic assertions about drugs and support the assumption that drugs possess a subversive identity in contemporary culture (Bidder 2001).

Drug zeros: death and popular music

To be a drug zero is to be dead. Within contemporary popular music, drugs have been a major cause of death or withdrawal from the music industry as a result of health problems. There has been a close link between death and modern popular music, starting with the nineteenth-century 'murder ballad' at executions (Clayson 1997) and continuing with Robert Johnson, the blues guitarist whose pursuit of dangerous pleasures resulted in death aged 27 in 1938 (Bayles 1994: 189). Before rock 'n' roll, Hank Williams's 1952 hit 'I'll Never Get Out of This World Alive' set the tone for the myth of fast living and breaking taboos (Pike 1993). Drug-related deaths have been a consistent factor in popular music, for example:

* *Jazz and soul*
  Sonny Berman (1947), Fats Narvarro (1950), Wardell Gray (1955), Charlie Parker (1955), Billie Holiday (1959), Clyde McPhatter (1972), Phil Seaman (1972), Graham Bond (1974), Greg Herbert (1978), Marvin Gaye (1984), Art Pepper (1985)

- *Country and folk*
  Hank Williams (1953), Danny Whitten (1972), Gram Parsons (1973), Michael Bloomfield (1981), Paul Butterfield (1987), Robin Maclennan (1997)
- *Punk and new wave*
  Billy Murcia (1972), Sid Vicious (1979), Malcolm Owen (1980), Pete Fardon (1982), James Honeyman Scott (1982), Nico (1988), Andrew Wood (1990), Martin Hannett (1991), Johnny Thunders (1991), Kurt Cobain (1994), Kristen Pfaff (1995), Jonathan Melvoin (1996), Michael Hutchence (1997), Joey Ramone (2001), Dee Dee Ramone (2002).
- *Rock and pop*
  Frankie Lymon (1968), Brian Jones (1969), Dickie Pride (1969), Jimi Hendrix (1970), Janis Joplin (1970), Alan Wilson (1970), Jim Morrison (1971), Duane Allman (1972), Berry Oakley (1972), Nick Drake (1974), Mama Cass Elliott (1974), Robbie McIntosh (1974), Vinnie Taylor (1974), Tim Buckley (1975), Tommy Bolin (1976), Paul Kossoff (1976), Gary Thain (1976), Elvis Presley (1977), Keith Moon (1978), Lowell George (1979), Dave Bidwell (1980), Tim Hardin (1980), Carl Radle (1980), Steve Took (1980), Bob Hite (1981), Dennis Wilson (1983), Wells Kelly (1984), Gary Holton (1985), Phil Lynott (1985), Andy Gibb (1988), Rick Grech (1990), Will Sinnott (1991), Jeff Porcaro (1992), Shannon Hoon (1994), Nicky Hopkins (1994), Jerry Garcia (1995), Jeff Buckley (1997), John Entwistle (2002), Zac Foley (2002), Layne Staley (2002).

Alongside this illustrative list of drug-related deaths it is also possible to construct another list of musicians whom I shall call the 'undead', whose careers have stopped or been interrupted as a result of their drug consumption. This has also given rise to the cultural phenomenon called celebrity rehabilitation, where high-profile musicians enter drug clinics. The musicians who have publicly recognized they have had a drug problem include: Marc Almond, Elton John, David Bowie, David Gahan, Brian Wilson, Pete Townshend, Eric Clapton, Syd Barrett, Boy George, Keith Richards, Peter Perrett, Peter Green, Danny Kirwan, Joe Perry, Steven Tyler, Topper Headon, Keith Leven, Shaun Ryder, Nick Cave, Sly Stone, Dave Crosby, Stephen Stills, Hugh Cornwell, Lemmy, Courtney Love, Michael Head, Jason Pierce, Noel and Liam Gallagher, Brian Harvey, George Michael, Julian Cope and Richard Ashcroft (Kent 1994).

Both drug casualties and drug deaths are highly romanticized in the world of popular music by the media, fans, musicians and the industry. In short, sufferance and sacrifice sell units. The drug-induced deaths of pop stars establish new 'consumer shrines' that feed on and promote personal and artistic mystery, suggesting that an individual's demise is not a closed book. This is followed by endless repackaging of existing material, remixes or releases of unsanctioned songs. In this hero worship of the dead or the undead, the artist becomes a saintly figure and the reality of their life and drug use becomes distorted. Drugs are seen as a demonic higher force that took the artist away because they were unable to cope with the mundanity of the ordinary world. Their drug consumption is seen as the dominating force of their creativity when in reality it may have destroyed their visionary talent. For example, Sid Vicious murdered his girlfriend Nancy Spungen and died of a heroin overdose[50] and Syd Barrett of Pink Floyd, a saintly figure of English psychedelia,[51] had an LSD obsession which later developed into schizophrenia. Their real life is silenced by the metaphorical power of their drug consumption. Each is romantically defined as too destructive for the world or too fragile for the world: canonized as rock–drug martyrs, close to madness or closed by death and unable to reply.

Anti-drug songs

Punk journalists Julie Burchill and Tony Parsons (1978: 76) saw cannabis as encouraging 'affluent complacence'. Within popular music there has been a range of famous musicians who have upheld an anti-drug stance. These include Cliff Richard, Bruce Springsteen, Frank Zappa, Chris Martin, Nicky Wire and John McLaughlin. For these individuals drugs are seen as wrong or are associated with weak self-discipline where musicians lack control and direction. Drug abstinence is supported by some musicians who have a mythical reputation for drug consumption: for example, Andrew Innes of Primal Scream argues that drugs and studio time do not mix.[52] Certain types of drug prohibition are operated by musicians when undertaking recordings[53] but outside the studio drug consumption takes up its mythical position: for example, Mezz Mezzrow's *Really the Blues* (1946) and Julian Cope's *Head-On* (1994) and *Repossessed* (1999)[54] are crammed full of 'wild' drug narratives about playing music and being fully 'spaced'. Anti-drug stances and voluntarily self-imposed limits on drug consumption during the production of music are acknowledged positions within the world of popular music but fail to receive public attention.[55]

A selection of anti-heroin songs could include: The Velvet Underground's 'Heroin' (1966), John Lennon's 'Cold Turkey' (1969), Black Sabbath's 'Hand of Doom' (1970), Neil Young's 'Needle and the Damage Done' (1972) and James Brown's 'King Heroin' (1972). Each of these songs presents a negative understanding of the experience of the drug. In contrast, the Stranglers' 1982 hit 'Golden Brown', which reached number two, suggested a more open and hypnotic representation of heroin. Three important anti-drug songs from the late 1960s are Canned Heat's 'Amphetamine Annie' (1968),[56]

Gil Scott-Heron's 'Home Is Where the Hatred Is' (1971) and Steppenwolf's 'The Pusher' (1969) from the film *Easy Rider*. Anti-cocaine songs[57] have included Curtis Mayfield's 'Freddie's Dead' and 'Pusher Man' from the 1972 film *Superfly*. Three major anti-drug hip hop songs are the 1984 top ten hit 'White Lines (Don't Do It)' by Grandmaster Flash featuring Melle Mel, Public Enemy's 'Night of the Living Baseheads' (1988), a critical focus on crack usage and De La Soul's 'Say No Go' (1989). Within acid house there has been Phuture's 'Your Only Friend' (1987), where a voice impersonating cocaine warns that you may end up with no friends except for cocaine itself. Pulp's number two hit 'Sorted for E's and Wizz' (1995), a double A-side with 'Misshapes', attracted attention from the tabloid press but the media failed to under-stand that the song was critical of ecstasy. Inaccurate assessments of drugs and popular music are common[58] due to the complexity of the message delivered.[59]

Two contrasting examples of anti-drug stances in punk and drum and bass are Straight Edge and 4 Hero. In America during the early 1980s Straight Edge, a musical subculture, emerged as an offshoot of hardcore punk in opposition to the 'sex, drugs and rock 'n' roll' myth. The Straight Edge punk lifestyle is defined by an absence of drug consumption and takes its name from a song written by Ian MacKaye and performed by Minor Threat (1981). To remain drug free and 'keep your edge' is the ideal alongside belief in animal rights and vegetarianism (Irwin 1999; Wood 2003). The Straight Edge doctrine of self-control and discouragement of drug use in more recent years has evolved into factions, some of which align with politically right-wing stances such as 'pro-life' abortion views and the Drug Free America campaign. The Straight Edge focus on individuality and white masculinity has brought a rather militant and self-righteous aspect to their style which, ironically, corresponds to the US government's programme of the 'war on drugs'.

In 1990 the drum and bass artists 4 Hero had an underground hit called 'Mr Kirk's Nightmare'. The song describes how a police officer calls at a house to inform a father of the bad news that his son has died of a drug overdose and could he accompany the officer to the station to identify the body. At the end of the tune the final statement is repeated twice. The fast metallic beats and disturbingly twisted vocal present a horror film atmosphere. Martin James (1997: 16–20) details that 4 Hero's dislocated tune was part of 'dark core', in opposition to commercial happy hardcore raves. 4 Hero continued to pioneer the cold dark sound with the EP 'Where's the Boy' (1992). The four tracks: 'Cooking up ya brain', 'Bunning,' Time to get ill' and 'Where's the boy? (Trial by Ecstasy) trace out the theme of death by heatstroke, which entered public consciousness as the explanation for a spate of E-related deaths'. It is unsurprising that 4 Hero are non-drug using musicians within the dance scene (Reynolds 1998:196).

Drug as a public relations exercise

Drugs are used as a public relations exercise by record companies and by musicians to promote and advertise debauchery, street credibility, creative individualism, risk, freedom and anti-authority attitudes. Here drugs and rebellion seem far from subversion and appear more related to safe predictability and conformity. Drugs are also used to promote moral standards, encouraging anti-drug attitudes. Recently, the successful R & B artists Destiny's Child have been seen wearing low-cut outfits with the logo of D.A.R.E. To Resist Drugs as part of their publicity shots.[60] Record companies and musicians consistently use drugs as a PR exercise, employing the specialist strategy of personal and intimate confession to suggest that an individual has been hurt in life.

The personal struggle is a human interest story. One of the leading personal stories of 'my drug hell' in the 1980s and 1990s was Boy George's *Take It Like A Man* (1995). This successful biographical and career relaunching economic strategy was subsequently exploited by George Michael and Robbie Williams. In 1990 Michael, following the confessional route, wrote *Bare* with journalist Tony Parsons and was able to dictate the manner in which drug accusations were directed at him, for example, making the front page of the *Daily Mirror* on 10 November 1997 with his personal cannabis revelations. Another dimension to the drugs as public relations exercise is to reveal the longstanding sensitivities which show the artist struggling with his oeuvre and emotional life. Williams featured in the tabloids but first on the cover of *The Face* magazine in January 1999 talking about his heroin and cocaine problems. He is presented as the nation's favourite: Elton John (self-declared ex-cocaine addict) helped him come off drugs; he has a close relationship with his mum; and he has 'chatted' with Prince Charles. Williams was reborn as an iconic star, no longer a boy band wonder. He became Mr Entertainment by promoting the idea that he was a confessional-based drug hero.

Two leading contemporary drug heroes have been Noel and Liam Gallagher of the rock group Oasis. On a populist level Noel and Liam are two of the most favoured names for babies. Liam Gallagher was arrested for possession of cocaine on 9 November 1996 and later in January 1997 he was released with a caution for possession of a class A drug. His release brought furious criticism from Conservative MPs such as Sir Teddy Taylor, Barry Legg, Sir Gerald Vaughan, Tim Rathbone and Lady Olga Maitland. Meanwhile, in September 1997 the Verve had a number one hit single with the song 'The Drugs Don't Work'. The song was incorrectly considered by George Howarth, a Home Office minister, as an example of an anti-drug message. The contents of the song have no reference to recreational drug use. It is a highly personal song by Richard Ashcroft, lead singer of the Verve, describing the emotional consequence of the cancer drugs which failed to cure his father's disease.

The debate about the meaning of the song lyrics became dramatically altered in October 1997 when Noel and Liam Gallagher were interviewed by DJ Steve Lamacq on Radio 1's *Evening Session* and proceeded to expound their assertion that 'drugs do work'.[61] What is most relevant about the Gallaghers' intervention is that Noel Gallagher is a friend of Ashcroft and would certainly have known of his father's illness and the true meaning of the song. However, what became publicly presented through BBC radio was a deliberate encounter with northern wit. The media seemed blind to the inverted jocularity which allowed Noel and Liam Gallagher to spin out their mischief making while allowing them to appear 'cool' drug heroes.

At the start of 1997 Brian Harvey, singer with the boy band East 17, who had over 12 top ten hits, made the front pages of most tabloids with his comment that ecstasy is 'a safe pill and it ain't doing you no harm'. Harvey's drug statement made during an interview for Independent Radio News at *Top of the Pops* fits the drug hero formula in that he advances that drugs are a heaven not a hell. He quickly became the object of a modern-day heresy campaign led not merely by tabloid journalists and anti-drug campaigners but also the Prime Minister, John Major. However, unlike other pop artists who have made positive statements about their drug use, Harvey failed to become a drug hero and quickly slipped into becoming a drug zero (Shapiro 1999). This was the result of his public retraction broadcast on the television programme *London Tonight*. Importantly, to be a drug hero in popular music you need to be intelligent; during 1997 the *NME* always referred to Brian Harvey, the 'former plumber and sweet shop assistant, as not the brightest of people'.

Although Noel Gallagher defended Harvey's honesty about his drug use, it was the end of East 17 and his solo career stalled.[62] Harvey was mercilessly condemned on the front page of the *Daily Mirror* in their 17 January 1997 'Ecstasy Shock Issue', and became a stepping stone to attack Noel Gallagher as a result of his refusal to denounce his 'drugs are as normal as a cup of tea' statement. Gallagher was criticized by Conservative MP Tim Rathbone, chair of the all-party Drug Misuse Group, the Home Office Minister Tom Sackville and Paul Betts. Gallagher succeeded in becoming a drug hero because he used the opportunity to demonstrate his articulate position by specifying a harm reduction approach, arguing: 'I urge all youngsters to educate themselves about the harmful side of drug taking.'[63] Rather than retract his statement, Gallagher called for 'an open and honest debate about drug abuse', adding that he condemned politicians as hypocrites for the 'criminalization of drug users.'[64] Gallagher, Harvey and other popular music artists were criticized in the *Sun* of 17 June 1997 in an editorial headlined 'Stop pop and fashion icons preaching drugs to our kids'. The paper's comment referred to drugs as 'black propaganda' and stated: 'Society must condemn them. Or drugs will destroy us.' Whilst the *Sun* may wish to appear to uphold morality, it can never resist its own obsession with absurdity: the following month the tabloid delivered a joke story about drugs on the front page, headlined 'Drugs Bunny: pet hooked on pot', showing the cartoon character Bugs Bunny smoking a spliff.[65]

A recent example of drugs as a public relations exercise to give credibility to a waning image, offering a momentary boost of apparent deviance, came on 21 March 2001 when the *Sun* exposed the pop group S Club 7 on the front page as 'Spliff Club 7', when three members of the pop group were caught smoking cannabis. The drug did not harm S Club 7, who subsequently went to number one with 'Don't Stop Movin''. The *Sun* and other tabloids used irony and absurdity when highlighting the pop teen heroes' use of cannabis, which is in marked contrast to the usual moral panic paradigm, calling them 'Reefer the Stars'. Having been caught using drugs, the pop stars learnt the lesson from Brian Harvey's witch trial and immediately offered an apology: 'We have been very stupid. We know we've made a mistake and we're very sorry.'[66] When S Club 7 were interviewed on Select MTV to confess their sins and show humiliation, the *Sun* journalist Dominic Mohan asked the programme to play 'The Drugs Don't Work'. Instead of playing Richard Ashcroft's song that, as we have seen, has no connection with illicit drugs, the programme played the future number one hit 'Don't Stop Movin'' and the event was turned into a public relations exercise.

Drugs and musical structure: the code of trance

In 1968 Andrew Curry coined the term 'drug music' to describe the music performed by Bob Dylan and the Beatles. Drugs have been used by musicians as a means of relaxation but also as a means of breaking traditional musical borders and creating combinations of textures and phrases. The popularizing of drug experiences and drug imagination through drug-oriented musical references has enabled musicians to explore different ways of constructing sounds. The use of intoxicants allows musicians transformations by extending consciousness to make connections with personal or collective cultural struggle. The relationship between drugs and music is one means whereby young people explore the cultural politics of consciousness. Chris Cutler (1985) argues that the use of drugs should be understood in terms of encouraging experimentation with sound. His analysis of music and drugs occurs at a political level. He maintains that drug-influenced music with its 'optimistic sound' shows social awareness and demonstrates the need for cultural change. Subversive music speaks of political resistance and articulates material and identity politics of youth. The link here is that drug references in music can suggest an openness and drug references in culture enable alternative lifestyles and ideas to be pursued for pleasure, conflict or as a way of life. Popular music creates imaginative opportunities for listeners to engage with a diversity of experiences and drug-influenced music is a means to aurally convey the hallucinogenic encounter. The precise aspects of the affinity between drugs and musical structure relate to the musical codes and their relationship to drug meanings (Curry 1968; Taqi 1969). In other words, the music produced is an equivalent to the experience of intoxication.

Building on Middleton and Muncie's (1981) analysis, Sheila Whiteley (1992: 8) develops the concept of psychedelic musical codes to describe the relationship between drugs and music. She argues that 'musically psychedelic coding focuses on alternative meanings and involves a correlation of drug experience and stylistic characteristics'. Whilst anybody without drug experience can listen with pleasure to music produced by the Beatles, Pink Floyd, Gong, Parliament, the Orb, the Aphex Twin, Lemon Jelly or LTJ Bukem, Whiteley (1997: 136) suggests that certain 'styles are written for audiences using psychedelic drugs where . . . similarities are present in the music [and in] the influence of drug experiences' (1997: 139). She states that these include: first, the manipulation of timbres, blurred, bright, tinkly overlapping associated with the intensification of tripping; second, the upward movement in pitch which compares with the experience of being high; third, the characteristic use of harmonies lurching and oscillating which change focus; fourth, the sudden use of regular or irregular rhythms suggesting sudden surges of rhythm and the free floating of the beat suggesting both the rush of a drug but also the trance-like condition of soundscapes and layering textured sound; finally, the shifting textual relationship of foreground and background, which acts to disorientate conventional musical structure, offering new enhancements from new technology employed in music and also through the process of hallucination (1997: 140). For Roy Baumeister (1984: 344) popular music develops features derived from the effects of drugs on an interactive level where 'the drug create[s] mental states with certain preferences and receptivities' and 'the music [takes] on features that [correspond] to these mental states'. A key attraction within popular music is the degree of repetition, the constant reiteration of harmonic rhythm – from the early blues and later rock to contemporary dance music the musical patterns are suggestive of a trance-like condition.

The universal condition of trance for Gilbert Rouget (1985: 316) is closely linked to music 'as a result of emotional power' acting in conjunction to produce a state of possession. He specifies that trance can be induced solely by drugs but also the combination of music with drugs can undoubtedly sensitize a person to trance possession. Rouget maintains that music and trance is a dynamic process (1985: 65–7) where the exact purposes of the drug and the music may be different: sometimes the drug acts as a stimulant to dance; at other times dance acts as a means to counteract the effects of the drug. Where drugs are deliberately consumed he says that 'an intensification of musical perception is consciously sought' (1985: 88). Rouget suggests that it is not strictly comparable to view music and drugs to be of the same order to produce trance-like conditions. His argument is that music and drugs act singly or in combination to trigger the 'strange mechanism' of trance. In this sense trance selectively acts physically and mentally through music and drugs as an external agent or as part of an integral group experience. Anatole Broyard (1948: 723, 725–6) argues that 'jive music and tea [marijuana] were the most important components of the hipster's life ... where "waking" life is compensated for by trance ecstasy'. The relationship between drugs and popular music can be seen as one where cultural meanings are stored and wrapped in visual and aural symbols of subversion and pleasure.

The importance of trance in relation to the musical structure is that it can be suggestive of mystery, spirituality and an induction into different states of mind. Middleton and Muncie (1981: 78) argue that drug consumption as a subject and an experience impacts on musical and cultural characteristics, whereby knowledge within drug culture can settle on music. They state that 'the meaning of drug usage is affected by the meaning of the associated music'. Popular music is related to drugs in a number of ways: a psychedelic song is one that the songwriter describes as being produced, derived or an articulation from an experience or imagination of an 'altered state'. Many artists announce that they have written songs or recorded entire LPs under such conditions,[67] including Pete Townshend (Marsh 1983: 229–30), Syd Barrett (Whiteley 1997: 128), the Beach Boys, Happy Mondays, Mercury Rev, the Flaming Lips and Grandaddy.[68] These musicians are making creative reference to the drug imagination hidden behind coded metaphors or argot where the music seeks to resemble the condition of intoxication, for example, through psychedelic lyrics or a wobbly bass. The song or piece of music is written and produced to make sense to the listener only when they enter into a condition of hallucination, for example Jason Pierce's Spaceman 3 album Taking Drugs to Make Music to Take Drugs.

The beginning of dance culture's acid house scene is closely linked to drug music and the forging of new musical styles which reflected the different types of drugs (Bidder 2001). In the US 'Acid Trax' by Phuture (1987) had little reference to drugs; however, in 1988 in England the hits by D-Mob[69] and Bomb the Bass[70] brought wider attention to drugs through their connection with the Shoom smiley-face logo and the emergence of illegal warehouse parties (Collin 1997). The five drugs associated with dance culture – ecstasy, speed, cannabis, cocaine and LSD – are 'mood enhancers' and in general have influenced the cultural production of popular music.

Hillegonda Rietveld (1998a: 165) argues that 'Dance drugs as a body of technology have not only contributed to the way house music is consumed, but also to the production of particular formal aspects of this music.' Her argument is that within different musical genres it is possible to identify the specific influences each drug has on styles of music. We can identify calmness and relaxation in music linked to cannabis, which in turn is linked to the impact of LSD in relation to exploratory adventures combined with 'stoned' humour and the notion of a journey where structures get loose. Simon Reynolds (1998: 315) argues that trip hop should be considered an adjunct to rave culture. He states: 'Like rave music, trip hop is based around samples and loops; like techno, it's the soundtrack to recreational drug use. In trip hop's case, that drug is marijuana.' The spacey, if slightly paranoid, 'spliff tempo' of trip hop, while being mellow, is an attempt to go beyond DJ dance culture. As Ulf Poschardt (1998: 297) confirms, the trip hop sound 'is aimed at the roof of your head' or as Broyard (1948: 724) noted in reference to jazz bebop, it 'was cerebral music'. The trip hop pace and focus is on consciousness rather than the body and follows the hallucinogenic journey of intoxicated music (Bennett 2001).

With amphetamine the word 'speed' defines the principal need of energy. As a result the faster pace of the beats is related to the intoxication as beats in techno and then gabber moved to 150 beats per minute (bpm) and higher. With drum and bass there can be a furious percussive pace where tracks can reach 320 bpm, which rejects the basic 4/4 time of house music and relies on fast 'break beats'. The drugs speed and cocaine have been associated with drum and bass and fit the heavier irregular bass line and the more frenetic experience of the drug dancer (Metcalfe 1997: 178). The uneven and slightly jagged style of drum and bass mirrors the shorter highs and lows of the cocaine experience: thus the musical style is changing and different. Ciaran O' Hagan[71] elaborates Stuart Metcalfe's ideas further, in that he identifies a clear series of divisions between drug use and different styles of dance music. For him the chemistry set of music and drugs is closely related to the cultural dynamic of the drug 'set and the setting'. Techno remains a musical form with hallucinogenic potential shown through both the music and flyers advertising shows, house remains soaked in ecstasy culture, while the garage scene and drum and bass have a closer connection with sexualized aspirations[72] shown through the decline of ecstasy use and the growth in taking amphetamine and cocaine (James 1997). From here the close association between drugs and dance music becomes consolidated and articulated as drugs begin to influence not merely the visual images and song lyrics but also the musical structure in terms of beats per minute to reflect the use of ecstasy, as well as in terms of relaxation with the arrival of 'chill out' music and marijuana. Drugs impact on the fast and slow tempo of the music and relate to the person's expectations of what the drugs will do according to the location, both physically and socially (Zieberg 1984).

Conclusion

In this section I have explored how certain styles of music and artists promote the subversion of legitimate meaning through drug music via hidden codes, argot and trance. This can take the form of innuendo, parody or a celebration of substances through a homage to hallucination, or take a more critical response against discrimination and poverty. The aim has been to suggest that drugs have an impact on the culture and structure of popular music. Theoretically it is the musicians' experience of drug consumption and their critical reflection on intoxication which acts as an aid in their production of music. Or at other times the consumption of drugs can result in the musicians' death or inability to produce songs. They become a drug zero. From the beginning of popular music there has been a broad range of anti-drug songs and credible musicians who have spoken against drugs. Anti-drug songs rarely provide simple solutions or describe easy answers, because they invoke contradictory real-life experiences. For drug prohibition the challenge is to incorporate these narratives into education as a means to engage with young people. Drugs have been an integral part of popular music for over a hundred years. They reflect the historical struggle of certain people and their diverse forms of resistance from humour to hegemony. Drugs within popular music possess to some extent a heroic position. The contradiction that drug prohibition has to tackle is that even where musical icons have died as a result of drug use the artist retains power, credibility and influence.

4 Youth subcultural theory
Deviance, resistance, identity and drugs

Subculture: introduction to a chameleon theory

The chapter will be concerned with the politics of youth subculture theory and the way in which different theories of subculture explain drug use. The concept has been attractive as a model for explanation in sociology by a diversity of theoretical positions because it assesses a group which is different from the mainstream and which pursues and acts out its own cultural solutions. In sociology the concept of subculture has been used as a means to understand meaningful action, 'learned problem solutions' and identity formation as a series of practices at an individual or collective level. Subculture is not macro theory; it is what Robert Merton (1957) described as 'intermediate theory', between grand narrative and 'grounded' everyday life.

Within sociology and criminology, according to Parker et al. (1998: 156) two theories have dominated explanations of drug use: first, developmental personality theories, which insist that drug use is a sign of abnormality; second, subcultural theories, which explain drug use as form of criminality or moral turpitude to account for deviance. I shall argue that the concept of subculture is a chameleon theory which possesses different and opposing definitions, from its use as a deficit model to describe 'subnormal behaviour' to its use as a concept to express resistance, vitality and consumer choice. Further, the concept of subculture possesses an ability to change its hue according to the sociological paradigm, but it also retains elements of previous approaches.

This chapter is divided into the following sections: first, I shall look at the theoretical origins of subcultural theory in work of Émile Durkheim and the Chicago school, which saw deviance within a social context of normality. Second, I shall examine the structural–functionalist approach, which defined subcultures as deviant outsiders. Third, I shall assess the psychoanalytical origins of the British theory of subcultures and its development by the Centre for Contemporary Cultural Studies (CCCS). Finally, I shall analyse the postmodern theory of subcultures.

Normality and deviance: the Chicago school and Émile Durkheim

In the development of subcultural theory it is useful to make the distinction between American and British theories of subculture. The formal academic study of youth began in America at the University of Chicago on the basis of undertaking empirical sociological research. From 1913 under the direction of Robert Park and later with Ernest Burgess the Chicago school began to construct ethnographic maps of the social and cultural territories of the city with its diverse populations (Bulmer 1984). Ned Polsky (1967: 124) suggests that Park's training as a journalist and his interest in popular culture made him focus on experience in his attempt to understand cultural difference and the subjective meaning of action. Park was a student of Georg Simmel (1858–1918) at Berlin; for Simmel the purpose of sociology was to 'capture moments' in order to understand the interaction and formation of groups (Scott 1995). Reflecting Simmel's concern to describe everyday 'configurations' of people's lives, Park concentrated on studying conflict and social change through an exploration of the city to discover the formation of urban social groups. This could be proposed as the beginning of subcultural studies, focusing on the 'youth's own story' (Shaw 1927, 1930; Burgess 1923). The Chicago school looked to understand young people from within an ethnographic context derived from normal conditions of urban social life (Downes and Rock 1982: 66).

Émile Durkheim's academic objective was to establish the legitimacy of the sociological approach. Therefore in *The Rules of Sociological Method* (1895) his intention was to break with psychological understandings of deviance and see deviance as a normal response by ordinary people to their experience of social divisions. Durkheim suggests that the deviant is a member of society; his social theory of deviance opposed the biological and pathological approaches developed by theorists such as Cesare Lombroso and Enrico Ferri (1901). In *L'uomo delinquente* (1895) Lombroso proposed the theory of criminal physical abnormality, a biological account of deviance which describes criminals in terms of primitives, savages and animals. The popularity of this theory of deviance has remained constant. Drugs are described as a social evil corrupting young people leading them into lax morals and crime. Deprived of their agency the drug consumer is defined as 'feeble-minded', suffering from mental defects closely linked to immorality. The drug deviant is placed on an evolutionary scale near the bottom. The drug user is defined as a subhuman or subnormal who can live only in groups or subcultures.

What was 'normal' for Durkheim and 'ordinary' for the Chicago school were the ways in which individuals and groups construct and negotiate social and cultural meaning. It is extremely doubtful whether Durkheim would have described subcultures as anomic. Durkheim looked at collective ritual in terms of the degree of consensus it created. Subcultural activity is about restoring order to the lives of young people. Subcultural formation is the solution to anomie: the subculture is the norm (Sprott 1958: 71). A subculture's deviance strengthens its internal group relations, creates solidarity and maintains order; anomie does not cause deviance, it is deviance which is the solution to anomie (Thrasher 1927: 3; Waller 1932: 180; Whyte 1943). The Chicago sociologists identify the social space, morality and bonds which groups perform through hard times. Their aim was to explain the social and cultural context of deviance without reducing young people's actions to symptoms of psychological inadequacy. Vivien Palmer's (1926: 341) concern was to argue for fieldwork as a primary source of knowledge to influence theoretical understanding, through what Clifford Shaw (1927: 150) describes as a combination of qualitative approaches to assess the total situation and conceptualized by Edwin Sutherland (1924) in his theory of differential association, which emphasized the normality of deviance. The work of the Chicago school occurred during the era of prohibition in the United States, where they sought to explain forms of behaviour within the context of social normality. Therefore consumption of illicit substances was interpreted as an expression of a person's position in the social structure and their relationship with the community.

Creation of the deviant outsider: functionalist subcultural typologies

A major figure in the development of American subcultural theory is Robert K. Merton. He was a research student of Talcott Parsons, whom he greatly admired, and his key project was the correction of Parsonian functionalism. He introduced his social theory of deviance first in 1938, and extended and revised it in 1957.[1] Merton does not use the concept of subculture in his original paper,[2] nor does he refer to the Chicago school's work on deviance.[3] The sociological value of Merton's theory of deviance derives from his argument that deviance results from the interplay of culture and structure in society. He argues that individuals in different social class positions in the social structure do not possess the same opportunity of realizing the shared values of success, and this situation generates deviance in terms of an individual's adaptation to the goal of success. Social hierarchy is identified as causing structural strain for the individual. Thus Merton identified social class as a causal factor in the generation of deviance. His argument was that any movement away from the set pattern could be labelled as deviant and an index of lack of socialization, i.e. anomie. This theory of deviance from the norm became the template for subsequent subcultural work in America and

Britain (Carson and Wiles 1971). Succeeding functionalists developed theoretical models to show that youth who refused to adapt to the norm, i.e. the goals of success via institutional means, were not part of society and were to be categorized as deviant outsiders (Cohen 1956; Cloward and Ohlin 1960).

During the dominant period of American functionalist sociology, theorists sought to reposition the contribution of the Chicago school to make it appear beholden to functionalism for revealing its inadequacies. Merton (1957: 179) argues that A. K. Cohen's (1956) theory of subculture is 'in a direct line of continuity with the earlier studies by Shaw, McKay and particularly Thrasher'. Short (1960: xli) states: 'Some may wonder why Shaw and McKay (1927) did not hit upon the notion of delinquent subculture since with Thrasher (1927) they were responsible for a large portion of the data upon which contemporary formulations rest ... it remained for Cohen (1956) to introduce the notion of delinquent subculture.' The functionalist argument is that youth studies proper could not begin until functionalist social theory dominated sociology and introduced the concept of subculture. The concept was now used to describe 'bad' or dysfunctional parts of society, including drug use; thus deviance moves away from being understood as a 'normal' feature of diverse communities. The functionalist concept of subculture saw drugs as emerging from subcultures whose values opposed 'conventional' society. Drugs became seen as a problem or threat to the equilibrium of society.

Cohen (1956) popularized the term 'subculture' and brought it into extensive use in youth studies. His theory of subculture as solving problems was influenced by Clellan Ford's (1942: 557) approach to culture (Plant 1975: 122), which Mike Brake (1980: 5) incorrectly identified as the earliest usage of the term 'subculture' (Lee 1945; Gordon 1947). This error was continued by Sarah Thornton (1997: 1–12) in *The Subcultures Reader*, where she argues the term was first coined in the 1940s and was unfamiliar to the Chicago school under Park. The concept of subculture was known to members of the Chicago school; for example, Palmer, in her *Field Studies in Sociology: A Student's Manual* (1928: 73), details the importance of gaining 'maps of subcultural groups'. She notes that 'subcultural groups ... display variations in the prevailing culture'.

Cohen used Merton's theory of anomie to structure his idea that it was the cause generating deviant behaviour in combination with a Freudian understanding of aggression and frustration. Cohen's theory of deviance is best described as the 'gang-into-subculture' theory, which is dependent on a psychological understanding of the subject. He adapted Merton's theory of anomie by applying the structural correspondence of differentiation within anomie to subculture. Cohen transferred the framework of Merton's theoretical argument concerning cultural goals and institutional means to his development of the concept of subculture, transforming Merton's scale of 'individual adaptation' to construct a new typology of collective adaptation.

Cohen extends the basic idea of Dollard et al. (1939: 1) that 'the occurrence of aggressive behaviour always presupposes the existence of frustration', arguing that an 'important function of the delinquent subculture is the legitimization of aggression' (Cohen 1956: 131). For Dollard et al. (1939) their analysis of status frustration is directly linked to the experience of schooling, a core element in Cohen's theory which later uncritically formed the basis of polarization theory in the British sociology of education (Lacey 1966, 1970; Hargreaves 1967; Sugarman 1967; Ball 1981; Hammersley 1985). In Cohen's subcultural theory the aggressive behaviour of working-class youth is seen as a result of not possessing middle-class status, owing to their class position; the structural strain causes the problem of status frustration. For him this becomes visible when working-class youth realize they do not possess the means to access legitimate middle-class culture. At the time, Cohen ignored the growth of middle-class drug use and its high-profile popularity amongst the bohemian literary elite of the Beat movement.

According to Cohen, status failure at school becomes internalized by the social group, who 'react to form' their delinquent subcultural goals based on a reversal of the values upheld by the dominant middle-class culture. 'React to form' is derived from Freud (1913: 244), who identified a series of hidden defence mechanisms of the ego – motivating forces 'in mental life which bring about replacement by the opposite in the form of what is known as reaction-formation'. Cohen's theory of subculture uses Freud's theory of the subconscious mind as a means to consciously solve problems for working-class young people, who are at the bottom of the class structure where avenues to success are blocked. Subcultural solutions are the result of class conflict where working-class youth suffer status frustration; in an attempt to resolve this young people replace the 'normal' goals of society with their own alternative set of values and norms to achieve success, called the 'collective solution', and thus is born the delinquent subculture.[4] Two leading American critics of the functionalist theory of subculture were Howard S. Becker and David Matza. For them the real problem of Cohen's theory of subculture was its inherent class discrimination and failure to explain the law-breaking activities of the middle and upper classes. Taylor et al. (1973: 107) state: 'Anomie theory stands accused of predicting too little bourgeois criminality and too much proletarian criminality.' Cohen's subcultural theory failed to explain middle-class deviance because the privileged did not lack status, they possessed it. Young middle-class deviants were never defined as pathological because they were not working class. American subcultural theory, with its uncoiling Freudian spring of inversion for problem solving, promotes an appeal to 'common sense' which has great attraction as an explanation to account for delinquency such as drug use. David Downes (1966: 67; see also Mannheim 1965) was the first theorist[5] to question the American subcultural solution proposed by Cohen. He located his research in the ethnographic tradition of the Chicago school, reasserting 'the ordinariness of most gang behaviour'. Downes (1966: 63) argued against the British importation of American subcultural theory to the 'English experience' (Bernstein 1977: 168). For him deviance was a natural response defined and regulated by the cultural norms of the community, it was not a symptom of psychological deficiency.

The British theory of subculture

British subcultural theory has consistently relied on psychology and psychoanalysis to explain the social. Two psychologists who played a crucial part in the developmental phase of the British theory of subculture were Cyril Burt with *The Young Delinquent* (1925) and John Bowlby with *Forty-Four Juvenile Thieves* (1946). Burt's (1925: 300) contribution to the concept of subculture is in terms of transferring elements of Lombroso's evolutionary theory of deviance into a series of cultural descriptions which refer to young people who enter deviant groups possessing defective morals showing pathological traits (1925: 40). This has significantly continued through the representation of drug users as some type of throwback. Burt's description of young deviants (1925: 302–5) offers depersonalized images; for example, speaking about a school truant called Tommy: 'In looks he was a typical slum-monkey. His sloping forehead, his diminutive snub nose, his prominent jaws and lips were suggestive of the muzzle of a pale faced chimpanzee.' Burt sees deviants as 'dull' and 'untrainable animals' who are mentally defective due to their interest in intoxication; their behaviour is defined as 'troublesome', resulting from their 'inborn backwardness'. Building on the work of Burt, the Wood Report on Mental Deficiency (1929),[6] largely written by E. O. Lewis, asserted that a large proportion of the mentally subnormal were of a type termed 'subcultural'. It was argued that at school the 'educationally subnormal' form marginal groups possessed of low levels of intelligence and are found amongst the lower social classes in subcultures (Susser 1962). These case studies, Stephen Humphries (1981: 19) argues, were directly misleading and used a 'faulty methodology for measuring intelligence and personality and failed to situate behaviour in the broader class context of poverty, inequality and exploitation'.

Whilst Burt produced biological theories of deviant youth drawn from social Darwinism in the first part of the twentieth century, Bowlby advanced more therapeutic theories of deviance for the 1950s. Bowlby's psychoanalytic theory of deviance served as a model for further research concentrating on the principle of 'inadequate socialization' as the reason for young people joining subcultures. In *Forty-Four Juvenile Thieves* (1946) he developed his analysis of the psychopathology of the 'affectionless character'. The 'affectionless personality' refers to a deviant young person who is said to be suffering from the emotional effect of deprivation from maternal affection in the early years of life. Bowlby's idea was that maternal deprivation was the cause of youth delinquency; he argued against Burt's biological theory to advance that nurture was to blame for the 'affectionless personality'. The maternal deprivation theory was fully developed in *Child Care and the Growth of Love* (Bowlby 1953: 38), where he says that 'separation of a child from his mother during the first five years of life stands foremost amongst the causes of delinquent character development'. Juliet Mitchell (1975: 228) states: 'In the effort to rebuild the family the equation went delinquency = latch key kids = having been abandoned by its mother in infancy to crèche or evacuation. From now onwards appeals to maternal guilt vied with the political exploitation of the economic situation to keep women at home ... we learnt that a person sucked his emotional stability literally with his mother's milk.' Bowlby's work quickly became orthodoxy and Madeleine Klein (1965) argues that Bowlby's theory of the affectionless personality was applied within the majority of studies on working-class subcultures during the period.

The post-Second World War development of psychoanalytical approaches to juvenile delinquency under Kate Friedlander (1947) and Bowlby (1946, 1953) retained reverberations of the old positivist tradition of Lombroso. A series of studies emerged during the 1950s which argued that subcultural formation by working-class youth revealed their inability to integrate in society. Subcultural formation was identified as a form of deprivation where individuals lacked intelligence and emotional development. The major studies included Bagot (1941), Fergusson (1952), Spinley (1953), Jephcott (1954), Mays (1954), Morris (1957), Kerr (1958), and Trasler (1962). Throughout these studies young people who formed subcultures are described in terms of animal metaphors and in the language of health and disease. David Downes (1966: 111) critically accuses these British theorists for their use of subculture in combination with psychoanalytic deprivation theory 'to erect an "omnibus" theory of "inadequate socialization" as the origin of delinquent behaviour'. The psychoanalytic underpinning of the British theory of subculture is not too dissimilar from the American theory of subculture elaborated by A. K. Cohen, which uses Freud's theory of 'reaction formation' as the basis for the subcultural solution of collective deviance. A defining feature of the early British use of the term subculture was to label individuals as misfits and 'subnormals'. With the intervention of psychoanalysis, the negative labelling approach intensified so that by the 1950s and 1960s deviant drug users were labelled as 'addicts', 'junkies', 'freaks', 'junk pushers' and 'dope fiends'. During this period the concept of subculture enabled theorists to differentiate between behaviour they defined as 'normal' and behaviour regarded as 'immoral'.

Subcultural magic and the 'imaginary'

From the late 1960s the British National Deviance Conference began to criticize American subcultural theory, and criminologists David Downes, Stan Cohen, Jock Young, Laurie Taylor and Paul Rock prepared the way for the development of a more indigenous and sophisticated form of British labelling theory which interpreted youth subcultures in terms of social class relations and social change. The psychological underpinning of the concept of subculture was questioned, and in an attempt to break the association of subculture with pathology Phil Cohen (1972: 30) argued that it is 'important to make a distinction between subculture and delinquency'. Thus his theory of subculture explained drug use as a 'recreational' part of a subculture's signifying practices.[7] The twin ideas Cohen introduced to subculture were 'imaginary relations' and 'magical solutions', through an Althusserian reading of Jacques Lacan's concept of the 'imaginary' and Claude Lévi-Strauss's concept of 'myth' (Cohen 1997: 48–50). Using one of Louis Althusser's theories of ideology as a 'real' and unconscious force seducing people via hidden determinations, he rearticulated Lévi-Strauss's theory of myth into an explanation of how subcultures magically resolve social contradictions through multiple narratives of bricolage in the form of style, symbols and ritual.

The position of psychoanalysis is particularly influential in Phil Cohen's theory of subculture and can loosely be compared to the Freudian psychoanalytic elements within earlier theories of deviant subcultures introduced by A. K. Cohen and John Bowlby. Lacan seeks to redevelop Freud's theory of the unconscious mind to account for human action. He maintains that the unconscious is structured like a language, where meaning is not fixed and instability is all around us. The unconscious can be described as a powerhouse of symbolic order and shifting alliances. On this basis youth subcultures are interpreted as a language: the meaning of their style is imaginary – that is to say, it is 'real' in that it derives from their contradictory class position but young people are not fully aware of this repression; it is only fully 'realized' in their semiotic displays of subcultural style. Working-class youth through their subcultures attempt to resolve ideological contradictions which remain hidden or unresolved in the parent culture. Phil Cohen (1972: 23–4) states that 'subcultures are symbolic structures and must not be confused with' the young people themselves. For him the youth in subcultures 'attempt to realize, but in an imaginary relation, the condition of existence'. Thus Cohen argues that the class position of subcultures is central, saying that subcultures were 'produced by a dominated culture not a dominant culture' (1972: 30).

For Cohen subcultures are harbingers, recreating new forms of solidarity, albeit retrieving old solidarities of the traditional neighbourhood, destroyed during post-war redevelopment. The problem of the hypothesis that subcultures can achieve a 'magical' integration with past forms of solidarity through a refocusing towards and with the adult working-class struggle is that youth are denied autonomous action; they are defined as a filter for wider adult class conflict. Cohen has argued that 'in certain senses I have over-played or made too deterministic the relationship between subcultures and parent culture'.[8] In an attempt to provide autonomy to youth subcultures Phil Cohen specifies the importance of style as a system of transformations which are 'selected and invested in subcultural value' (1972: 23). The sub-culture is defined in terms of its relationship not to the labour market, but within working-class leisure practices at a cultural level. Cohen makes the distinction between real relations, i.e. where the parent culture is engaged in the contradictory struggles of the labour process, and imaginary relations, i.e. where the youth subculture is engaged in struggle through the creation of stylistic meaning and identity. On this basis youth are engaged in magical solutions at an ideological level in the leisure sphere rather than in material struggles experienced by the parent culture at the economic level. Social class rather than gender is the key to understanding Cohen's subcultural theory, which focuses on style as a series of cultural expressions, including drug consumption, offering symbolic politics, leaving material problems for youth unresolved other than at the imaginary level of leisure.

Subculture becomes class conscious: resistance, signifiers and hegemony

A major contribution brought by the Center for Contemporary Cultural Studies (CCCS) to youth studies, *Resistance through Rituals*, was to systematize the topic as a field of academic discourse. The cultural studies approach to subculture theory was innovative, although Stuart Hall (1980a)[9] has argued that many sociologists at the time of the centre's founding were hostile to 'cultural studies' (Blackman 2000). The approach used in *Resistance through Rituals* is to read youth cultural style as a text, to interpret each subculture through its creation of meaning. The basic assumption is that youth sub-cultures belong to the working class, deriving from the experience of sub-ordination. Subcultural activity is interpreted as a form of symbolic politics to particular class and cultural experiences. It is useful to note that a range of theoretical positions on subcultures exists within the text and the leading theoretical paper itself is self-reflective and cautions readers about the lim-itations of an ideological understanding of subcultures. This diversity of theoretical importations from Marxism and structuralism used by the CCCS resulted in a highly intricate analysis. In summary these concepts are:

1. *Style* – as defined by Roland Barthes, it is read as a text through complex semiotic analysis to reveal hidden meanings within sub-cultures.
2. *Resistance* – initially elaborated by Louis Althusser, it is understood

as an activity which occurs in a site or space, such as a subculture, which holds the potential to create, recreate or win relative
autonomy.

3. *Bricolage* and *homology* – these two theoretical concepts derive from
   the work of Claude Lévi-Strauss. They were applied by the CCCS to
   give a new and different understanding of how value, meaning and
   internal order are subversively created and recreated within subcultures. (Levi-Strauss 1958, 1966, Hebdige 1979:113, Willis 1972.)

4. *Hegemony* – development of Antonio Gramsci's theory of how social
   consent is managed enables subculture to be seen as a subject of
   negotiation between forces of incorporation and resistance. The
   CCCS's refinement of the concept of hegemony could reveal how
   social struggle is an active engagement by class cultures in a dynamic
   relation between subordinate and dominant orders.

The CCCS subcultural theory identifies drugs as a normal practice of subcultural groupings, which is reminiscent of the Chicago school's understanding of deviance as a normal expression within an urban community.[10]
The subsequent valorization of subculture as the meaning of style enabled the
CCCS theorists to describe drugs as an intentional recreational practice which
promoted resistance and refusal. Thus the CCCS theory of subculture enabled
drugs to be seen not as a social problem but as signifier of subcultural identity.

The CCCS sees subculture as a concept which can reveal counterhegemonic processes, where youth subcultures are formed in contradiction
and engage in cultural conflict as a site of struggle. Subculture is applied
theoretically as a device within the complex Marxist base-and-superstructure
problematic. European theorists are employed to redefine the concept of
subculture as a potential space for youth as a creative agency to occupy. The
CCCS in its elaboration of the Marxist metaphor created a macro theoretical
model for the general reading of micro subcultures (Hall and Jefferson 1975).
However, 'literary ethnography' was substituted for direct empirical observation as a means of obtaining evidence for their theory (Blackman 1995).
The interpretation of meaning, i.e. what the subculture represents, is
achieved through semiotic analysis. There is no empirical observation of how
subcultures at an interactional level struggle to develop a culture of resistance
through youth style. For Stan Cohen (1980: xxvii) 'too much of the theory
masks a curious value distortion. The subculture is observed and decoded, its
creativity celebrated and its political limitations acknowledged – and then the
critique of the social order constructed'. The concept of subculture as a subordinate culture is placed against dominant culture, giving the abstract model
movement and contradiction. Although youth style is 'ethnographically'
traced to the youth subculture(s), the concept of subculture is defined
at the outset in terms of a hegemonic relation to the dominant culture.

The abstract concept of subculture is defined as oppositional, possessing potential strategies for resistance. Without ethnographic studies on subcultures in *Resistance through Ritual* the CCCS aim falls short of bringing the social back into theory. The subcultural response of youth is related to masculine structural features of hegemony at the level of class, culture and generation, but not to women and race (McRobbie and Garber 1975; Hebdige 1979; Davies 1984; Griffin 1993).

The concept of subculture is taken by Dick Hebdige to a different level as a theoretical device using Lévi-Strauss's concepts of bricolage and homology. As a result subculture breaks free of its social class expressions and becomes a complex structuralist tool enabling endless opportunities for interpretation with little political force. The priority given to subcultural style as creative resistance is a legacy of the Leavisite tradition of literary interpretation. Hebdige is the bearer of this legacy; he seeks to establish a popular aesthetic and show working-class subcultural practices within a framework of 'high culture'. On this basis creativity can only occur through small groups (youth subcultures) for reasons of creativity itself (Filmer 1977: 73). However, not all working-class youth fully enter subcultures: the Leavisite interpretation is elitist, as only those youths in subcultures are seen as the select group who possess the 'real' creative potential to challenge bourgeois order.

Subculture: an emergent critique

The first contemporary challenge to the CCCS theory of subculture came from within by Paul Willis (1972: xlv–xlvi).[11] He is critical of the concept of subculture, saying: 'There has not been a vigorous analysis of the status of the culture a subculture is supposed to be "sub" to. The notion implies a relative positioning which seems to give an altogether misleading sense of absoluteness and dominance of the main culture.' Neither does Paul Willis apply the concept of subculture in *Learning to Labour* (1977), referring instead to counterculture with its obviously greater political connotations. Building on Willis's argument, my own study *Youth: Positions and Oppositions* (Blackman 1995) sought to develop an alternative concept to describe young people through the theory of youth cultural forms. The reason for not applying the concept of subculture did not rest on the variations between different competing definitions, but on the capacity of the concept to explain youth groups in action, in both their internal and their external relations. The category of subculture homogenizes youth and fails to allow for local variation. The theory of youth cultural forms is conceptualized in terms of specialized positions, social relations, specialized semiotic and signature, which integrates the three aspects into a coherent picture. The driving force of the theory was that 'status positions' influence and generate forms of action, which enable young people either to conform or take part in resistance towards authority.

Status positions revolve around intellectual capacity, class identity, displays of subcultural style, expressions of feminism, degrees of autonomy, advancement of sexual confidence and use of aggressive violence. In this theory social class remains an important variable but it is not the determinant one, it is a crucial factor amongst others. In different social contexts any one of these status positions may secure a primary position, with gender relations playing a major role in all forms of communication.

Further criticism of subcultural theory comes from Sarah Thornton (1995: 8), who applies subcultural theory through the adaptation of Pierre Bourdieu's concept of cultural capital. She argues that the CCCS theory of subculture is 'empirically unworkable', but also suggests that youth subcultures are created by the media. Her use of Bourdieu's ideas is creative, but she limits her understanding of subculture in terms of 'taste cultures' and appears to underplay Bourdieu's analysis of class in favour of a more postmodernist preoccupation with superficiality as a driving force within subcultural capital (Hollands 2002). In Thornton's study drugs are mentioned as crucial to participation but there is little analysis of the meaning of drugs for youth in the subculture. Subcultural capital is used by Thornton to confirm class, gender and status discriminations between 'true' subculturalists and the mainstream in a negative sense; those without subcultural capital are thus inferior and lack taste. Thornton (1997: 163) describes the operation of subcultural capital in Weberian terms, stating that it is a 'means by which young people negotiate and accumulate status within their own social worlds'. The emergent critique of subculture by Willis, Blackman and Thornton is based on the concept's inability to account for 'lived experience' linked to ethnography. In general, it is possible to argue that Weberian theory and methodology have formed the basis of the current revision to subcultural theory.

Postmodern theories of subculture

This section will be concerned with critically examining the development of postmodern subcultural theory, which is premised on arguments from three key social theorists: Max Weber, Jean Baudrillard and Michel Maffesoli. Ideas extracted from these thinkers have been used in combination to argue against what is described as CCCS 'theoretical orthodoxy' (Muggleton 2000: 73) and also to construct new terms to replace the concept of subculture such as 'neo-tribe' and 'lifestyle'. The high point of postmodernist revision to subcultural theory has been achieved by Muggleton and Weinzierl (2003) and Bennett and Kahn-Harris (2004). A key starting point for the postmodernist critique of the CCCS comes from Gary Clarke's paper 'Defending Ski-Jumpers' (1982). He questions 'the value of decoding the stylistic appearances of particular tribes' (1982: a) and from his own position at the CCCS he stressed that there was a reluctance to consider the different degrees of commitment to a subculture 'since any discussion of life chances is regarded as a "Weberian deviation"' (1982: 8). A major concern for postmodern subcultural theorists is an attempt to construct a new canon of discourse linked to one of the founding figures of sociology, Weber, via the French sociologist Maffesoli. Rob Shields (1996: iv) in his foreword to Maffesoli's *The Time of the Tribes* says that he offers a 'Weberian perspective focusing on the meaning of social interaction for participants'. Clarke's use of the term 'tribe' to describe subcultures and the legitimacy he specifies for a Weberian approach have been considerably influential in the post-CCCS development of subculture theory.

A leading voice of the British postmodern approach to subcultures has been Steve Redhead (1990, 1993, 1995, 1997). His criticism (1995: 88) of subcultural theory has been accusatory and rhetorical; for him pulp fiction '[has] told us more about the "feel" of contemporary youth culture than hundreds of pages of sociology of youth'. He dismisses the CCCS theory of subculture as a fantasized academic creation, arguing that 'it is seen to be no longer appropriate' (Redhead 1997: x). He states that 'subcultures were produced by subcultural theorists, not the other way around' (Redhead 1990: 25). This critique has been explored by Antonio Melechi (1993), Hillegonda Rietveld (1998a), Steven Miles (1995: 36), Ben Malbon (1998: 279), David Muggleton (1997: 201) and Andy Bennett (2000: 24), who have confirmed Redhead's assertion either by specifying the exact quotation or commending his contribution. For postmodernists, subcultures react imaginatively through consumption and identity to construct creative meanings which can be liberating from subordination. Postmodern subcultural theory seeks to move away from models of social constraint and places greater emphasis on agency in the search for individual meaning in subcultural practice. The postmodern milieu of spatiality and cultural pessimism valorizes locality and the power of subcultures to imaginatively reappropriate global commodities for emancipation. This new 'postmodern' work on subculture has been described in MacDonald et al. (2001), Cieslik (2001) and Chatterton and Holland (2003) as creating problems for sociology because of the apparent reluctance to integrate social structures into the analysis, promoting instead an individualistic understanding of the social.

'Subcultural disappearance' and 'post-subcultures'

At Manchester Metropolitan University the aim of Steve Redhead (1997: 2) has been to champion what he calls 'Popular Cultural Studies' as a new discipline, to 'borrow liberally from' ideas of key postmodernist thinkers such as Jean Baudrillard in order to critique the sociology of youth as 'a genre of writing ... fast becoming a cliché' (Redhead 1995: 11–12). Redhead sampled Baudrillard's thesis of the 'end of the social' to reject the CCCS radical tradition and the concept of subculture and to critique sociology in general (Redhead 1995: 76). He argues that subcultures are part of the emancipatory project developed by modernist theorists belonging to the past and should be discredited. Redhead relies on Baudrillard for his disciplinary critique of sociology and subculture. Barry Smart (1990: 407) states: 'Baudrillard's proclamation of the demise of sociology may be regarded as fundamentally flawed in so far as it is based on an impoverished conception of both the discipline and its subject matter.' Redhead (1990: 23–4) applies Baudrillard's notion of an 'end' to explain that there will be a closure to youth subcultures because orthodox theory suggests they evolve 'in a linear fashion'. Ironically, having announced the end of subcultures, he then announces the new aim to be that 'postmodern youth culture can be excavated by way of some of Baudrillard's signposts' (Redhead 1993: 5).

Redhead and others explore subculture through Baudrillard's (1983: 2) notion of simulation, where there is 'the generation of models of a real without origins or reality: a hyperreal'. For Baudrillard postmodern society is based on the hyperreal, where the distinction between what is real and what is imaginary collapses, leading to the notion that simulations can be experienced as more realistic than reality; hence Redhead's claim that pulp fiction is better than empirical work in youth studies. On this basis Redhead (1993: 23–4) proceeds to argue that there are no 'authentic subcultures' and that 'this "depth model" is no longer appropriate ... to analysis [sic] the surfaces of (post) modern culture, a culture characterized by depthlessness, flatness and "hyper-reality".' Using Baudrillard's notions of postmodernity, Redhead (1993: 17) defines subcultures as 'free-floating' signifiers which enhance differentiation of individual experience. Redhead's aim is to avoid grand narratives as this would suggest determinism or imposition. Although he speaks profusely about ethnography, there is no empirical data in his work; this makes his theory of subculture subject to the very criticisms he levels at the CCCS. By defining subcultural activities as wholly hedonistic and preoccupied with surface appearances, young people become identified as being shallow themselves. Twenty-first century youth subculture is not merely an age of superficial plunder; rather it has spawned a multiplicity of diverse and interconnecting subcultures which mark festivals as a site of difference and unity: an inclusive collective action. In this sense Redhead's postmodernist theory of youth subculture is itself superficial and lacks critical reflection, because empirical reality supports the view that youth culture is more complex, diversified and meaningful than Redhead allows. The new emphasis on difference and pleasure fails to give young people rights or agency; nor does it critically recognize the structures and institutions which seek to impose marginal status on the young.

Antonio Melechi (1993) and Hillegonda Rietveld (1993, 1998a) elaborate Redhead's discussion on subcultural hedonism in relation to drugs and develop Baudrillard's notion of the 'real' being lost to an image. Speaking about the acid house subculture, Melechi (1993: 37–8) argues: 'Those who sought to understand this subculture in terms of a politics of usage and identity completely missed the point.' For him this subculture is about 'escape'; 'the self is lost' when the 'whole subculture attempts to vanish'. Melechi theorizes the act of apparent subcultural 'disappearance' as a strategy of resistance, which resides only at the level of the individual. Rietveld (1998a: 196) develops the idea of the 'spectacular disappearance' applied to subculture, stating: 'The concept of the self has been untied, losing its socially constructed identity like some unnecessary luggage.' Here the postmodern theory of subculture puts pleasures first, arguing that individual sensation is found in empty kitsch, intoxication and hedonism: new forms of self-expression where drugs and different types of dance music allow young people to implode with the pure joy of individualistic consumerism.

Rietveld (1998a: 196) and Melechi's (1993: 32–3) theory of subculture – as an act of disappearance – is achieved by exchanging Baudrillard's ideas on the 'ecstasy of communication' with the ecstasy of drug consumption in subculture. Their theory is also defined by the notion of the tourist gaze. It is through tourism that the 'self is lost' and this equates with the act of drug consumption in dance culture to signal abandonment and experience the 'act of disappearance'. Thus Melechi and Rietveld's theory of subculture is causally linked to achieving intoxication through drug use so as to experience the trance-like condition, combined with Baudrillard's (1988) notion of the meaningless superficiality of post-tourism. In postmodern subcultural theory drug use has lost its negative label and becomes valorized as a means to search for vitality, meaning and pleasure.

David Muggleton (1997, 2000) follows Redhead's interpretation of Baudrillard to assert that post-subcultures are now concerned with 'surface' and self-authentication. Muggleton (2000: 47–9) defines post-subculturalists as revelling in choice 'no longer articulated around ... the structuring of class, gender or ethnicity'. Thus subcultural identity is understood by him as 'free-floating signifiers' torn away from social structures. On this basis he argues that 'there are no rules'; following Redhead's assertion he proclaims there are no authentic subcultures (2000: 47). However, if you look at the case studies presented in Muggleton (2000), the mods and the punks, it is clear that they conform to precise subcultural regulations. It is not a case of no rules, as Muggleton suggests; it is perhaps more that shifting boundaries may enable individuals to exhaust subcultural style and move on to a different one.[12] Muggleton's interpretation (2000: 49) insists on an individualistic appreciation of subcultures, asserting that 'subcultures are just another form of depoliticized play in the postmodern pleasuredom'. This emphasis on 'surface qualities' and diverse affiliation is suggested to give priority to subjective meaning, allowing individuals agency. Following the postmodernist assumptions that there has been a growth in generalized culture and a blurring between elite and popular culture, it is then argued that social structures have become unstable where choice is everything. Muggleton argues (2000: 48) that 'postmodern subcultural identities [are] to be multiple and fluid. Constituted through consumption, subcultural style is no longer articulated around the modernist structuring relations of class, gender and ethnicity'. Whilst claiming subcultural agency in terms of consumption and individual autonomy Muggleton (2000: 45) strips youth of their creative edge by announcing the end of subcultures. He states: 'Subcultural styles have two options: they can feed off each other ... destroying their own internal boundaries in the process; or indulge in the stylistic revivalism.' In other words, he suggests there can be no new subcultures, only forms of hybrid nostalgia.

A major weakness in the theory of subcultural disappearance is that the policing of rave subculture was not invisible. No subcultural participant at events during the 1990s could help but be aware of the different political forces which opposed the subculture (Bidder 2001). Dance subculture faced three main forms of state intervention: from the Prime Minister, John Major, and the Conservative government's legislative programme, which sought to repress and to regulate the subculture; from the tabloid media, which sensationally reported on the subculture to attract readership; and from the police through the Pay Party Unit, which sought to stop acid house parties. Simon Reynolds (1998) argues that throughout the 1990s popular youth culture was in perpetual self-invention as a dynamic cultural force, fragmenting but projecting a collective voice. Part of the radical element to contemporary dance subculture has been its integral connection to other forms of DIY protest, including free festivals, movements to legalize cannabis, anti-nuclear groups, the Reclaim the Streets movement and anti-road groups, through specific dance collectives such as Exodus and Spiral Tribe. These disparate forms of protest have been brought together via demonstration against 'capitalism'. For western governments and media such non-traditional alternative lifestyles were understood to represent values which were in opposition to the mainstream (Hutnyk 2000). The loose coalition between the various DIY cultures, forms of protest, travellers and the dance scene gives the impression of an identifiable international youth subculture (McKay 1998).

Subcultural 'tribes'

The sociological theories of Michel Maffesoli have been central to the development of a subcultural theory which employs the concept of the 'neo-tribe'. The work of David Muggleton (2000), Ben Malbon (1999), Andy Bennett (2000) and Kevin Hetherington (2000) advance Maffesoli's concept of tribe as a means to describe young people's groups under conditions of postmodernity. Maffesoli (1996: 76) argues that 'neo-tribalism is characterized by fluidity, occasional gatherings and dispersal', suggesting that this could be applied to 'punk or retro fashions', i.e. subcultures. He states (1996: 98) that the tribe 'is without the rigidity of the forms of organization with which we are familiar; it refers more to a certain ambience, a state of mind, and is preferably to be expressed through lifestyles that favour appearance and "form"'. Maffesoli's ideas promote pluralization in opposition to the constraints of total theories, which he describes as a 'conceptual framework imposed by the 19th century' (1996: 157). He sees great value in relativism as a destabilizing force impacting on the 'pretensions of universality'. However, in parallel with the CCCS theory of subculture, he suggests (1996: 51) that tribes are political forms which do not withdraw into narcissistic individualism but can challenge 'the logic of domination . . . belonging to the dominant classes'.

Postmodern subcultural theorists employ Maffesoli's concept of the tribe to suggest the existence of a 'postmodern age and postmodern sensibilities' (Bennett 1999: 607). Here the concept of tribe acts as a carrier for postmodern theory or ideology. The postmodern subcultural theory of neo-tribe is closely linked to theories of consumption and lifestyle which posit the centrality of choice and individualism as key factors in identity formation. Drugs are theorized as a feature of subcultural choice, simply part of consumer capitalism (Harrison 1998; Hammersley et al. 2002, Jackson 2004). The idea is that neo-tribes confirm our sense of identity and individuals take pleasure in the hybridity of consumerism. The centrality of choice in postmodern theories of subculture argues that social categories such as class, sexuality and ethnicity are too reductive and universalistic. The reluctance to consider the way in which choice is also imposed on young people by capital, structures and institutions fails to give voice to different young people's experiences of marginality (Shildrick 2002). On this basis postmodern theories of subculture do not address or critique the relations of dominance and subordination exercised through social and cultural structures of society.

Bennett (2000), Muggleton (1997, 2000) and Malbon (1998, 1999) seek to argue that subcultures are 'fixed', in contrast to 'neo-tribes', which are 'fluid'. They put priority on local variation and the micro focus of 'everyday' contexts which shape subcultural affiliation. Malbon's work is closer to that of Melechi and Rietveld's, due to the emphasis he places on drugs as a key feature of the subcultural experience, but he also elaborates a more sophisticated theory of subcultural disappearance called 'oceanic experience' drawn from Toop's (1995) idea of an 'ocean of sound'. Malbon suggests that he wants to 'rethink resistance', but there is little critical discussion of resistance theory or cultural struggle. Malbon suggests (1998: 280) that resistance cannot be understood as 'a struggle with a dominant hegemonic culture'; for him resistance is located 'in the most minute subtleties of clubbing'. Drugs are an integral part of his theory of subculture but he fails to place drug consumption within the political context of state control. As a result Malbon also ignores the fact that club culture has consistently and incestuously celebrated drugs as a form of resistance to authority. The form that this resistance takes may be contradictory, but it is clear that the dance–rave subculture has a history of revolt even where there have been attempts to turn this pleasurable revolt into support for the dominant culture, such as through mainstream tourism and leisure. Malbon is highly critical of subculture representing resistance, preferring to stay within localized cultural analysis focusing on the politics of subjectivity. There is a sense in which Malbon, Muggleton and Bennett employ the assumptions of postmodern theorization as offering fluidity and individual difference, then transfer this description on to subculture as a means to demonstrate the existence of diffuse groupings called 'tribes'.

Lifestyle theory and the loss of the group

Steven Miles (2000) and Andy Bennett (2000) show great disaffection with the concept of subculture and seek to elaborate the concept of 'lifestyle' in its place. They argue that consumerism allows young people to construct alternative lifestyles through local and global strategies where in local settings they can use, appropriate and transform cultural commodities for their own authenticity. In essence, it is argued that lifestyle theory places new emphasis on local practices and through local culture youth lifestyle strategies attach new and different meanings onto global commodities. Miles and Bennett are seeking to highlight the emancipatory potential of 'critical' consumption for young people serving as a basis for 'stability in an otherwise unstable world' (Miles 2000: 10). Underlying Bennett and Miles's work is a hostility towards Marxism and its influence creating 'moribund conceptions of youth sub-culture' (2000: 5). Neither theorist engages in a critical assessment of what type of Marxism informed the CCCS subculture theory. Miles's criminological accusations of the CCCS theory are inaccurate in the sense that Phil Cohen specified the purpose of an epistemological break between deviance and subculture. Bennett (2000: 25) uses Weber's critique of Marx to argue that people in status groups claim honour by pursuing patterns of consumption and lifestyle to criticize the CCCS, but he does not consider Gramsci's theory of hegemony in the Marxist theory of subculture. However, on closer examination it is possible to argue that both Bennett and Miles depend on certain Marxist ideas for their assertion that subcultures hold the potential of emancipation.

Bennett argues (2000: 27) that lifestyle theory places new emphasis on 'understanding how collective cultural meanings are inscribed in commodities' which enable young people 'to construct their own forms of meaning and authenticity'. This idea is derived from Walter Benjamin's understanding of modernity through his 'micrological approach' and 'redemptive critique'

(Sontag 1979). Benjamin's style was to focus on small pleasures to understand the pulse, portability and power of a commodity, somewhat like an ethnographer looking at subjects through a cultural microscope. Benjamin's 'redemptive critique' examines small commodities to find potential freedom and emancipation embedded or inscribed in the cultural object. He identifies commodity fetishism as achieving a mass effect, transforming culture and society into a totality on the basis of a dialectic possessing division and emancipation simultaneously, whereas Bennett prefers to remain at the level of 'local scenarios', suggesting that young people can 'inscribe' their own localized meanings on global culture. However, Bennett's lifestyle theory remains built around wider social categories such as age, sex, status, ethnicity, etc. These categories are closely linked to purchasing power and disposable income, which are themselves closely associated with social class and thus social structure plays a significant role in shaping consumption through limits and constraints. Bennett's preoccupation with the power of the local culture to reinterpret meaning is valuable but cannot be seen as equivalent to the discursive power of global media institutions based on the accumulation of capital (Morley 1995: 313). Consumption is not available to all and thus is a marker of inequality. Young people can be resistant and attempt to challenge dominant values, but young people's encounters with social exclusion and zero-tolerance drug policy show that consumption is a chimera of choice in constructing subcultural identities. Young people desire subcultural expressions and commodities which are themselves defined by the power of the market. Bennett's priority on consumption at the expense of production misrecognizes youth marginality under postmodernism. Youth consumers may have developed into a specialized subcultural market niche but capital actively denies youth economic stability, which prevents them from participating in cultural consumption.

The work of Steven Miles is comparable with that of Bennett to the extent that he proposes a theory of lifestyle based on a critique of the CCCS theory of subculture and identifies consumer culture as offering individuality for young people. Miles's interpretation is more structural; he argues that 'lifestyles are not individualized in nature but are constructed through affiliation and negotiation ... Lifestyles are, in effect, lived cultures in which individuals actively express their identities, but in direct relation to their position as regards the dominant culture' (Miles 2000: 16). This argument is a reconfiguration of the CCCS theory of subculture with its implicit use of Gramsci's ideas where he asserts the desire to speak about the dominant culture in terms of institutions such as school, the labour market and 'power structures' (2000: 9). For him youth identities are constructed through stable commonalties: 'through consumer goods, which allows them to feel unique' (Miles 1995: 42). It is clear that Miles wishes to promote an understanding of youth subcultural identity as stable, which offers agency, but he sees adherence to particular forms of collective solidarity as more ephemeral due to conditions of postmodernity. The attention of both Bennett and Miles is on in-dividualistic identity and individual performance in subculture where 'young people do identities rather than have identities'. They no longer see the term 'group' as possessing permanent qualities (Bennett 1999: 605; Miles 2000: 18). They ignore the collective response by young people over the last ten years at festivals, raves and anti-capitalist demonstrations, where diverse and unified forms of subcultural identities and affiliations have performed rituals of resistance.

Postmodern subcultural emancipation: the bricoleur's critique

Postmodern subcultural theory has raised significant theoretical and metho-dological issues and brought more sensitivity towards an understanding of subcultures. It wants to argue that youth are engaged in creative and oppo-sitional activities and claim emancipation is obtainable, but in what sense? Postmodern subcultural theorists rely on an individualized understanding of the 'bricoleur' acting with conscious vitality and critical agency. For Claude Lévi-Strauss (1966: 21) the bricoleur 'speaks not only with things ... but also through the medium of things'. Crucially, for him the bricoleur is engaged in collecting and using structured material from society, with knowledge mak-ing the act of reconstruction an informed process where participants possess awareness in order to challenge society. For Lévi-Strauss (1966: 33) bricolage is a cultural strategy to reverse and reorder meaning so as to use 'so many indestructible pieces for structural patterns in which they serve alternatively as ends or means'. The bricoleur is engaged in intellectual and concrete emancipation anchored within social and cultural structures of the local la-bour market and globalized commodity fetishism. In postmodern subculture theory the bricoleur enables young people to be creative, to challenge mar-ginality through collective drug use and illegal events, such as described by Steve Redhead, Antonio Melechi and Hillegonda Rietveld; through making alternative local music, described by Andy Bennett; through style, described by David Muggleton; and through participation in legal and illegal forms of consumerism, described by Steven Miles and Ben Malbon. In their explicit or implicit use of Lévi-Strauss's idea of the bricoleur, postmodern subcultural theory has significantly broadened the CCCS theory of subculture by placing emancipation as an integral feature of subcultural practice at the level of the particular.

A weakness of the new theoretical developments of subculture derives from its place within an ideology of postmodernism. In its refusal to address a collective subject, postmodern subcultural theory has been a source of political rhetoric and a supply of ammunition for the political right to oppress expressions of diversity and difference (Scruton 1998). Postmodern subcultural theorists in their preference for plurality, difference and otherness seem unaware that postmodernism, according to Aijaz Ahmad (1995: 45), 'is imperialist at its very base'. These cultural preferences have been incorporated into the cultural logic of marketing contemporary subcultures, strengthening the capitalist mode of production where drugs are used as a marketing strategy for products. In its imitation of the commodity form, postmodernism deludes us with play while imposing the 'crippling austerity of the market place' (Eagleton 1995: 68).

Postmodern subcultural theory reduces 'real' subculture to surface signifiers without authenticity where identity is determined by choice. In postmodern analysis spatiality and locality are given special attention, but this becomes disconnected from local structural processes, leaving young people with exaggerated individual autonomy, which decentres their political understanding of globalized material divisions. A result of the personal and private being seen as valuable is that postmodern subcultural theory presents an individualistic understanding of subcultures which fails to see how social space and locality is structured by capital as a universalistic form of exploitation. Subcultures are lived and experienced through hierarchical structures where struggle is played out against social categories such as class, gender and ethnicity that interpolate the social identities of individuals in subcultures. Postmodern subculturalists have been seduced by the micro-politics of bodily performance and intoxication and appear unable to access the broader social processes which subcultures inhabit. The approach lacks critical self-reflection; it claims to be against universals, because these constrain and deny individuality, but it constantly asserts universal moral prescriptions such as plurality instead of singularity, fluidity to fixity, hybridity to sameness, etc. (Eagleton 2000: 82).

Under postmodern analysis subculture returns to a Mertonian interpretation of individual adaptation to neo-liberal economic and social policies. Priority is given to the individual to absorb and choose subcultural style, to explore personal emancipation and self-fulfilment. This individualistic appreciation of subcultures appears to ignore the collective basis to subcultural practice and performance. Emancipation is retained within postmodern subcultural analysis as a form of personal expression where individuals can engage with global commodities to redefine meaning in order to support their individualized subcultural practice. Postmodern subcultural theorists fail to understand that these local variations have national and international connections which have supported subcultures from the 1950s[13] to the twenty-first century.[14] Subcultures may celebrate locality but they also possess an international context which is both local and global against forces of domination.

In its celebration of localism postmodern subcultural theory fails to see the commonalities of collective positions amongst local subcultural groups within a nation and across states. Speaking about the subculture of hip hop, George Lipsitz (1994: 31) maintains that local variations of hip hop across different nations can affirm wider international solidarity. Subcultures work within contradictions, producing tensions and hostilities as a result of incorporation into global capitalism. Postmodern subculturalists remain silent on the material marginality of youth, while romancing the cultural marginality through postmodern and postcolonial theory. Drug consumption is seen as individualized choice without a historical or cultural context, defined as a fashion accessory with no focus on drug meaning or control regulation. Postmodern subcultural theory releases the power of the local and personal wanting to argue that emancipation is individual, but young people in subcultures experience constraint as their stylistic appearance, drug use and bodily representations become normalized as mass-commercialized products. Postmodern subcultural theory wishes to retain the notion of emancipation, but through denouncing universals as oppressive it ignores the power of capital. Thus without a means of understanding collective forms of oppression postmodern emancipation remains a 'speculative exercise' (Eagleton 1995: 66).

Conclusion

In this chapter I have argued that the concept of subculture has a long legacy in sociological theory; its longevity relates to its power of explanation and its attraction relates to its apparent immediacy and relevance to the social world. On this basis the concept has had popular appeal for different and opposing sociological paradigms. For the Chicago school the early use of the concept of subculture reflected their ethnographic concern to map diverse social relations within urban communities. The American school of structural functionalism saw subculture as a means to explore criminality and categorize subcultures as deviant. The initial British theory of subculture emerged from positivism and biological theories of adolescence, but was soon dominated by a psychoanalytical interpretation, where it was used to explain an apparent social inadequacy. The cultural studies approach to subculture saw it as a means to critique society and address issues of conflict and social change. In Marxist and structuralist theory subcultures became part of a critical vanguard to challenge bourgeois order and celebrate creative resistance to authority. The postmodern theory of subculture has taken on a Weberian appearance, where status and spatiality are seen as providing individuals with opportunities for increased freedom in consumerism and fluid identities. The postmodern theory presents an individualized understanding of the subculture as simulacrum, where no authenticity exists and individuals free-floatingly signify any identity. Each sociological approach has used the concept of subculture to explain drug use, which in turn supports the legitimacy of their discourse. Drug consumption has been accounted for as an ordinary feature of social life, a dysfunction for the individual and society, an example of mental deficiency, personality failure and social stigma, an expression of symbolic refusal and a sign of informed consumer choice and identity formation.

5   Drug normalization
A historical and contemporary critique

This chapter examines the drug 'normalization' thesis, looking at its application within government policy, academic discourse and the media. The concept of drug normalization has become a popular notion to describe recreational rather than problematic drug use. The theory possesses flexibility and is attractive as it can be used to support opposing positions in the drug debate. It comfortably fits into drug prevention policy to account for increased drug consumption, so supporting more punitive controls. At the same time greater drug availability and widespread coverage of drug issues within the media and popular culture suggest that drug use is no longer a deviant practice but an activity undertaken by ordinary people. Contradiction is at the centre of the term's application: in its academic usage the term offers an explanation for non-deviant drug use, whilst television programmes and tabloid newspapers tend to focus on sensation and scandal to reinforce the label of the drug user as 'other'. This chapter will start by looking at the evidence of drug use within ancient and classical culture and argue that drugs have played a more significant role in human development than previously acknowledged. I will examine the first use of the term 'normality' as applied to drug use and assess the role of the media in promoting drug representations within popular culture. Here I shall argue that drug normalization has become what Foucault describes as a 'discourse of regulation'. The final section will critically assess the theoretical relationship between drug normalization and postmodernism.

A weakness of drug normalization theory has been its focus on the contemporary, where it lacks a historical context to understand drugs in society. Evidence suggests that every past society has used and explored drugs as part of its cultural practice and social life, which indicates that drugs are an integral part of our human nature (Rudgley 1999). Drug consumption has been a feature of common and ritual life and to this extent it represents part of normalized activities by individuals within communities. Drugs have played and continue to play an important agricultural and commercial part in the generation of wealth. The illicit drug economy is enhanced by its legal–cultural support system, which puts forward diverse images about drugs that promote different messages of drug normalization. Psychoactive drugs are more popular than ever in contemporary society, but this taste for intoxication within everyday life is not new; it can be traced to our ancestors and their heritage of preparing and using drugs. Understanding previous drug consumption in past societies provides knowledge to assess the present situation.

Ancient society and drug normalization

Long before Christianity both cannabis and opium were well established in ancient culture and society. For example, in China there has been a continuous history of cannabis cultivation for about 6000 years (Li 1974b). Both plants grow easily in the wild and can be described as social plants: through their domestication they serve a range of purposes for a community, including food, medicinal and material usage.[1] Discovery of the remains of these drugs reveals that they are some of the oldest cultivated plants associated with humanity. The earliest use of paper made of hemp was found in a grave in Shensi province dating from before the reign of Emperor Wu (104–87 BC) (Li 1974a: 294). Such plants brought forward a welfare and technological revolution during the neolithic period, when farming developed and leisure became a cultural factor in social life. Medicine has its origins closely linked to magic in early cultures. Hui Lin Li states (1974b: 447): 'The use of the plant in medicine, especially as a hallucinogen, was apparently associated with the extensive practice of shamanism in north eastern Asia.' To induce sleep, or as an anaesthetic, cannabis and opium offered neolithic people the opportunity for hallucinogenic experience. The earliest pharmacopoeia specifies the effects of cannabis. Hui Lin Li (1974a: 295) argues that the famous *Pen-ts'ao Ching*, attributed to the legendary Emperor Shen-nung (*fl.* c.2000 BC), was compiled in the first or second centuries AD, but was undoubtedly based on traditions from prehistoric times. It states that '*ma-fen* (the fruits of hemp) if taken in excess will produce hallucinations [literally 'seeing devils']. If taken over a long term, it makes one communicate with spirits and lightens one's body.'

The earliest Indian literary reference to cannabis occurs in the *Atharva Veda*,[2] written between 2000 and 1400 BC, where hemp is an ingredient in a potent drink referred to as *soma*. Chopra and Chopra (1939: 33) state that, according to the old Hindu poems, 'God Shiva brought down the hemp plant from the Himalayas and gave it to mankind.' In ancient India the earliest synonym for cannabis is *bhanga*; formally Shiva's title is Lord of the Dance but one of his other epithets is 'Lord of Bhang'. Within Indian culture cannabis is seen as sacred, closely related to divination and holding stimulating and euphoric properties. The early use of cannabis within Chinese and Indian societies reveals it to be understood as a powerful substance for achieving a range of integral cultural experiences from ritual divination to social intoxication.

The broad location of the first cultural use of cannabis is suggested by

Merlin (1972) and Rudgley (1993) to be the steppe zone in central Asia. The evidence of hemp use found at neolithic sites points to the importance of cannabis as a social plant which followed the cultural movement of people from east to west. Scythia was a large ancient area of south-eastern Europe and Asia composed of different communities drawn to the west. At Pazyryk Valley in central Siberia, evidence from Russian archaeologists uncovered frozen tombs revealing sculpted artefacts of high aesthetic quality and evidence of the use of hemp for intoxication. These were equestrian people who formed a domesticated society through dairy production and cultivation of cannabis for clothing, while artisans produced elaborate utensils, rugs and textiles (Artamonov 1965; Pokorny 1970). The Scythians who occupied the southern part of Asiatic Russia between approximately 700 and 300 BC operated a complex trade network and were militarily successful. The charred remains of hemp seeds found by the Russian archaeologist Sergei Rudenko are what is left after dried leaves of the cannabis plant have smouldered into disintegration.

In 5 BC, Herodotus (Book IV, pp. 73ff.) details that the Scythians built tents for the ingestion of cannabis smoke, saying that they delightedly 'howl with joy, for the vapour bath'. Herodotus also describes how the use of cannabis as a custom is found among people living on the islands in the river Araxes. He states:

> The inhabitants, when they meet together in companies, and have lit a fire, throw on the fire as they sit round in a circle; and by inhaling the burning fruit that has been thrown on, they become intoxicated by the odour, just as the Greeks do by wine; and the more fruit is thrown on, the more intoxicated they become, until they rise up to dance and betake themselves to singing.[3]

Scythian culture is credited with the origin of the Indo-European name for hemp, *kavvabis*,[4] which Carl Linnaeus formally categorized in 1753 as *Cannabis sativa*. This credit has brought negative accusations against Scythian culture which both Sherratt (1991) and Rudgley (1993) see as a means of deprecating neolithic culture as the basis of European civilization in favour of the rationality of Greek and Roman society.

The Classical Age, Homer and drugs

From the Classical Age, we can see in Homer the description of drugs associated with deception, fearlessness and luxury, establishing sets of contradictory experiences, where mythological characters encounter intoxication giving rise to human indifference and inability to control emotion, action or reason.

In the *Odyssey*, Helen of Troy served a drug called nepenthe to battle-weary Greek warriors. Homer (1980: 40) states:

> Then a new thought came to Zeus-born Helen; into the bowl that their wine was drawn from she threw a drug that dispelled all grief and anger and banished remembrance of every trouble. Once it was mingled in the wine-bowl, any man who drank it down would never on that same day let a tear fall down his cheeks, no, not if his father and mother died, or if his brother or his own son were slain with the sword before his eyes. Such were the cunning powerful drugs this daughter of Zeus had in her possession; they had been a gift from a woman of Egypt, Polydamna wife of Thon.[5]

The poppy was well established in Greek society and used for a number of purposes. Levinthal (1985: 563) says: 'In Greek cities of that time, opium was sold in the form of opium cakes and candies as well as beverages of opium mixed with wine.' Homer suggests that the negative potential of powerful drugs comes from elsewhere than Greek society, representing an attempt to blame social corruption in one society as the result of outside influence. Merlin states that it was the early Egyptians, whom 'Homer regarded as a nation of druggists' (1972: 61).

Hayter (1988: 20) suggests that opium symbolized natural processes. She says that the drug was used 'to bring forgetfulness of the sorrow of the dying year and to share, by a short winter sleep of the emotions, in the death and rebirth of the plants – the juice of the flower bringing the men who drank it back into its own vegetative nature'. The origin of this interpretation of opium as a symbol of decline and rebirth, a plant of joy within nature, derives from the cult of Demeter in Greek mythology, focusing on redemption from death, where Demeter sets out in search of her daughter Persephone, and arrives at a place called Sicyon, previously called Mecone, the city of poppies. In the fields she slits the seed heads, gathers colourful wild flowers and then tastes the oozed gum, causing her to forget her sorrows. Hayter continues that the Greeks 'sometimes portrayed her holding a poppy in her hand instead of a sheaf of corn, and the flower adorned her altars and its drug was perhaps used in her rites at Eleusis' (1988: 20). The Eleusian mysteries can be seen as one of the oldest religions in the west which is centred around intoxication. Lee and Shlain (1992: 66) argue that 'for two millennia pilgrims journeyed from all over the world to take part in the Mysteries and drink of the sacred kykeon', while for Graves (1961) these ancient Greek insights into paradise derived from intoxication have been distilled and brought into Christianity on the basis that visions are a historical representation but unnecessary in the contemporary world. Hofmann et al. (1978) maintain that drinking the spiritual potion focuses individuals on the symbolic act of renewal within the life cycle and that Plato, Aristotle and Sophocles were active participants at these rituals.

The theme of responsibility and control is further elaborated in Homer, where Odysseus is forced to rescue three of his sailors after reaching the land of the lotus eaters, a population described as drug users (1980: 101). He writes:

> I sent away some of my comrades to find what manner of human beings were those who lived here. They went at once, and soon were among the Lotus-Eaters, who had no thoughts of making away with my companions, but gave them lotus to taste instead. Those of my men who ate the honey-sweet lotus fruit had no desire to retrace their steps and come back with news; their only wish was to linger there with the Lotus-Eaters, to feed on the fruit and put aside all thought of a voyage home. These men I then forced back to the ships; they were shedding tears but I made them go. I dragged them down under the thwarts and left them bound there. The rest of my crew I dispatched aboard with all speed, so that none of them should taste the lotus and then forget the voyage home.

The narrative suggests that drugs alter personality through a change resulting from intoxication, which makes individuals unable to see reason and clarity; this places drugs in opposition to humanity. In Homer drugs change rational people into cowards and deserters who do not conform or follow orders. Drugs are presented as a burden or obstacle to returning, located on the outside where danger and ruthlessness are at hand.[6]

Opium was firmly integrated in Greek culture. Levinthal (1985: 563) argues that opium's 'medical use could never be separated from its "recreational" use by people without any physical complaint'; it had a diversity of uses extending from pleasure to pain. However, the range of potential applications has slowly been reduced and reversed. Opium no longer signifies Homer's forgetfulness; it has been inverted to symbolize a day never to be forgotten: Remembrance Day. Opium has also lost its original connection with life and rebirth, with medicine and recreation, and with sleep as Virgil describes in the *Aeneid*.[7] The contemporary meaning of opium is now focused on the dead of wars. Through the visual representation of the poppy, opium has only one meaning, the symbol of permanent sleep: death (Scott 1969).

The distortion of our historical understanding of drugs is also Vivian Nutton's concern. She highlights how drugs were linked to historical misrepresentation in Roman imperialism through the accounts of Pliny (23–79 AD). Nutton (1985: 140–1) says that the official morality tale put forward by Roman history claims that the end to the military victories of Hannibal's Carthaginians over the Romans at Cannae was brought about by 'the Carthaginian warriors [who] eagerly descend on Seplasia'. In Capua, in southern Italy, the area known as Seplasia was so famous that it gave its name to the whole ancient drug trade. But according to Roman accounts she notes it was 'far from being the place for a decent physician to visit, it was frequented by gilded youths with dandified manners'. The result was that the Carthaginian army became weak to the luxury of drug consumption and were unable to defeat the Romans again. Nutton's point is that drugs are cited as morally harmful when imperial control was under threat, but are also used as a means to label or discredit other groups' or people's identity.

Victorian academics and the representation of drugs

A key scientific endeavour of the nineteenth century was to gain control over what we understand as the Stone Age, by positioning it as far removed from the Classical Greek and Roman period, thus relegating it as a starting point in civilization. In popular illustrated guides to archaeology and antiquity there is an absence of references or focus on drugs consumed by people in the Stone Age. Introductory texts produced by English Heritage (Barton 1997), Constable and Robinson (Adkins 1998) and Hamlyn History (Kennedy 1998) continue the theme of silence on the use of intoxicants during the Archaic period, where there is no reference to opium, cannabis or even hemp. Popular archaeological texts have successfully eliminated the important role of drugs within neolithic culture. The term 'Stone Age' is a nineteenth-century creation by C. J. Thomsen, who in 1836 first popularized the notion with its three different periods.[8] This idea is now part of received wisdom and serves to establish a large gap between the present time and the past age. The neolithic is the final period of Stone Age, covering the period 4500 to 2300 BC, during which humanity had developed a farming economy and its technologies produced utilitarian and cultural objects. These prehistoric peoples possessed considerable knowledge of animals, plant life and astronomy: their achievements are found in artefacts, paintings and their own burial remains. For people and their cultures during the neolithic period, drugs, including the fly agaric mushroom, cannabis and opium, were part of their social and cultural life (Sherratt 1991).

The legacy of the archaeological neglect to focus on intoxicants is also found in anthropology. In both disciplines, bourgeois Victorian morality was influential and has shaped our understanding of the past through an exclusion or revision of the meaning drugs held within primitive cultures. Ancient and primitive cultures were defined as 'savages' by male academics who regarded themselves as civilized. The revelations by traders, colonial administrators and explorers that these cultures used drugs for intoxication affirmed their privileged assumptions that these people were brutal and uncultured. These negative understandings of primitive cultures were also a result of the elitist institutional context which anthropology encountered in late nine-teenth-century England.

Victorian academics gazed upon primitive cultures and sought to confirm their own beliefs about the high point of their own science and morality. According to Inglis (1975: 17), the refusal by the dominant white intellectual tradition to accept the importance of intoxication and a state of ecstasy reached by the shaman had consequences which led Edward Tylor and James Frazer to use disguised or alternative phrases to describe drugs. This process of qualifying meaning continued into the twentieth century, where Edward Evans-Pritchard's work described the drugs used by shamans as 'medicine'. The modern myth is that prehistoric people lacked the skills and sophistica-tion we possess. Neolithic and contemporary primitive cultures which em-ployed a framework of myth, magic and intoxicants were defined as backward. The medical profession of the British scientific establishment identified the newly understood condition of divination or a 'drug trance' as a certifiable form of mental illness (Inglis 1975: 18). The use of drugs within primitive societies when discovered by missionaries, for example, David Li-vingstone, was also interpreted as an induced form of hysteria having at its basis a form of divination which represented a threat to monotheistic religion (Inglis 1975: 109; Du Toit 1980). The existence of shamans to speak of drug-induced experiences was held by the Church to represent possession and the potential for decadence, as described by Eliade (1951). European imperial nations held contradictory views on drug use amongst indigenous peoples. Roman Catholicism condemned intoxication as the work of the Devil and missionaries claimed it brought a degeneracy of morality to 'uncultured' people; in reality their concern was whether drug use would make people politically restless and question their new imperial governors (Leonard 1942).

Within anthropology, Bronislaw Malinowski's dislike of the primitive people he studied is well known through the posthumous publication of his field diaries. For Lévi-Strauss (1966: 3) Malinowski presented an un-sophisticated interpretation of culture and relied on stereotypes to degrade our assessment of past people. Lévi-Strauss argues that we hold a debt of inheritance to neolithic culture, which forms 'the basis of our own civiliza-tion'. Through reinstating the Stone Age as part of the beginning of human culture, it is also possible to argue according to Rudgley (1993: 14–15) that 'prehistoric human populations had all the faculties necessary to discover and use psychoactive plants'. Drugs have had a larger role in the evolution of human culture than has been previously acknowledged by academics.

One useful starting point to explore the position that drugs have been denied a history is the work of Marlene Dobkin de Rios (1984), who examined the use of hallucinogens from a cross-cultural perspective, focusing on 11 ethnographic studies of different peoples' uses of intoxicants: Australian abor-igines, the reindeer-herding people of Siberia, Plains Indians of North America,

Nazca fishermen of coastal Peru, New Guinea highlanders, Mochica of Peru, ancient Maya, Aztecs of Mexico, Incas of Peru, the Bwiti sect of the Fang in north-western equatorial Africa and urban Amazonian Mestizos of Peru. Dobkin de Rios's study is useful in that it demonstrates how a range of diverse non-western preliterate societies engage in patterns of non-abusive psychoactive drug use. Where the cultural meaning of substances derived from plants has been incorporated into the social organization of society, their beliefs, hopes and values are seen as being influenced through intoxication. It is not that drugs form a dominant part of these cultures, but that they have shaped the people and their culture and are an integral aspect of their heritage. She argues that early western anthropologists and travellers saw drugs as something less dignified than is fitting or customary, presenting other cultures in a condescending manner. Focusing on the cultural context in which there is ritual use of drugs she examines the process whereby forms of cultural solidarity and cohesion in society are brought into being. For Strassman (1987: 91) this represents a strengthening of social bonds and a 'means of the reaffirmation of certain cultural motifs during the drug experience'.

The importance of Dobkin de Rios's study is her critique of European thought (1984: 14); for her, drugs have an influence on ethical and moral systems of belief which challenge the applicability of simplistic notions of good and evil encapsulated in the Judeo-Christian tradition. One of the findings of her ethnographic work is that people's consumption of substances did not lead to drug addiction: 'we find little, if any, abuse'. She maintains that European colonialism brought degrees of cultural disintegration to indigenous people and, in particular, that drug use became subject to European hegemony, which sought to remove the position of drugs from within the community. For example, historically, when the Roman Empire adopted Christianity under Constantine all other religions were forced into exile. Walton (2001: 27) argues that the Dionysian cults of ritual intoxication were crushed or incorporated under the monolithic single deity of Christianity. The successful result of Christian propaganda, according to Lee and Shlain (1992: 66), was 'the destruction of documentary evidence by the church [concealing] the full scope of the ritual use of hallucinogens in Europe'. The dominant European morality has sought to define drugs in terms of a cultural separation, outside the norm, rather than an integral aspect of culture. Therefore, the white European influence on defining and understanding intoxication has been to remove drugs from their ritual, 'ordinary' or normalized position in society.

Drug normalization in nineteenth-century Britain

Contemporary historical analysis by Parssinen (1983) and Berridge and Edwards (1987) suggests that two aspects of drug normalization were apparent
in Britain during the Victorian period. Within working-class and middle-class
communities, not only was there diverse use of patent medicines mixed by
chemists and families themselves who compounded recipes derived from
previous generations, but there was also recreational drug use. The main form
of commercial opiate consumption was laudanum. It was Paracelsus who in
1520 promoted the idea of mixing opium, wine and spices, calling it laudanum, meaning 'something to be praised' (Levinthal 1985). Further examples
of opium included variations on infant 'quieteners', for example, Godfrey's
Cordial, often known simply as 'comfort' drops, opium pills, penny sticks and
square lumps. The cheapness of opium was an important factor in its widespread availability, but it was also recognized as a popular medicine and
opium consumption was part of popular culture. In Britain the established
and successful opium importers Jardine Matheson and Dent and Co., along
with the relaxation of duty on patent medicine, brought forth a flourishing
development of remedies which included opium, laudanum, cocaine and
chlorodyne. Certain medicines such as Dover's Powder or Daffy's Elixir had a
long ancestry, but there was considerable uncertainty between what were
medical and 'non-medical' remedies.

From the early 1800s there were innumerable medicines which included
opium and an expansion of chemists supporting the tradition of self-medication under the new era of customer power.[9] Berridge and Edwards (1987:
22) state that by the nineteenth century 'a number of provincial wholesale
houses established themselves, often developing as specialist businesses from
grocers who found drugs their most profitable line'. Opium, laudanum and
other drugs were available virtually without restriction from grocers, chemists, public houses, general stores and back streets. Berridge and Edwards
(1987: 25) estimate the number of people selling drugs in the 1850s to be
between 16,000 and 26,000 and that this figure is likely to be a substantial
underestimation. Self-medication was an accepted cultural practice, along
with the cultivation of opium and hemp in Britain, to the extent that it
became a celebrated and ritualized feature of British life. The cultivation of
opium in Britain followed a traditional pattern: the Society of Arts awarded
gold medals, the Caledonian Horticultural Society offered prizes for sophoric
medicine, for example, the opium lettuce, while the most successful opium
cultivators were rewarded with financial prizes. Jones (1800: 178) describes
how to successfully propagate opium in England, showing the important role
of child labour in the process of harvesting the drug:

> Each of the children being provided with a tin cup, having one
> handle, so contrived as to fix itself to a girdle fastened round his
> waist, with a common gardening knife scraped off the opium that
> appeared upon the heads in a soft ash-coloured substance.

The acceptability of opium within the established medical profession is
documented by Payne (1900) in his biography of the famous Dr Thomas
Sydenham, whose own remedy, known as 'Sydenham's Laudanum', was
widely available in the nineteenth century.[10]

It is often suggested that recreational consumption of opium began after
Thomas De Quincey's publication of *Confessions of an English Opium Eater* in
1821 (Harding 1998: 3). The use of opium as a pleasurable stimulant was
widespread amongst the Romantic poets (except Wordsworth), where drug
use was identified with middle-class luxury and leisure (Jay 2000). Parssinen
(1983: 42–6), using data from local chemists, argues that as early as 1801 in
the areas of Nottinghamshire and Lancashire opium was taken by large
numbers of working-class women and the practice of drinking laudanum was
especially prevalent amongst large sections of the poorer class. Samuel Taylor
Coleridge in a letter of 1808 notes that 'the practice of taking opium is
dreadfully spread – throughout Lancashire and Yorkshire it is the common
dram of the lower order of people – in the small town of Thorpe the druggist
informed that he commonly sold on market days two or three pounds of
opium and a gallon of Laudanum – all among the labouring classes' (Berridge
and Edwards 1987: 105–6). Writing in the *Lancet* in 1845 Samuel Flood notes
that on Saturday night in Leeds 'in the public market place . . . are to be seen
. . . one stall for vegetables, another for meat and a third for pills'. Opium was
a regular feature of Saturday night and the culture of the public house. In
1863 Dr Henry Hunter reported to the Medical Officer of the Privy Council
that many of the men in south Lincolnshire 'never take their beer without
dropping a piece of opium into it. To meet the popular taste, but to the
extreme inconvenience of strangers, narcotic agents are put into the beer by
the brewers or the sellers' (Berridge and Edwards 1987: 39).

Furthermore, the following year Hunter reported that 'a well-accustomed
shop will serve 300 or 400 customers with the article on a Saturday night'
(Parssinen 1983: 49). In 1885 a letter to the editor of the *British Medical Journal*
reported that the town of Whittlesea, in Cambridgeshire, had a population of
3700 and supported five druggists whose primary business was the sale of
opium. Berridge and Edwards (1987: 45) conclude that 'shop counters in the
Fenland towns were loaded every Saturday night with three or four thousand
laudanum vials'. Opium was the cheap intoxication for dance and pleasure
and as an aid to relief from routine physical hard labour.

It is possible to overromanticize the tradition of self-medication and recreational drug use but it was a result of material limitations experienced by the poor.

The acceptability of drug use from within the labouring classes was challenged by the bourgeoisie under the guise of the public health movement. The campaign possessed a multiplicity of targets but none was more emotional than criticism of working-class child-rearing practices, through what is generally referred to as 'infant doping'.[11] Parssinen (1983) argues that although opium is undeniably connected with the deliberate intervention to bring about the death of some infants, the drugging of young children was part of the stark reality of working-class labour and domestic life in the nineteenth century. Working-class parents employed infant sedatives on the basis of economic survival. They also used opiates themselves on the same basis for relaxation or as a stimulant after work, hence the expression 'pick-me-up'.[12] When Marx used the phrase that religion 'is the opium of the people' (1843: 244), the comparison is clear: both were cheap and easily accessible. He saw religion and drug use as forms of 'protest against real suffering'. Conventional historical accounts and moral reformers of the period fail to mention the oppressive material conditions of working-class family life. Moral reformers link high usage of infant doping with a medical condition related to the mother's absence at work, supporting their own privileged middle-class assumptions.

Contemporary drug normalization

The first modern sociological application of the term 'normality' applied to drug consumption was put forward by Alfred R. Lindesmith (1938: 597), who argued that theories of drug use 'tend to be moralistic rather than scientific' and accused drug prohibitionists of defining drug users as 'defective psychopaths'. He specifies that this negative and misinformed view about drug use is not only widespread among psychiatrists but is popularly held as well. Lindesmith's point is that scientists, educationalists and the media have constructed a 'monstrous person' called the drug user who is not real but a 'figment of the imagination' (1938: 204). In an attempt to challenge this 'body of stereotyped misinformation', he looks at international data on drug use and argues that more than half of drug users have 'no criminal records of any kind prior to addiction' (1938: 204) and two-thirds of drug users show 'no appreciable changes in their general behaviour as a consequence of addiction'. Thus he sets out the case for 'the normality of the drug user', arguing that one of the key factors of drug use is the cultural milieu, especially the culture of the group to rationalize and situate motivation for drug use. From the outset, the term 'drug normalization' has been used as a means to critique inaccurate descriptions of drug users or, as Lindesmith (1940) states, to expose the creation of 'dope fiend mythology'.

In sociology, normalization was a central research question within ethnomethodology which refers to the process of understanding everyday life (Douglas 1971). One significant advantage of the normalization thesis with regard to recreational drug use is its potential temporarily to remove the moralistic and pathological understanding of drug consumption by placing it within the realm of cultural norms as a social practice. Removal of *a priori* blame allows drug use to be understood within a social and community context rather than placing it outside society. It is in this sense that prohibitionists may dislike the term normalization because it suggests that drugs should be understood as one feature within people's lives, that is to say an everyday experience. The concept of normalization does not suggest that drug taking is a widespread activity; it seeks to understand drug use as an action of everyday life for certain sections of the population.

Normalization is a useful concept because it refers to human behaviour which exhibits some degree of regularity. In a Weberian sense social human actions are common expectations governed by agreement on formal and informal rules. Critically, then, normalization does not necessarily refer to actual social behaviour, because the term refers to a series of possible social expectations about cultural behaviour. This gives rise to potential disagreement between dominant groups who wish to impose one set of norms and other subordinate groups who consider that their social behaviour is equally norm-based, although different from that of the dominant culture, thus creating conflict over social expectations (Rock 1973: 84–6).

The theory of drug normalization outlined by Parker et al. (1998: 152) is specific: they state that it 'refers only to the use of certain drugs, primarily cannabis but also nitrites, amphetamines and equivocally LSD and ecstasy. Heroin and cocaine are not included in the thesis. Similarly chaotic combination drug use and dependent 'daily' drug use form no part of our conceptualization'. They argue that there are six dimensions to the normalization thesis: drug availability, drug trying, drug use, being drugwise, future intentions and cultural accommodation of the illicit. Drug normalization describes the process of an apparent increase in the availability of drugs, but also indicates the possibility of an increased acceptance of drug use. Thus normalization suggests drug use has become more conventional and integrated into certain people's lives. The evidence put forward for drug normalization by Parker et al. (1998) is broadly twofold: statistics which specify large numbers of young people who claim to have used drugs in terms of frequency and regularity; and changes in culture which they identify as being more drug centred. A key rationale for government drug policy is the assertion that there has been an increase in drug usage, therefore the normalization thesis comfortably sits within the framework of control. The Conservative policy of 'Tackling Drugs Together' (HM Government 1994: 35) asserted that 'drug misuse is a major and growing problem'. The subsequent Labour government consolidated this understanding in 1998 with 'Tackling Drugs Together to

Build a Better Britain', which also saw the launch of an American-style anti-drug coordinator or 'drug tsar'.

Media populism and drug normalization

The pinnacle of drug 'normalization' at the onset of the twenty-first century was the rave celebration held on New Year's Eve 1999 by the Ministry of Sound at the Millennium Dome in London. During the last two decades, television and the press have been central players in the delivery, promotion and relay of ideas linked to drug normalization. In the battle for viewing figures, both the BBC and television companies belonging to the ITV network have taken part in what could be described as 'soap drug wars'. Drug stories are an important feature of drama and realist documentaries, but drugs in soap operas occupy a special place because of programme longevity. The claim that soaps deal with real life has resulted in the inclusion of drug narratives, which in turn attracts viewers and increases audience figures through the performance of topical issue stories. Thus the portrayal of drug normalization on the screen results in high ratings and relevance, making the programme appear popular. It cannot be simply argued that soaps promote drug use, because by their very nature soaps provide polysemy or multiple messages and meaning. The power of the soap opera derives from its mode of populism – its claim to be immersed in popular culture.

In the last 20 years television soap opera, serial drama and situation comedy have consistently brought drugs into people's lives. Zammo Maguire in *Grange Hill*, Leanne Battersby and Jez in *Coronation Street*, Lucy Benson and Rob Hawthorn in *Hollyoaks*, Mary the Punk, Martin Fowler and Nick Cotton in *EastEnders*, Jimmy Corkhill in *Brookside*, Ferdy in *This Life* – the list of characters is virtually endless. Drugs get portrayed as bad and wicked in *The Bill* or *London's Burning*, cool in *Sex and the City*, *Absolutely Fabulous* and *Queer as Folk* and become mainstream in *Only Fools and Horses*, where Delboy jokes that 'Rodney's been on the wacky baccy', or in *EastEnders*, where Dot Cotton's consumption of herbal tea is seen as a source of drug humour. During the 1970s the situation comedy *Open All Hours* with Ronnie Barker and David Jason saw the hilarious introduction of the 'dope cake'. In 1995 Channel 4 presented a cannabis showcase called 'Pot Night', which included many aspects of comedy including the American situation comedy *Roseanne*; also the British comedian Lily Savage demonstrated how to make hashish cookies on 'Lily's Cooking'. The recent success of young comedian Sacha Baron Cohen's creation Ali G, with his ludicrous and witty inversions of serious subjects, could be described as the real-life 'Spliffy'.[13] His constant punning and double entendres about smoking 'weed' have been incorporated into contemporary youth culture. Although appearing to be marginal and part of late night risk television, his appearance in Madonna's 'Music' video and the widespread impersonation of his style across British television reveal he is a mainstream character, especially since his film *Ali G Indahouse* (2002) and appearance on the BBC's interview programme *Parkinson* (2002).

Soap opera and situation comedy actors who have appeared on screen for decades bring familiarity and enable viewers to become embroiled in the drug stories and drug humour, making drug normalization a homely experience. This led the *Sunday Express* on 13 February 2000 to accuse television soaps of portraying drugs as fashionable, announcing: 'TV soaps "push drugs"'. The irresistible rise of drugs within television soaps is often argued by producers and characters as being information based and preventative. However, there is a concentration of action into a single character or series of characters who promote excitement, anger, fear and sympathy. This concentration is the artificiality of the soap, creating an exaggerated narrative in condensed time with cliffhanging episodes and interweaving story lines which sustain suspense. Here the drug narrative becomes part of the thrill, where entertainment, death, criminality, sex and downfall are covered in the drug drama. The soap drug wars thrive on stereotypical 'bad' figures. This conforms with genre theory, where certain characters are identified as possessing recognizable markers and thus fit specific categories and stereotypes. According to Lévi-Strauss (1966) we understand the world through an acceptance of binary oppositions. In soaps the drug issue is real but the narrative is exaggerated through a series of predefined opposites which reduce the complexity of social life. The drug user is defined as bad, the drug dealer evil, and the drug lifestyle chaotic, in contrast to the good, honest and the well-organized non-drug taker. The essentialism of drug soap wars can either result in confirming an audience's assumptions about drugs or producing scepticism and hostility from 'drugwise' viewers who see through these artificial constructions.

The popular symbol of drug normalization during the twenty-first century has been the 'celebrity drug dabbler', from Bill Clinton to the disgraced Conservative peer Jeffrey Archer. Television personalities, soap opera actors and their fictional characters are regularly featured in the tabloid press and their coverage of drug problems and drug scandals. The unfolding and blurring narrative of the 'TV star's drug nightmare' is exploited by the press as a personal interest story which merges on- and off-screen images, as with the presenter Angus Deayton. Two useful examples which the press have slavishly followed are Michael Barrymore and Danniella Westbrook. The press have pursued each of these TV personalities for their extravagant drug lifestyle in the manner of a 'never-ending story'. In Barrymore's case the tabloids present drug use as a gateway for further sensations focusing on homosexuality, criminality, murder and desire to mix socially with the 'lower classes'. With the case of Westbrook, an actor from *EastEnders* who severely damaged her nose, losing her septum from extensive cocaine use, the press coverage has conformed to the beauty-and-the-beast duality. Her beauty as an attractive woman has been placed alongside the ugliness of her self-inflicted damage through negative labels such as 'mono-nostril'. The tabloid coverage of each personality has specified that drugs were a 'normal' part of their 'fast lives' and on this basis normalization is used as a causal explanation for their downfall. Here drugs become a metaphor for personal and individual tragedy, which the media 'trickles down' in flavoursome soundbites, keeping the audience and reader warm with the delight of expectation.

Drug normalization within the media follows a complex pattern. The dominant tendency amongst the tabloid press is to describe TV personalities and soap opera stars as drug victims and 'weak characters'. Here the drug problem plays a secondary role in terms of their perceived weakness, where the drug story is used as a carrier to heighten other social fears, such as male homosexuality or the 'fallen woman'.[14] An important feature of the Barrymore and Westbrook examples is the media presentation of them as 'true stories' of personal failure that possess universal interest and eternal truths.

'True confessions' want to shock, in a similar way to moral panics, to prompt disgust in people by showing how degraded celebrities can be in their drug excesses of their 'normal' lives, such as in the *Sun* on 16 December 2002: 'Tracy: my cocaine hell'.[15] High-profile media celebrity drug confessions take the form of self-publicity, selling the celebrities' image. A range of drug media confessions have come from the Premier League football player Paul Merson, the former England rugby union captain Lawrence Dallaglio and members of the aristocracy such as Prince Harry, Tom Parker Bowles,[16] Lord Frederick Windsor, Tara Palmer-Tomkinson and Alastair Irvine, son of the Lord Chancellor.[17] The true confession is assumed to be of public interest, where each celebrity is given approval or public support because of their presence at anti-drug campaign launches. Drug confessions are also a strategy to rebuild a television career, as with the case of Richard Bacon, the *Blue Peter* presenter who went on to work for *The Big Breakfast* on Channel 4. In 1998 he made the front pages of the tabloid press for 'snorting cocaine'. What is of interest is the manner in which the tabloids reported the sacking of the *Blue Peter* host. For example, the *Sun* of 21 October 1998 in a series of headlines offered numerous innuendoes such as 'Here's one they made earlier', also using the 'pulped' *Blue Peter* book with headlines 'Pot it?' and 'Racing the dragon'. The articles inside the *Sun* by Stafford Hildred and Trevor Kavanagh ridiculed BBC children's television as being drug centred and attacked the BBC in general, revealing that drugs are an important medium through which more significant political targets can be attacked by right-wing journalists.

Drug coverage of celebrities within the tabloid press takes its own form of soap opera where there is no closure as snippets or tasty teasers are continually presented or represented. In the last ten years Noel and Liam Gallagher of the band Oasis, the celebrated heroes of the 'chemical generation', have actively lived out an online biography with drug prohibitionists and the tabloid press. Remarks by Noel or Liam Gallagher that promote drug normalization should be recognized within the framework of a soap opera, where irony plays an important role.[18] Tabloid newspapers and television contribute to the 'normalization' of drug use through amplifying and sensationalizing the extent of drug use amongst public entertainers and the scale of the problem it represents: statistics and verifiable evidence are the least of their concerns when promoting a moral crusade. From William Randolph Hearst to Rupert Murdoch, newspaper owners have used the public's preoccupation with figures from entertainment as a means to increase circulation (Silver and Aldrich 1979). Historically the newspaper medium has been intimately linked with moral crusades and political hegemony. As Young (1971: 179) points out, the media 'selects events which are atypical, presents them in a stereotypical fashion, and contrasts them against a backcloth of normality which is overtypical'. The misperception of drugs polarizes society into an unrealistic conforming majority and a deviant minority. Today this is achieved through the repetitive performance of actors in TV soap operas, television personalities, film stars, pop idols, and selected 'ordinary people' who have 'fallen victim' to drugs. The representation of a catalogue of stereotypes is a constant theme which constitutes the media's normalization of drug use. Media drug 'normalization' does not offer greater understanding of drug issues; rather, it works in tandem with 'othering' or negative labelling, which services the myths and ideology of 'drug war' prohibition.

Drug normalization as a discourse of regulation

The assertion that drug normalization equals drug epidemic is a key feature of the drug prohibition message to increase moral and punitive regulation. Government legislation on drug prevention requires a popular portrayal of drug normalization in order for the intervention of drug prevention strategies. Within public statements made by media and government, drug normalization is understood to mean drug acceptability, suggesting an increased casualization of drug use. It does not refer to Howard Parker's specific concern with increased 'soft drug' use. Media and government spokespersons have consistently blamed youth culture figureheads from Timothy Leary to Noel Gallagher as responsible for this casual attitude towards drugs. Drug normalization is an opportunity to play on respectable fears, demonstrated by front-page tabloid newspaper headlines such as 'it could be your child'. For Foucault (1975: 308) government and the media provide support for discourses of regulation (law and medicine) which are preoccupied with discipline as a means to exercise a normalizing judgment. Government and the media employ what he calls 'the power of normalization' to categorize the drug user as a type of deviant; this behaviour becomes classified and made into objective law, which regulates people at the expense of difference. The drug consumer is categorized as a delinquent threatening society, whereby government can exercise legitimate power to regulate whole populations; normalization is thus concerned with conformity and prescription. Foucault states (1975: 184): 'It is a normalizing gaze, a surveillance that makes it possible to qualify, to classify and to punish. It establishes over individuals a visibility through which one differentiates them and judges them.' Defining the drug user as criminal or immoral acts as a warning to respectable citizens, to remind them to be constantly vigilant and hostile towards the so-called drug deviants. Not only are drug takers individualized and deemed answerable for their own actions, but also their apparent lack of self-responsibility means that they are untrustworthy and require disciplinary incentives. This self-blaming approach cuts the drug user off from society. It separates them from the community because it asserts that the drug user is trying to destroy the community (MacDonald and Marsh 2002). Government policy promotes images suggesting that drug users are unreliable figures. This uncertainty is then used by the media to demand constant surveillance of the drug deviants. Therefore punitive policy towards drug issues is deemed rational, necessary and possessing public support.

The problem faced by government is that acknowledgement of increased drug usage may work in favour of conditions to introduce more punitive drug law, but it also works in the opposite direction, suggesting that a large number of people regard drug use as normal. This contradiction destabilizes the power of the normalizing gaze because the drug deviant is no longer simply categorized as belonging to 'an entirely different world, unrelated to familiar, everyday life' (Foucault 1975: 286). Instead, the drug consumer is at the centre of the social world. The rationale used by the drug consumers is that they are pursing individual choice and consumer autonomy, claiming that their actions support the dominant ideology of capitalist values and norms. The legitimacy of the drug consumers' actions is therefore based on acceptance of the prevailing principles of choice, difference and diversity. In contrast, negative language constructs of drug normalization in the mass media and academic discourses induce fear and mystery. South (1999: 12) argues that the dominant discourses of drug prohibition, enforcement and regulation are medicine, psychiatry and international law, which define and set cultural and legal boundaries. This dominant discourse is a particular construction by institutions of power. It differs over time and needs to be seen as a regulatory framework which seeks to impose hegemony. The morality of public policy and the objectivity of science articulate an understanding of drug consumers which defines their dual status as both outside and inside society. This double positioning establishes a tautology of 'othering'. It enables the legitimate discourses to define drug users as not normal, i.e. outsiders, while at the same time it has the authority to invoke disciplinary procedures to reform or punish individuals before they are allowed to return to society after 'adjustment' to become 'normal' insiders.

Drug normalization and postmodernist theory

The leading critics of the normalization thesis have been Michael Shiner and Tim Newburn. They correctly maintain that the concept oversimplifies drug consumption by young people. Their criticism of drug normalization is threefold: first, it exaggerates drug use; second, it is based on a biased research method; third, it rests on an ideological theory of postmodernity.

Shiner and Newburn (1999: 145) identify the two leading advocates of the normalization thesis as Howard Parker and Frank Coffield, whom they accuse of empirical exaggeration through their focus on lifetime contact with drugs rather than current usage. Shiner and Newburn maintain that non-drug users outnumber the young drugtakers and assert that drug use is a minority practice. In order to prove this they examine four different quantitative data sets from Britain and the USA, together with their own study, to conclude that there is 'little to support the contention that youthful drug use is a normalized feature of contemporary post-industrial societies'. The concept of normalization is applied by Parker and Coffield from within the symbolic interactionist tradition in an attempt to be non-judgemental, to examine the motive and response of the drug user as an active subject. Shiner and Newburn argue that this qualitative paradigm which supports grounded theory is an ideological construction, in the sense that data is used to support a preexisting theoretical position, in other words 'normalization'. They suggest that the normalization thesis follows too closely the voice of the researched, i.e. drug consumers, in a biographical or descriptive sense and presents the data as naturalistic. Shiner and Newburn argue (1997: 511) that the normalization thesis presents a partial view where 'drug use by young people is becoming so common that it is no longer regarded as a "deviant" activity by them'. They go on to state that 'this trend should not be treated uncritically'. Thus Shiner and Newburn suggest that the 'normalization thesis' promotes a sympathetic, even positive understanding of drugs.

However, the normalization thesis is not about an uncritical acceptance of drug use in society; it is a concept which may enable a better understanding of patterns of drug consumption. On the basis of using a grounded theory approach, the concept of normalization carries the voice of the drug consumer, who describes their range of experiences from positive to negative. Parker et al. (1998: 159) argue that the validity of their account rests on a 'grounded strategy' where truth is seen to derive from the voice where 'respondents have spoken to us'.[19] Unlike in quantitative approaches, to undertake valid qualitative research it is necessary to gain rapport and trust. The relationship basis to ethnographic studies leads positivist researchers to claim that the research is being guided by the research subjects themselves. For these reasons drug prohibitionists may find this approach unacceptable or even ideological.

Shiner and Newburn criticize drug normalization within postmodern social theory. Their argument is that '[fears that]illicit drug use is a normalized feature of postmodern youth culture are clearly exaggerated' (1999: 147). They suggest that the postmodern condition may have resulted in prioritizing consumption over production, where drugs are just another consumable, but this social change has not resulted in increased drug consumption. In essence, their argument is that postmodernity is not a causal factor in patterns of higher drug use by young people. Shiner and Newburn's argument against what they see as Parker's postmodern theory of drug normalization is flawed partly by their own limited understanding of postmodernity and also by Parker's own acknowledged uncertainty of the postmodern condition (Parker et al. 1998: 22). Parker sees the normalization thesis as 'consistent' with the individualization thesis developed by Beck (1992). It seems that they want to retain an argument which possesses structural inequality, but also want to define normalization as a local and individual concept within a theory of risk society. They openly admit to having sidestepped some of the difficulties in this debate. Their approach is to combine Howard Becker's notion of career applied to drug use as a recreational and rational action, with a postmodernist assessment of risk culture to suggest intention and agency. However, Beck's individualization thesis has a tendency to psychologize risk (France 2000), reducing such actions to the personal and diminishing the significance of structural inequality and the ideological power of the dominant order.

Parker locates young people's drug use within a generalized framework of postmodernity, but does not specify whether postmodernity is an ideology, or a form of social change. Postmodernity is taken as given rather than critically investigated, resulting in a confusing analysis partly drawn from ideas developed by Jean-François Lyotard and Jean Baudrillard. This lack of clarity is further heightened in Shiner and Newburn's attempt to understand Parker's theoretical backdrop. Shiner and Newburn trawl through a broad range of postmodern theoretical signposts, optimistically hoping to hit the target. Lyotard and Beck are named, but the assumptions and ideas are derived from an amalgam of thoughts derived from Fredric Jameson and Baudrillard. Taylor argues:

> Shiner and Newburn appear to produce a circular argument, based on a somewhat limited and confused conceptualization of what constitutes 'postmodernism'. They offer no clear definition of what they

mean by the term, whilst the thesis that any condition of post-modernity must depend upon 'a significant break with the past' which they use to test the validity of the conclusions of other commentators would appear to be deficient.

(Taylor 2000: 351)

Parker's idea of drug normalization is to get beyond the narrow understanding of deviance linked to subcultures by showing that drug use has become part of mainstream normalized youth culture. Shiner and Newburn (1997: 512) argue that the drug normalization is theoretically 'underpinned by a subcultural perspective in which the liberal permissiveness of youth culture is contrasted with the conservative restrictiveness of the adult world'. They maintain that there is a 'subcultural basis' to the normalization thesis. Here subculture is applied as a theoretical term which retains strong links with deviance and crime. For them drug use is not part of 'normal' (majority) youth culture due to its conceptual location as a deviant minority practice belonging to the subculture. At the same time they see the rave dance culture as a subculture playing a 'special position within the normalization thesis' (517). But they seem to be unaware of dance culture's size, longevity and diversity. Indeed Saunders (1995), Malbon (1999), Pini (2001) and Jackson (2004) argue that dance and its associated drug use can no longer be described as a minority subculture, but has to be understood as a majority youth culture. On this basis the drug normalization thesis offers one useful explanation of the increased drug consumption amongst a more widespread youth culture (Shildrick 2002).

Shiner and Newburn's theoretical interpretation of youth culture is un-developed with no reference to free market capitalism's profit from drug culture (Blackman 1996b). Nor do they examine the drug references of sub-cultural style, popular music or icons from popular culture who have spoken and written about their drug use. In an attempt to suggest they have examined contemporary youth culture they cite the journalist Matthew Collin. Rather than critically assess Collin's work as a feature of the production of drug normalization within popular culture, they describe it as 'florid' and therefore miss the point of his study and fail to position it within the normalization debate.[20] Shiner and Newburn's analysis is a useful beginning to deconstruct the ambiguities of the normalization thesis, but it is weakened by their moralistic tone and reluctance to engage with the political construction of drug policy formation. Drug normalization cannot be verified by statistics alone, because the drug user has historically been described through an ideological conception of 'othering', which has been part of the prohibition campaign.

Conclusion

In this chapter I have demonstrated that our understanding of drugs has been subject to silence, revision and denial. I specified examples from Ancient, Classical and Victorian society which have deliberately distorted the use of drugs as a means to discredit populations and cultures and impose an imperial hegemony. I further considered the contemporary historical work on nineteenth century working-class and middle-class self-medication and recreational drug consumption, its everyday context and integral location within horticultural shows, weekend leisure practices and economic oppression. The historical analysis shows that drugs have been a consistent cultural factor in social life, which drug prohibitionists and moral reformers have sought to revise or destroy according to their notions of rationality.

The current drug normalization debate is shaped by two conflicting discourses which understand drugs in terms of cultural separation or cultural integration. Drug prohibitionists see the notion of normalization as a threat to drug prevention, its rationality, dominant authority and legitimate control. Prohibitionists position drugs outside society and understand normalization as a threat to the community. The media have played a major and contradictory role in promoting and supporting drug normalization as a discourse of regulation upheld by punitive government drug policy. Drugs are given a negative label but, paradoxically, this negation also possesses chic attraction, rebel status and market potential, alongside prohibitionists' efforts to deny drugs a place in the understanding and development of society. The recent emergence of the normalization idea is one means put forward to advance the understanding of drug use in society to overcome the moralizing judgement of describing drug users as 'other'. The normalization thesis is an untidy concept. It has problems in relation to overgeneralization, it lacks the ability to distinguish between different drugs and different drug users and also supports the ambiguous distinction between soft and hard drugs. This idea is not the answer to understanding drug use, but it does represent a small advance away from the dominant pathological and moralistic approaches.

6 Schooling and substances
A critical approach to drug education

The American anti-drug film *High School Confidential* (1958) directed by Jack Arnold opens with Jerry Lee Lewis bashing out young people's rock 'n' roll music, thereby defining the target audience of the movie. It is the story of Tony Baker, played by Russ Tamblyn,[1] an undercover police officer posing as a drug dealer at his new high school, Santo Bello. Tony moves from cannabis to cocaine to heroin, then some of his fellow students die. The film, released by MGM, is a standard morality tale of drugs, teenagers and schooling, focusing on drug abuse. In essence, the film portrays the 'gateway' theory of drug use, where cannabis leads to heroin use, which results in promiscuity leading in parallel to tragedy. *High School Confidential* was taken seriously by the Federal Bureau of Narcotics (FBN), warranting additional direction from its head, Harry Anslinger (Stevenson 2000: 41). Michael Starks (1982: 63) says: 'Although intended as anti-drug propaganda, the film has become a comedy classic.' The transformation of *High School Confidential* from a serious film about the dangers of teenage drug use to 'cheesy' camp trash reveals that drug education can become the subject of humour and therefore lose the original intention for which it was devised. The film is now released on video and DVD and is making money again, but on the basis of comedy, not drug prevention.

This chapter will be concerned with drug education within secondary education. Initially I shall look at current British drug education policy and also explore its rationale, delivery in the classroom and location within the curriculum. I will then examine a series of issues facing drug education. These include the conflict between education and prevention approaches; the feasibility of developing a scientific model of drug education; and the opposition between peer pressure and peer preference to account for drug use motivation. Finally I will assess the consequence for schools of becoming the new site of primary prevention concerned with abstinence.

British government drug policy: increased concern

According to government policy drug education is required because there has been an increase in drug use amongst young people. The extent of the contemporary problem is specified within government documents as follows:

- use of drugs in society has become more widespread
- the age of the first-time user of drugs is falling
- an increase in drug seizures by customs and police
- a rise in the number of deaths resulting directly from drug use and an increase in 'drug-related' death
- an increase in crime which is 'drug related'.

These claims are supported by a series of key statistics from the Home Office, Drugscope and the police,[2] while at the same time two government White Papers[3] acknowledge that accurate measurement of drug use is difficult to substantiate due to its 'covert nature'. The Health Advisory Service (2001: 7) states that 'data concerning trends in drug use provided from police and clinical populations, self report national surveys, indicate in general an upward trend'. Robert Power (1998: 3) says: 'We can say that at least 25% of the general population will have used illicit drugs at some point in their lives. This is approximately 10 million people between the ages of 15 and 69.' Further support that drug use is increasing comes from independent research (Dorn 1992; Parker et al. 1995; Wibberley 1997; Power 1998; Taylor 1998; Coggans et al. 1999; Plant and Plant 1999; Wyvill and Ives 2000), where it is commonplace for academics to begin by detailing evidence that suggests a growing number of young people are using drugs (Parker et al. 2001).

During the 1990s and early twenty-first century the government has used the apparent growth in drug use as the basis for its increased interventions focusing on drug prevention and drug education. The picture of widespread drug usage has been consolidated by visual and literary representations in popular culture associated with the expansion of ecstasy and dance culture (Collin 1997; Reynolds 1998; Push and Silcott 2000). The increased presence of drugs within society is described in the drug literature as 'drug normalization' and within the popular media as the 'chemical generation'.[4] Government and media have taken up the notion of drug normalization as shorthand for drug acceptability to describe the social condition of Britain. The consequence has been an urgency to write drug policy documents and deliver drug education. Over the last ten years there has been new drug control legislation and a mass of policy initiatives which have brought drug education to the centre of public policy.[5] A key factor of the increased drug acceptability argument has been the suggestion that drug consumption in Britain has become more diverse and now includes young women, ethnic minority groups and youth from rural locations (Ettorre 1992; Henderson 1997; Parker et al. 1998, 2002; Pearce 1999).

The present government position on drug education is based on the distinction between primary prevention and secondary prevention. Primary prevention, according to the DFE circular *Drug Prevention and Schools* (1995: 3), is 'stopping people from taking or experimenting with drugs in the first place'.

Secondary prevention, according to the circular, is 'treatment and re-habilitation to help those who are misusing drugs to stop'. As can be seen from these definitions, primary prevention and secondary prevention are largely concerned with abstinence. In general, primary prevention techniques emphasize abstinence while secondary prevention leans towards bringing drug use within the control of the individual to limit dangers, propose moderation and stop use.

The main providers of drug education in school are the police, teachers, parents, peers and invited guests, who deliver it within a multi-agency framework which emphasizes evidence-based practice, developing a whole school approach. Drug education has two locations within the National Curriculum: first as a statutory requirement in the subject of science; second as part of the new statutory programme of personal and social health education (PSHE) and citizenship. At Key Stages 1 and 2, PSHE and citizenship are non-statutory, while at Key Stages 3 and 4 citizenship has statutory orders and will be taught as a foundation subject separately from PSHE. Pupils will also have the opportunity to take a short course GCSE in the subject as a result of its gaining statutory orders. In addition, some schools may opt to deliver drug education within tutorial time. PSHE is defined in the Education Reform Act 1988 as 'an essential part of the curriculum' and at each key stage curriculum guidance materials detail the learning objectives specific to drug education.[6] A further development undertaken by the Labour government has been the launch of the National Healthy Schools Standard (NHSS) in 1999, whose aim is to support quality standards in PSHE and citizenship in order to provide increased integration of these subjects in the curriculum, which will in turn help to promote drug education in schools. Thus, the current government drug policy is based upon a multi-agency approach to what is understood as a social problem with multiple causes.

Drug education approaches

The various approaches to drug education follow disciplinary boundaries defining drug interventions according to medical, psychological or sociological theories. Drug education approaches are often combined but can be broadly categorized on the following bases:

1. *Medical or psychological drug education approaches*
   - information or factual
   - deterrence
   - self-empowerment
   - decision-making skills
   - refusal skills
   - behavioural.

2. *Sociological or cultural drug education approaches*
   - diversionary or alternative activities
   - situational education
   - peer education
   - cultural
   - life skills
   - harm reduction.

The quality, effectiveness and appropriateness of British drug education varies widely and has been criticized by government and independent research (Ofsted 1997, 2000; Plant and Plant 1999; Bishop et al. 2001). O'Connor et al. (1998: 52) state: 'The foundations of drugs education have been challenged in terms of both their assumptions about the causes of drug using behaviour and the objectives of their procedures.' Because drug education suffers from a credibility problem this in turn has become its motor for change, where the emphasis is to develop ever new approaches or different combinations of interventions. Drug education is subject to fashion swings. The current movement towards less prescriptive anti-drug messages has meant drug education becoming more flexible to deliver diverse forms of intervention and promote active participation. In the search for the new approach, not only is drug education caught in a circular treadmill, but it fails to address a central problem: that the kernel of drug education retains a primary-prevention message. The current emphasis given by the Labour government is first early drug education for children, starting at 5 years old, and second to deliver drug education within a social and life skills framework.[7] There is considerable overlap within these approaches and in practice schools may teach a mixture. The development of a drug programme suitable to each school is essential but increased specialization among schools creates problems for effective evaluation across diverse forms of drug intervention (Allott et al. 1999).

Information-based programmes assume that young people will not use drugs if they are given the facts, especially the dangerous, negative and unpleasant ones. The information, factual and deterrence approaches are based on a medical and psychological understanding of drug use and defined in terms of exhortation, namely 'Just say no', and also include the Leah Betts video 'Just an Ordinary Kid', and the British government TV and billboard campaigns against drugs such as 'Heroin screws you up'. It is difficult to justify this approach in educational terms because its basic function is to discipline young people with a shock horror story. There is some evidence to suggest that fear-arousal campaigns linked with an information approach may increase drug experimentation (De Haes and Schuurman 1975; Kinder et al. 1980; Plant 1987; Beck 1998). The information approach has developed to include peer-led education with the aim of making information more credible.

Information which focuses solely on the negative aspects of drug use tends to be ignored or seen as biased by young people, who may already possess information to the contrary concerning pleasurable aspects of drug use. However, the information approach is still relevant as a drug education strategy because of its role in developing knowledge and encouraging learning.

A key part of drug education is to provide the appropriate level of drug information at the appropriate age. The rationale for early-age drug education from 5 years old is based on the assumption that exposure to negative meanings and messages about drugs prior to drug consumption enables young people to foster anti-drug attitudes. This approach rests on a commonsense theory of negative incubation and conforms to Julian Cohen's (1996) notion of drug education as propaganda for children. The essence of the early drug education approach is explained by Plant and Plant (1999: 387), who say that 'with little pre-existent knowledge' about drugs such interventions 'would make attitude alteration potentially easier'. This form of drug education seeks to erect negative barriers of drug knowledge as a resource strategy to enable young people to refuse or challenge pro-drug stances which they may encounter later in life. The originality of the approach derives from the idea of providing drug education before drug experience. However, there is little which is innovative about this form of drug education, which conforms to the abstinence model.

The intention of early-age drug education is to provide a foundation of critical fear arousal, before children get access to a broader, more complex range of drug representations which could undermine or contradict the early negative message. Early-age drug education is clearly related to the decision-making approach. Ultimately the early-age approach defines young people as lacking skills to make rational choices about drugs. Its philosophical basis is deprivation theory: the theory seeks to be in advance of 'inadequacy' by establishing negative attitudes prior to drug encounters. Early drug education and the decision-making approaches speak about choice but it is clear that the assumption of an 'informed choice' is pre-established as 'No'. The real danger of the early drug education approach is in the learning context of exchange, openness and trust in the classroom: because young people are being told to believe, or not to do, something before they are aware of it, this could led to resentment or the feeling that they have been indoctrinated.

Social and life skills

The social and life skills approaches include the following: peer resistance/ peer-led education, decision-making and confidence skills and diversionary alternatives. The aim is to promote new attitudes and values, such as developing a health-promoting school highlighting the attractions of a drug-free lifestyle, which in turn will generate personal responsibility and strong moral beliefs. This approach involves making important connections within the local community with relevant agencies which come into contact with young people outside school hours. The life skills approach has become a popular preventive because it fits within a holistic approach looking at the overall context of the young person's actions. An additional factor which has led to life skills gaining more attention has been its concern to incorporate harm reduction messages and promote more realistic objectives.

The diversionary–alternatives approach in drug education also seeks to enable participation and choice. It aims to provide access to experiences that meet the same needs as drugs. The approach cannot be easily adopted for the purpose of performance targets in achieving measured reductions in drug prevalence because it starts with no pre-given message of drug prevention. It shares more in common with harm minimization than primary prevention. The strength of the diversionary approach is its flexibility and adaptability, which makes it an easy target for criticism (Davis and Dawson 1996).

In Britain, the USA and Australia the development of life skills drug policy is based on a notion of 'gateway drugs' and its central aim is to delay the onset of drug consumption. The assumption is that if experimentation can be delayed prior to the introduction of life skills education this may enable young people to build up their social competence of drug refusal and to shorten the time available to develop a drug career. In Britain the gateway theory played an important part in the evaluation of Project Charlie[8] by Hurry and Lloyd (1997), which examined the positive impact of life skills approaches on primary school pupils.[9] Hurry and Lloyd (1997) regarded their study as too small in terms of its sample for wider application, but they were convinced that the life skills approaches required reinforcement sessions to consistently repeat the anti-drug message (Lloyd et al. 2000: 113). In the USA school-based drug education using life skills approaches has evolved into a series of high-profile preventives. A number of drug prevention projects have received favourable attention, such as Project ALERT (Adolescent Learning Experiences in Resistance Training) and Project DARE (Drug Abuse Resistance Education), both of which fit into the prevention strategy of bolstering peer resistance through the context of creating anti-drug norms. Due to the longevity of these drug education programmes they have been modified and revised, which can make them more difficult to compare (Gorman 1998).

DARE began in Los Angeles in 1983 and was subsequently imported into Britain during the 1990s, first by the Nottinghamshire police force (Whelan and Culver 1997). DARE has been subject to many appraisals, the majority of which reveal initial promise but conclude that the project has limited effectiveness (Ringwalt et al. 1991; Ellickson et al. 1993). The assessment of DARE by Clayton et al. (1996) specified that it had no lasting effect on young people's drug consumption, and it was not meeting its stated objectives. There remains considerable doubt not only about DARE but also about the formal evaluations themselves undertaken on the different programmes across the United States (Rosenbaum et al. 1994). In Canada, Sheppard et al. (1985: 4) reported on a drug education programme in Ontario delivered to over 5000 pupils from 1977 to 1983. Their conclusion was that the drug education had little impact but they add: 'We would not expect a student to learn new geographical or mathematical concepts in one or two lessons, and therefore, why would we expect him/her to learn about drugs with such minimal exposure?' They caution against the involvement of 'committed people' in drug education and call for better programmes, more evaluation, longitudinal research and greater awareness of the pro-drug messages within popular culture.

In Australia during the 1980s the government launched a massive drug education media programme, headed by the Prime Minister, Bob Hawke, called 'Drug Offensive'. The effectiveness of this intervention was questioned by Makkai et al. (1991: 75), who argued that the success of the campaign could be measured in terms of the large number of people who came into contact with the drug prevention messages, but that it was too short an intervention to have a real impact and was undermined by the homogeneity of the anti-drug message, which was negatively received by young people. Also in Australia, the evaluations of the drug education programme 'Life Education' showed no evidence that it delayed either experimentation or initiation (Hawthorne et al. 1995). The Life Education programme delivered by mobile Life Education centres is also noted in Lloyd et al. (2000: 117) to have been 'eclectic' and 'contentious'. Most controversial of all is that its 'teachers are trained to avoid discussions of illegal drugs' (Plant and Plant 1999: 394). In the UK an overview of school-based drug education was undertaken in Scotland, where 25 per cent of secondary schools were surveyed. Coggans et al. (1991: 14) found that 'drug education had no effect on attitudes to drugs or use of drugs but did improve knowledge'.

In the USA, UK, Australia and Canada evidence from evaluation studies on drug intervention programmes appears to show that drug education is not achieving its objective in reversing drug prevalence. Gerard Hastings and Martine Stead (1999: 3) argue that these large anti-drug campaigns seem to 'have reinforced already held views about drugs and not influenced those at high risk of using drugs'. Given the negative assessment of the effectiveness of different drug education interventions, it is important to ask: Why does drug education continue? The unconvincing results of these drug education programmes seem unlikely to halt their delivery. The problem is assessed as being located elsewhere: for example, the failure is not the drug education programme but the lack of creative and interactive teaching methods; or the weakness is linked to the underlying theoretical model, which requires revision;

or the failure is dismissed because there has been no detailed and systematic evaluation. The continued legitimacy for drug education seems to rest on a strange combination of science and faith. The enthusiasm for such programmes is not related to their cost effectiveness or successful outcomes. Drug interventions produce their own justification supported by government departments and media agencies, where the apparent popularity of drug education seems to derive from a self-belief in public prevention morality.

Drug education or prevention – towards the new managerialism?

In twenty-first-century Britain, a new style of drug education has emerged promoting itself through national quality standards, multi-level organizational commitment, and specified outcomes. The new focus is on 'safety from harm' with PSHE and citizenship working alongside the NHSS. The removal of the ex-chief constable as the drug co-ordinator, the decriminalization of cannabis and greater opportunities for rehabilitation for heroin users suggest a movement towards educational objectives with a harm reduction focus.

The new government strategy, 'Tackling Drugs Together to Build a Better Britain', is set out in terms of managerial efficiency and military effectiveness. It defines itself in terms of transferability and comprehensive strategic service, in other words the local and national mechanisms to initiate and deliver drug education suggest totality. From the Home Office and Departments for Education and Health, to the drug action teams and teachers, delivery of drug education is described in terms of quality evaluation, such as monitoring, targetting and planning, which set the pace alongside more positive metaphors such as partnership, inclusion and participation. These institutional arrangements represent the new human-science approach of drug education, where the language of business and the market operates the principles of drug education. The dominant image of the new drug education is its priority on the individual and self-responsibility, putting forward a new approach to 'human relations'. The new emphasis has been achieved by incorporating notions of harm reduction within the framework of education and prevention. This has been reflected in documents produced by the Standing Conference on Drug Abuse, the Drug Prevention Advisory Service and the Advisory Council on the Misuse of Drugs which speak of the advances of harm reduction and the value of community partnerships in understanding and dealing with drug issues. The lessons learnt from dealing with HIV and AIDS have also been used as evidence to highlight this new, less prescriptive basis to drug education. Drug prevention agencies have moved towards incorporating elements of this less judgemental style of intervention to drug misuse as part of community safety.

Although drug education and drug prevention are complementary fields of practice, Coggans et al. (1999: 28) identify distinctions between them. They see drug prevention in terms of 'dependent forms of substance use ... and psychiatric disorders' whilst drug education is identified as 'preventing people from harming themselves'. It is suggested that a possible conflict exists between drug education and drug prevention in terms of aims, intervention strategies, teaching methods and outcomes. The opposition between drug education and drug prevention at a simple level is determined by the issue that drug information is not neutral (Blackman 1996b). Information in the public domain concerning drugs can be used by other agencies such as the media for the purpose of expressing political and moral ideologies. Prevention is based on the idea that information on drugs should be *against* drug use, whereas drug education considers drug information should be *about* drug use. The difference between information against and information about drugs demonstrates that drug knowledge is not objective. Calls for drug education to be 'objective' are all too easy to announce and they not only reflect an unrealistic vision of the social world, but also fail to understand the history behind the politics of prevention.[10]

The government drug strategy combines education and prevention without distinction. For example, the phrase 'good practice in drug education and prevention' has been used as a corporate logo on government drug education documents. Furthermore, guidelines on drug education have sought to demonstrate their less prescriptive nature, for example, the government publication series 'The Right Choice'. Drug education as specified by *The Right Approach* (1999) follows the behaviouristic outcomes model and managerialist framework, where benchmarks are set and criteria specified that form the basis for action plans. The abstraction of these models is self-generating and self-fulfilling, they make sense to the logic of the model irrespective of the social world.

Contemporary policy phrases such as 'the right choice', 'the right responses' and 'the right approach' correspond to a belief in the market and consumerism by focusing upon individual responsibility and initiative. The drug user is defined as being in opposition to community safety and destroying their own personal opportunity. By not taking the right choice the young person thus loses their place in society. The simplistic soundbite 'the right choice' differs little from the discredited slogan 'Just say no'. In effect the phrase 'the right choice' means the only choice; it is a prescriptive message with a predefined outcome and therefore not subject to negotiation. It is choice as presentational rhetoric without choice in reality. The punitive side of drug prevention with its priority on abstinence appears dominant in its influence, especially when delivering drug education in the learning context of a school classroom. Here prevention may be perceived as carrying fixed messages which are prescriptive and therefore reluctant to consider contradictions. Education, on the other hand, is seen as encouraging debate and openness about drugs, where messages are interpreted as revealing the complexities of social life. The new rationality of drug education may suggest choice, but ultimately the only message upheld is that of abstinence (Midford 2000: 442). The new emphasis on harm reduction approach is not harm minimization[11] but another variation of primary prevention. Harm reduction has become a 'soft way' of promoting drug deterrence, making it appear to carry the supportive ideologies of harm minimization, but has not advanced drug education away from prescription.[12]

Behaviour change, choice and outcomes

The government website Wired for Health states that information about drugs is 'wrapped in myths' and that this 'fiction gets in the way of the facts' and prevents young people from gaining 'information they can trust'. This statement is broadly true but the government seems to suggest that it has not previously contributed to drug misrepresentation. In Chapters 1 and 2, I demonstrated that historically information concerning drugs has often been inaccurate and biased. Furthermore, contemporary drug education has been similarly labelled as propaganda or dogmatic (Coggans and Watson 1995; Gorman 1998).

Consider three examples of drug education presented as information but clearly demonstrating bias. First, Alan Marlow (1999: 2–3) in his assessment of youth and drugs policy slips into moral language rather than academic argument when he uses terms such as 'alarming' and 'pernicious'. Second, Philip Robson's (1994) otherwise useful study includes Patricia Broughton's discriminatory and stereotypical illustrations of young people presented in terms of drug excess, racial othering, immorality, laziness, corruption and sexism.[13] Third, in David Emmett and Graeme Nice's book *Understanding Drugs: A Handbook for Parents, Teachers and Other professionals* (1998), we see drug misinformation delivered by professional drug prevention experts. It is an example of a well-meaning drug education text which lacks historical and cultural detail and supplies misinformation as fact. Let me briefly cite two errors in Chapter 2. First, they comment that 'western Europe has very little history of drug use' (p. 7). This is followed by the assertion that 'The use of such drugs[14] by ordinary people and in particular by young people was to remain almost unknown until after World War II' (pp. 7–8). The text is a contemporary example of prescriptive knowledge which Richard Ives (1997: 18) called a 'military manual for misguided war-mongers'. These examples of drug misrepresentation promote an understanding of drug consumers as people who are isolated from history, culture and social structures. They demonstrate that drug information is not neutral in its efforts to achieve behaviour change.

To achieve behaviour change is not merely difficult, it is an ethical question, related to what type of information a person can access and how their level of consciousness responds in the context of understanding such knowledge. The aim of altering behaviour can have a paternalistic tone but may also be adversarial, especially in relation to drug information and knowledge which is claimed to be accurate and truthful; for example, the *Talk to Frank* campaign 2003. Given that a central aim of the new drug education is to change behaviour, this means that programmes of drug education are measured only in terms of their effectiveness to achieve a reduction in drug consumption. Without a reduction in drug prevalence, it is thus assumed that drug education has failed to reach its performance targets. It is clear that drug prevention outcomes have monopolized the aims of drug education. Narrowly conceived measurements of effective drug education become a victim to young people's choice or freedom. This model of drug use effectively blames young people for their choice to consume drugs and for failing to listen to the rationality of the anti-drug message defined as right. Thus not only are young people seen as irresponsible, but also the teachers who provide drug education are further branded as failures for their consequent lack of success in curbing substance consumption by their pupils.

The establishment of rigorous performance targets for the reduction of drug prevalence may sound politically attractive but substantive evidence suggests that such narrow objectives cannot be achieved. This means that drug education is vulnerable to attack for its lack of effectiveness. Therefore inflated, unrealistic and over-burdensome expectations force drug education into failure; drug education requires more diverse forms of measurement and cultural recognition of drug differentiation. The fate of drug education is that it is given the measurement targets for drug prevention. This results in drug education being understood not as a process but as an outcome: successful drug education is thus measured by predefined performance targets of behavioural change.[15]

Outcome-based drug education is driven by a rational scientific model of management and measured by performance targets where the ruling ideas of drug education are defined on the basis of an agreed framework of quality standards. For Kathy Evans (2001: 2) drug education has been reduced to an initiative within the paradigm of prevention, her argument being that education seems to have lost autonomy. She declares that drug education should be part of a young person's 'right to education, part of the comprehensive process of enabling them to learn about the world around them and to analyze, understand and act within that world'. In the behaviouristic outcome model of drug education there is conflation between learning and skill.

Skill has been misappropriated within drugs education in an attempt to dissuade young people from drug consumption. Skill is understood as an individual task of refusal to accept drugs. Young people are seen as possessing skills only in terms of pre-established performance criteria and targets which can be measured by showing a negative attitude to drugs. This managerial approach to teaching drug education is predetermined; it is not the wealthy inheritance of current psychology but a replay of behaviourism where learning is laid down as an objective (O'Connor et al. 1998).

Drug education: models, media and 'monsters'

Jeffrey Wragg (1992) argues that the objective of models in drug education is to change drug use behaviour, through what is described as 'social engineering'. Whether the approach is medical, psychological or social, the purpose of drug education models is to provide a conceptual framework or underpinning for a programme of intervention. Thus a central feature of the drug education model is its philosophical and theoretical basis. A model is an abstraction which is used to explain the existence of social activity such as drug use, and the attraction of a model rests in its application to yield an answer. In British drug education we have seen the development of countless models and innumerable theories describing the motivation for drug use. In America the theoretical models developed to explain drug consumption are complex and multidimensional, specifying hypothesized relationships between exogenous and endogenous factors (Brown and Kreft 1998). Here these advanced conceptualizations focusing on the predictability of causes and consequences seem at some distance from drug users' understandings. As a result, the discussion of antecedents and outcome variables is resonant with the precise specifications of science and justification.

The legitimacy of the medical approach for treating problematic drug use has influenced the formulation of social drug education models in terms of demonstrating that drug interventions should be based on objective principles, frameworks, methods, criteria, outcomes, clarity, targets, strategy and evaluation. The key principles underpinning drug education point to its authority and legitimacy, confirmed by the forms of scientific management and targetted outcomes specified by its own rationality (Dorn and Murji 1992: 4). In the drugs literature, drug education models have a tendency to be discussed in abstract form, which is self-generating and growing in importance. For example, Suzanne MacGregor (1998: 193) states that 'models' are increasingly influential and 'cited as desirable to adopt'. She continues: 'There are calls for an "over-arching" strategy capable of matching multiple problems with multiple solutions.' What we see here is the ever-increasing desire for complex models which abstract the individual from their personal, social and cultural context. A further feature of the expansion of multi-complex modelling is the opportunity to suggest totality. Models of drug education have turned into a search for the Holy Grail, to create a comprehensive programme which incorporates all the necessary diversity and flexibility. John O'Connor and Bill Saunders (1992: 175) argue that the problem with theoretical models relates to 'an assumption of humans as overly rational beings who can be influenced, by brief exposure to drug education programs, to act in an objectively healthy manner irrespective of the circumstances'.

The failure to find an explanatory model seems to have resulted in the further intensification and successive development of new drug models which appear to be preoccupied with their own sophisticated rationality and reflexivity. The apparent desire for the creation of a total drug education model captures the imagination of drug prohibitionists; it indicates a desire for compulsion and homogeneity, showing little recognition or understanding of cultural differences. During the 1960s and 1970s it remained fashionable for scientists to conduct drug experiments on different types of animals in an attempt to unravel the potential negative effects of drugs for humans (Midford 2000). Biological and psychological approaches were often fused, such as in the work of Peter Witt et al. (1968) and Witt (1982),[16] providing drug prohibitionists with evidence of the chaotic impact of drugs in society. One of Witt's more bizarre research studies was to give spiders LSD (Jensen 2002).[17] It was found that high doses of LSD completely disrupted web building, but spiders would also construct complex three-dimensional webs. The interpretation offered is that without drugs spiders construct normal functional webs that sustain life; with drugs spiders constructed irregular and ineffective webs likely not to sustain life. The conclusion is that drug use will result in death. The example of 'stoned spiders' research demonstrates the positivist end of drug prohibition, which uses 'science' to achieve its behavioural objective of establishing a drug-free society. The implication is that so long as drug prevention identifies itself as a form of science, which seeks to build rational models to change behaviour, the purpose of drug education will be to feed the appetite of the monster created by drug prohibition.

During the twenty-first century young people pictured in the British National Drug Helpline poster 'Know the Score' are presented as half human and half monster. The depiction of young people at play combined with textbook-style dissection revealing the internal workings of the body falls within the fear arousal strategy but at the same time it is kitsch. The biological image of young people's bodily organs on display conforms to the dominant representations in contemporary Hollywood horror movies and populist TV such as *Buffy the Vampire Slayer*. In the context of youth culture commodified 'evil' has become an aspect of 'coolness', as for example with 'nu-metal' icons Slipknot, Marilyn Manson and Cradle of Filth.[18] The document 'Protecting

Young People' (H M Government 1998: 23) states that 'teenage icons have typically brushed with the riskier and seamier side of life'. What is meant by this general, vague and accusatory comment is not made clear. Drug education materials which use youth culture and drug culture reference points to deliver anti-drug messages attempt to break with traditional abstinence representations. Although the National Drugs Helpline is trying to capture the attention of young people in their leisure time, Damon Taylor (2000: 347) argues that these posters do the opposite by appearing 'to come straight from the schoolroom', thus repositioning young people in didactic education (Bishop et al. 2001).

The use of popular imagery associated with youth within the framework of drug education may encounter and produce contradictory learning outcomes. Modern media anti-drug campaigns have a long history in the film, advertising and television industries, where the dominant message has been abstinence supported by negative and stereotypical imagery of drugs and drug users as unhealthy, immoral and untrustworthy. In the United States and Britain evidence has emerged that media anti-drug campaigns have not only failed but may also have contributed to an increase in drug use (Shoemaker 1989; Davies and Coggans 1994). Media campaigns have been criticized as biased and dishonest in their preoccupation with 'blaming the victim', leaving individuals without support or guidance (Kiger 1995). National mass media campaigns, Martin Plant (1994: 61–2) argues, are a 'politically attractive' device to demonstrate that action is being taken, but in reality are merely 'exercises in propaganda or exhortation'. Thus we can identify two contrasting forms of manipulation of drugs, one for the purpose of increased punitive regulation and the other based on entrepreneurial opportunity to exploit youth through commodity consumption. Drug control policies assert their neutrality, drug education models assert their rationality and the commercialization of drug youth culture has enabled drugs to become a fetishistic commodity for profit.

The 'gateway' metaphor of drug consumption

For drug education the concept of the gateway is attractive because it works on common sense rather than intellect. From the 1930s Harry Anslinger proclaimed marijuana was a 'killer narcotic' leading to insanity and death. Rufus King (1972: 81) pointed out that soon Anslinger realized his vision of cannabis as the murderous weed was inadequate. Therefore Anslinger changed his discredited cannabis addiction theory from causality of death to a stepping stone or gateway to more dangerous drugs. The gateway is one of drug prohibition's most powerful metaphors. The sheer visualization of vast openness and free access to drugs illustrated by a gateway is all that is required.

Central to the life skills approach is reliance on the theory of gateway drugs. The notion of the gateway upholds that early use of legal drugs such as alcohol or tobacco and illegal substances such as cannabis are predictive of more serious drug consumption later in life. The assumption is that these 'less serious' drugs are the gateway to 'more dangerous' drug consumption. The gateway theory contains a strong commonsense rationality to it, and this makes the notion of the gateway appealing to explain drug use. The theory is used in drug education to argue that experimentation is more dangerous because it leads to problematic use: thus experimentation predisposes a young person to use other drugs. Gateway theory is correct in that cannabis use typically precedes introduction to other drugs, but evidence suggests that cannabis is not the cause of initiation into hard drugs.[19] A more accurate predictor of the movement into hard drugs is psychiatric disorder and a family history of psychological problems or alcoholism (Mack and Joy 2001). One of the contradictions of the concept of the gateway method rests with its potential to foretell the future, which in reality is based on retrospective drug recall by adult substance users. Evidence suggests that drug users who try to remember their past forms of experimentation or induction either conform to the researchers' own predefined assumptions or selectively remember what highlights their own self-image and identity (Bukstein 1995; Davis and Dawson 1996).

The explanatory power of the gateway theory has two major weaknesses. First, it identifies the origins of the individual drug user's problems as their involvement in criminal or deviant forms of behaviour. A significant problem with this idea is that deviance is defined only in relation to drug consumption; therefore non-deviant drug users are simply categorized with other deviants because their drug use is defined as criminal although they do not take part in any other form of deviance. Second, linking the gateway theory to life skills suggests that it can equip young people throughout the life cycle with strategies of personal confidence. This assumes either that young people lack the necessary skills to refuse a drug offer or that they deliberately choose to ignore the warnings and are therefore acting in a deviant manner. In the former case young people are defined as lacking knowledge, reason and information while in the latter they are defined as weak willed and pliable to negative influences from their peer group, who are then seen as knowingly deviant. Therefore, the motivation for drug use is defined according to psychological factors revealing the individual's pathology or abnormality.

The contradiction of the gateway theory is that young people are defined as deficient through possessing low self-esteem but are also defined as highly motivated and confident to consume drugs. The combined use of gateway theory and the life skills approach enables drug consumption to be understood as a deviant practice and causally linked to behaviour problems such as crime and delinquency. This is challenged by Coggans et al. (1999: 35), who claim:

'The majority of those who experiment with drugs or use recreationally will not develop a 'drug problem'. The explanation for most people's drug use will have less to do with personal inadequacies than with perceived positive goal attainments, such as valuing the drug experience for relaxation, stimulation, socializing, or other qualities.

The rationality of the life skills model is based on the assumption that young people lack personal and social competence and the drug education programme aims to compensate for this apparent absence by providing positive education. It is assumed that the correction to low self-esteem and improved decision making will allow the individual to learn skills and then choose not to use drugs. The explanation put forward argues that if a young person decides to use drugs they are inadequate at a social and psychological level. The theory specifies that the choice to consume drugs is not only wrong, irrational and immoral but demonstrates that the person is a failure in life (Coggans et al. 2002).

The gateway concept has informed the Social Exclusion Unit and the Connexions Service in their generation of typologies to account for drug use, which are in effect a new set of social pathologies. The government specifies that young people's drug problems are related to 'poor parenting', being 'in care', having a 'low income', living in 'poor housing', having 'low achievement' in school and living in a 'disadvantaged neighbourhood'. These risk factors are detailed in columns with the certainty of a precise science and in models, but flounder in confusion over the difference between a characteristic and a cause. Whilst evidence may demonstrate that some of these factors could contribute to young working-class people's consumption of drugs, the theories, models and typologies ignore the Home Office findings (Leitner et al. 1993) that show that higher income earners from the upper and middle classes are the biggest users of illicit drugs in Britain. The Social Exclusion Unit does not specify whether the young aristocracy who are using most drugs also have been in care, or were brought up in a deprived environment.

Peer education and peer preference

A positive aspect of the peer involvement approach in drug education is that it seems to be a popular style of intervention preferred by young people (Blackman 1996a; Shiner and Newburn 1997; Chapman 1998). The focus on peer education has been given priority by the government. Steve Parkin and Neil McKeganey (2000: 293) say that 'the concept of peer education has been endorsed by a variety of government bodies and expert reviews[20] of drug services and drug problems'. The rationale for peer education programmes is that young people will not listen to adults' views on drug prevention.

Therefore it is assumed that they will be more responsive towards people of a similar age to themselves. The proposition is that the shared attitudes and values held by young people act as a foundation of credibility which can then be used as a basis from which to transmit drug education messages. There is an expectation that peer educators will serve as role models on a local basis because they are already experts on their own community. Evidence suggests that there has been considerable success in the application of peer education in gay culture specifically related to the problem of HIV and AIDS (Shepherd et al. 1997). The assumption of peer education is that young people fall under the influence of peer pressure to use drugs; therefore they need to be taught skills in how to resist and say 'no' to drug use.

The rise of peer education corresponds with the new priority of research politics to give young people an active voice through offering forms of empowerment. Many of the ideas explored in contemporary peer education derive from recent youth work practice and attempt to establish young people's participation in youth councils (McCulloch 2000). In England an early development in peer education was the nineteenth-century pedagogic practice of pupils assisting teachers with lessons. This style of teaching was known as Monitorialism and was associated with Andrew Bell, an Anglican clergyman, and Joseph Lancaster, a Quaker schoolteacher. This early form of peer education was strictly designed to teach only limited knowledge where the information transmitted was mechanical and given; there was no space for individual understanding. This legacy has implications for teaching drug education. A key feature of this initial peer education, described by Richard Johnson (1976: 48) as 'the most coercive and negative moment in the whole history of schooling', was its cheapness. Parkin and McKeganey (2000: 301) note that peer education has an appeal due to its reliance on 'unpaid volunteers' making it 'relatively inexpensive'. They also raise the issue of how genuine is young people's empowerment and question to what extent are young people following a prescribed adult agenda. Niall Coggans and Jonathan Watson (1995: 217) demonstrate that the selection of peer educators can reflect the wishes of authority figures rather than of young people themselves. What the young peer educators are doing is affirming the power of the drug prevention programme rather than speaking with an autonomous voice. Evidence suggests that young people are being brought in as part of a teaching strategy to speak subjective local knowledge, but in their new role as peer educators they feel uncomfortable when they lack the specialist knowledge and training (Klee and Reid 1995; France 2000). This makes them vulnerable for exploitation, not merely as 'conduits for the adult's point of view' but as individuals who are used as a research instrument inside youth groups for the purpose of undertaking surveillance (Chapman 1998; Geddes and Rust 2000). Bangert-Drowns (1998) found peer-led education to be particularly ineffective, especially where the young people leading the project are slightly older than the target group. Lloyd et al. (2000: 121) concludes that peer education is 'largely ill defined and unproven'.

Implicit within the notion of peer education is the counternotion of peer pressure, which is a 'catch-all' phrase negatively defining young people as vulnerable to coercive persuasion. The political attraction of the concept of peer pressure is that you can blame young people themselves for their problem while assigning a battery of psychological theories as evidence of disturbed behaviour. Coggans and McKeller (1994: 19) demonstrate that peer pressure is a popular theoretical device used to drive deficit theory, which seeks to argue that peers take up drug use because they possess weak personalities. They state: 'There seems to be an all too widespread unwillingness to accept that people could be motivated to use drugs for reasons other than pathological.' Their contention is that the peer pressure argument is based not on proven evidence but 'speculative interpretations'. For them susceptibility to peer influence shows a general pattern of peer preference within friendship networks, not peer pressure. To employ the theory of peer pressure releases young people from their own destiny because they are defined as beyond control, even 'out of control', thus establishing the legitimacy of therapeutic interventions.

The growth in popularity of peer education schemes has occurred at a time when the concept of peer pressure has been critically exposed. Although the concept is derived from academic disciplines it is commonly fed back to young people who then use it to explain and interpret their own behaviour and deliver the responses that adult intellectuals require, reducing complex social relationship to simple causality. Charlie Lloyd's assessment (1998: 223) is that peer pressure theory has been incredibly 'naive'. Peer drug education programmes are also linked to sponsorship from private companies, such as BT, Granada and Prudential. Joan Bailey and Andrew Elvin (1999: 145) report on a drug peer education project set up under the Prudential Youth Action Scheme in Luton. This is part of the Labour government's drug strategy to encourage partnerships. However, Bailey and Elvin fail to reveal that the Prudential Group is a major shareholder in the SFI Group.[21] Nick Horley (1999: 32) states that SFI is the owner of 'Britain's biggest chain of lap-dancing clubs at which no stigma is attached to paying a woman £10 to give you a close look at her genitals'. The links between lap dancing, pornography and prostitution are described by Horley as 'tenuous'. Private industry's business sponsorship of drug education appears to see no double standard between, on the one hand, moral arguments to uphold drug prohibition to stop young people from harming themselves and, on the other, maximizing profits for shareholders through the massive expansion of SFI's 'For Your Eyes Only' sex shows,[22] where young women perform naked for the voyeuristic pleasure of wealthy businessmen.

Drug education as primary prevention: PSHE, citizenship and Connexions

Drug education has always been located within a moral framework but now schools and the youth support service Connexions, which operates systems of 'mapping' and 'tracking' people, have been attracted into taking on a leadership role as agents of primary prevention. The government documents *Protecting Young People* (1998) and *The Right Approach* (1999) specify the performance indicators introduced to monitor achievements and set universal targets for agencies involved in drug education against the following objectives:

- reduce the proportion of young people under 25 reporting use of illegal drugs in the last month and previous year (key objective)
- increase levels of knowledge of 5- to 16-year-olds about risks and consequences of drug misuse
- delay age of first use of illegal drugs
- reduce exclusions from schools arising from drug-related incidents
- reduce the number of people under 25 using heroin
- increase access to information and services for vulnerable groups – including school excludees, truants, looked after children, young offenders, young homeless and children of drug-misusing parents.

The new format of PSHE, citizenship and health for young people is promoted as local and interactive. The integration of the NHSS within schools, drug action teams and the Connexions service provides a more holistic and broader partnership to deliver drug education. The establishment of performance targets for drug education in schools and for the Connexions service to change behaviour demonstrates that the government demands successful outcomes from educational interventions. Drug education is expected to achieve results, it is not merely concerned with conveying information. It has moved into the realm of teaching primary prevention. Government pressure on education is not new but drug education may find itself a victim of rising expectations with unforeseen consequences. The current government policy promotes high expectations with its rigorous support for managerial quality standards and performance targets within an outcomes framework based on assessment of teacher effectiveness to deliver drug education. Yet this rationality may find itself a hostage to pupils who want to make an informed choice, i.e. to consume drugs.

Previously, the problem of locating drug education in PSHE was that the subject suffered from low status because it was free of examination and pupils failed to take the subject seriously. This freedom was formerly regarded as essential for PSHE's aim of delivering social education in a relaxed environment. Evaluations of drug education revealed that students claimed that learning was 'done to them' rather than with them taking an active part (Ofsted 1997; O'Connor et al. 1998; Wibberley and Price 2000). Here teachers and pupils experienced the linear sequence of a successive list of nos as not productive to the learning process.[23] One response to this perceived problem has been to make PSHE into a foundation subject and offer examination in the new subject of citizenship. The danger here is that social subjects such as PSHE and citizenship take on forms of prescriptive knowledge and outcomes to correspond with statutory subjects. The new framework may appear equally divisive in that pupils may see it as determinist and only concerned with model behaviour. Drug education is regarded by government as good for citizenship, demonstrating great faith in the power of education as a force for drug prevention. By making citizenship a foundation subject in the National Curriculum it takes on a compulsory identity, where rules and prescription are the daily diet for young people. Teaching citizenship through instilling values presupposes an agreed set of beliefs. When applied to drug education with its absolutist notions of prevention, citizenship seems more like an induction into what Andrew Marks (2001: 155) calls 'a grand behaviourist enclosure'. Students quickly realize that teachers want them not just to learn something but to accept something and change their behaviour. When young people leave school PSHE stops, but Sarah Ansell (2001) specifies that the Connexions service aspires to deliver PSHE within a youth work context. She raises serious doubts about the effectiveness of post-16 PSHE, especially where young people may hold negative views of figures in authority and see through pedagogic attempts to change their lifestyle, values and culture. Thus drug education in PSHE and citizenship may be understood by students as a mechanism that the school imposes upon them in an attempt to regulate their values, behaviour and ideas.

The Healthy Schools initiative of the NHSS can be seen as following the health promotion model through its populist approach of roadshows, special events and use of young people's language, for example, employing the phase 'wired for health' as a website address. An issue for drug education within PSHE and citizenship is that its association with health promotion approaches could place drug education within a potentially narrow framework. At the centre of health promotion is the ideal of a healthy society. While this aspiration can appear to be neutral, Alice Kiger (1995: 32) demonstrates that it is all too easy to assume that health values are generally held and acknowledged as the right values. Chris Wibberley and Sally Whitelaw (1990: 13) argue that health education drug interventions work on an individualistic basis 'centring on the need for behavioural conformity to prescribed social norms'. The guidance on health education in the National Curriculum reflects the view that health is an individual responsibility.

This moral ascendancy over the pupil is perpetuated in health education through statutory universal prescribed targets. The new provision of drug education is proposed as more participative and interactive, following a less prescriptive approach, but its target is abstinence. The dilemma for health education, PSHE and citizenship is that drug education delivered as primary prevention may fail to engage with young people (Denman et al. 2002).

Conclusion

Both the use of drugs and drug prevention are areas replete with complexity and contradiction, merging concerns about health with moral prescriptions; real risks with political agendas; social problems with stimulating and plea-surable experiences; notions of non-conformity with commercial interests. Young people hold a range of understandings about drug use as *either* harmful *or* pleasurable; and interpret anti-drug messages as *either* social control *or* legitimate concern for their well-being. Without clear recognition of such differences drug education slips into a dangerous simplification of issues. Drug education based on performance targets for the reduction of drug pre-valence will fail to have an impact on young people while it retains ab-stinence as its key message. Different positions on the status of drugs in society can be gained from the police, the government, the media, politicians, commercial retailers and the medical profession. This inconsistency allows young people to exploit perceived differences, enabling them to counter of-ficial drug education messages.

7 British drug reform
Towards responsive prohibition?

During the 1970s the United States began to reform its drug policy. Legalization and decriminalization of cannabis brought a new era to what Paul Rock (1977: 20) called 'the aegis of an ostensibly static set of official definitions'. But by the end of the 1980s the Republican President Ronald Reagan had reversed these policies. In the twenty-first century Britain is undertaking reform to its drug policy. This chapter will start by examining the opposition of drug policy reforms presented by the media through their high-profile coverage of the drug deaths of young women. I go on to look at the popular development of drug tourism connected with national and international clubbing. This is followed by an assessment of changes to drugs law introduced by the British government which include the commercial development of medical cannabis, the growth of cannabis self-medication, the reclassification of cannabis from class B to class C and the development of the cannabis coffeeshop. This chapter demonstrates that drug policies may encounter decriminalization and recriminalization according to wider political struggles and moral agendas.

The political right, drug zero tolerance and the free market

The front page of the *Mail on Sunday*, a British newspaper, on 8 October 2000 read 'We took drugs, say seven top Tories'. The Conservative politicians formed part of the Shadow Cabinet.[1] They were responding to Shadow Home Secretary Ann Widdecombe's declaration at the Conservative Party conference in which she announced a 'zero-tolerance' anti-drug policy. The right-wing British tabloids were reluctant to reproach these politicians, to criticize them as bad role models for young people, which is the case when popular music or film stars publicly admit to drug consumption. The *Mail on Sunday*[2] stated: 'All seven belong to that wing which demands economic freedom for business, but also believes that individuals should be given a corresponding freedom in their private lives.' The libertarian right, for example, Milton Freedman, argue that personal conduct such as drug taking is a matter of individual choice. Here we see the Conservative press and Conservative politicians clearly following a political agenda according to a neo-liberal economic and philosophical theory about freedom.

The political right have found it acceptable to promote individual rights for male Conservative politicians to take drugs, but when others consume drugs, in particular young women, the British tabloids have a more traditional focus and stress a degradation of morals in society. For Sheila Henderson (1997: 35) the drug melodrama of prohibition is about social and moral control 'to nurture this fear in the adult population as a whole'. For example, one of the most evocative drug headlines during the 1990s was addressed not to young people but to adults and parents. The *Daily Express* on 14 November 1995 warned: 'Drugs: the rotten core at the heart of Middle England'. Looking at the coverage of dead young women and drugs through the decade Karim Murji (1999: 71) argues that 'elements of the media treated the death of Leah Betts and the other cases as symptoms of a general social malaise'. The following section looks at the way in which the British tabloid press have presented a public gallery of dead young women to promote a political and prohibitionist agenda.

Public gallery of dead young women

Marek Kohn (1992) shows that the beginning of the media's interest in rousing public anxiety through the combination of drugs and young women starts during the period 1900 to 1925. He examines the cases of four young women whose tragic deaths were related to their drug use: Edith and Ida Yeoland, Billie Carleton and Freda Kempton, who were actresses, models and dancers. From the 'cocaine girls' of the 1920s to the 'ecstasy girls' of the twenty-first century, the drug prohibition movement has consistently used two contradictory images of women: one as the holy custodians of traditional family values; the other as evil 'seductresses' of society (Kohn 1997).

Recently, British tabloid newspapers such as the *Daily Mail, Daily Express, Sun, Mirror* and *Daily Star* have delivered front-page headlines about drug deaths accompanied by a series of photographs of young women who have died.[3] The visual representation of the young female drug victim follows a pattern which shows them as typically feminine and attractive. These photographs are then contrasted with pictures of the dead, revealing their swollen, bruised or bloodied bodies. For example, the cases of Leah Betts in 1995, Julia Dawes in 1998, Lorna Spinks in 2001 and Rachel Whitear in 2002 were heavily covered in the newspapers. The parents of Leah Betts and Rachel Whitear have taken a leading role in the presentation of their daughters' deaths through the production of anti-drug videos.[4] All the young women came from middle-class backgrounds and were preparing for or had undertaken college courses.[5] They were ordinary, pleasant, young white people, they were not criminals or delinquents but came from respectable families.

All the parents have released photographs of their daughters for newspapers to print and more recent articles refer to Leah Betts's death, either with a quotation from her parents, or a picture of Leah dying. On 29 March 2000 a photograph of Leah Betts made the front page of the *Daily Mail* in connection with a story concerning the downgrading of cannabis to a class C drug. The front-page lead story focused on Janet Betts's opposition to any relaxation of the current drug laws. The *Daily Mirror* of 1 March 2002 combined on the same page photographs of Lorna Spinks and Leah Betts on their hospital deathbeds and Rachel Whitear dead on the floor with a needle still gripped in her hand.

The media representations of Leah Betts, Julia Dawes, Lorna Spinks and Rachel Whitear are meant to be disturbing; we see them as beautiful, sometimes sexy, when they are pictured wearing skimpy dresses for 'going out' or as innocent children framed in their school uniforms. Both the 'sexy' and the 'innocent' representation are meant to evoke feelings of loss that these were young women 'cut down'. The charm and beauty in these girls' faces calls out to us to condemn drugs as the suggested cause of their death. The 'sexy' and 'innocent' pictures of these young women used by newspapers are contrasted with the bleak photographs showing a hospital bed with ventilator tubes inserted into a body, or a collapsed, distorted, black and purple body. These photographic representations are structured to heighten the contrast between the normality of an attractive young woman and the disfigured unrecognizable 'monster'.[6] The tabloids also deliberately disturb the 'sexy' and 'innocent' image: for example, the *Daily Star*'s front-page headline on 18 August 1998, 'Super E pill girl fights for life', tells the story of a 17-year-old 'teenage girl' who suffered from a collapsed lung and was rushed into hospital. Alongside this headline is a large semi-naked photograph of the British pin-up model Jordan (Katie Price) with the comment 'Take a last look lads', referring to the topless model's forthcoming operation to enlarge her breasts. The newspaper wilfully brings the two headlines 'fight for life' and 'last look' together by allowing Jordan's left leg, dressed in a black stocking, to penetrate with her knee the enlarged picture of an ecstasy tablet.

Alongside the different pictures of the young women are photographs of grieving and weeping parents who tell of their personal sadness. It is apparent that you feel great sympathy with the parents and the friends who lost their 'special person',[7] but Natasha Walter (1996) argues that the portrayal of dead young women within the tabloid newspapers is used to suit the purpose of the new agenda of anti-drug prohibition. The key issue is that 'dead girls' are not able to speak back. They chose to take the drug with friends, they were in pursuit of an intoxicated pleasure and demanded to enjoy life. Through being denied the power of speech and having others speak for them, this is not merely an act of discrimination but is also a factual misrepresentation. The French theorist Hélène Cixous in her work on women and voice argues that speaking 'is a powerfully transgressive action for women' (Shiach 1991: 22). Leah Betts, Julia Dawes, Lorna Spinks and Rachel Whitear have lost their right to speak not just by the reason of their death but because as young women they broke the taboo of taking illegal drugs.

Even where there has been a high-profile recovery from near drug death, as in the case of Helen Cousins who in 1996 was in a coma for a week, the subject, although alive, is not permitted a voice and remains silent. Helen Cousins's mother Janet read a statement from Helen which included: 'You realize that ecstasy isn't worth the dance with death.'[8] Sheila Henderson (1997: 32) states: 'Here was a young woman lucky enough to return from the jaws of death, a young victim who lived to tell the tale like the adult world wanted to hear it.' Unable to voice their opinions and preference, others now speak for them. Their silence is further reinforced by defining the young woman as a child, their autonomy gets denied; parents and newspaper collude in returning the young women back to girlhood. The *Daily Mail*'s front page on 14 November 1995, relating to Leah Betts's death, warned 'It could be your child' and the Daily Mirror of 1 March 2002, referring to Rachel Whitear's death, said: 'Heartbreak dad: Don't let this happen to your child'. In the cases of Leah Betts, Julia Dawes and Lorna Spinks their innocence is confirmed by the newspaper headline 'one single ecstasy tablet'. The press do not focus upon the young women's previous use of drugs, they are presented as innocent or 'foolish' about drugs. To offer contextual information such as that the young women positively choose to consume drugs or that they had previous experience of drug taking would counteract the construction of the young woman as naive drug victim.[9]

Leah Betts's media drug death: new-style personalized shock tactics

Before Leah Betts died in 1995 there had been ecstasy-related deaths of young women, for example, Claire Leighton in 1989, Paula Carrier in 1992, Corrinna Williams in 1993 and Julia Young earlier in 1995. Leah Betts's death could be described as a media death: it was not a private family event, her funeral was filmed for the video and according to Matthew Collin (1997: 295) 'her parents were determined to use her death as an anti-drug parable'. The cooperation between the Betts family and the media expanded into a major anti-drug campaign, through television interviews and a nationwide billboard campaign with the poster 'Sorted', created by advertising company Knight Leach Delaney. A black border frames Leah, smiling, with her shoulder-length hair swept back over her chubby cheeks, the large letters spell 'Sorted' and under the drug slogan is the omen: 'Just one ecstasy tablet took Leah Betts'. These posters were on every inner-city hoarding across the country. In opposition, the agit-pop anarchists Chumbawamba (1996) produced an anti-poster 'Distorted: you are just as likely to die from eating a bay leaf as from an ecstasy tablet'.

The poster was also distributed via their website. They argued that the Leah Betts 'Sorted' poster was produced by a private corporation which was 'selling capitalism showing a young corpse'. During the 1990s Leah Betts's parents became connected with the Conservative government's drug policy: Sheryl Garratt (1998: 316) states that they supported a private member's bill introduced by Barry Legg 'to allow dance clubs to be shut down immediately if there is proof of a serious drug problem on the premises'. Paul and Janet Betts were later photographed with Prime Minister John Major promoting anti-drug messages to a media audience.

The anti-drug crusade intensified with the video *Sorted: Leah Betts: just an ordinary kid*, commercially sponsored by Granada and BT. *Sorted* runs for 16 minutes and contains interviews with her parents, siblings and best friends with whom she took ecstasy. Few parents choose to become involved in public campaigns as a result of losing their daughter or son. Hope Humphreys (2001) questions 'why would any parent allow such a terrible picture of their child to be seen by everyone?'.[10] The usual reason put forward is to persuade other young people to learn from the disturbing image of death as a warning. In some cases parents may feel some necessity to try and punish their son or daughter's friends. Some parents have demanded that friends of the drug victim walk past the dying body in hospital;[11] others demand the death penalty for drug dealers.[12]

Consistent coverage on tabloid front pages of the tragic death of young women and the production of anti-drug videos reveal that there remains substantial mileage in the shock tactics approach. Paul Betts states:[13] 'Our release of the picture of Leah and the video we made afterwards has been hailed by young people as the best drugs awareness information package they have seen. I've been to over 3 200 schools, spoken to 2.3 million young people and 500 000 parents' (Hall 2002). Regarding the new anti-drugs video *Rachel's Story*, Pauline Holcroft, the mother of Rachel Whitear, makes a similar point when she says: 'The feedback we have got from parents is excellent. Practically 100% of children said it would make them think they couldn't do this to their families.'

The shock tactics approach has a long history in drug prevention, where the picture of an unknown young person who died from drugs was a common educational resource but often meant little to young people who did not know them. In contrast, contemporary shock tactics are based upon the media production of a public gallery of dead young women who are subsequently known to everyone. The grieving parents are the primary sources for the modern shock tactics approach based on the photographic opportunities they have provided for the media. For anti-drug campaigners shock tactics keep the spirit of their lost son or daughter alive, making it a personal and professional crusade. Janet Betts[14] states: 'If we can make a difference to just one person's life then we will feel she did not die in vain.'[15] While Paul Betts[16] says:

'What we must never forget is that if you just save one person's life, it's been worthwhile' (Hall 2002). Their belief in the shock tactics approach derives from their personal experience of drug death. Thus the living memory of their son or daughter is their motivating force. They do not 'feel better' by speaking to other parents or young people about the dangers of drug consumption because their loss remains permanent. For them the objective of the shock tactics approach lies with a minority of one; in other words if one person refuses to take drugs then shock tactics are a success. The strategy is driven by its apparent commonsense value, impossible to verify systematically; its appeal rests with heartfelt emotions.

Contemporary shock tactics are no longer impersonal, because through the media dissemination of the public gallery of dead young women, they are known to everyone: shock tactics become a personal strategy within drug prevention. The new style of shock tactics takes on sacred overtones; drug prevention becomes a religious experience with its fragile message from life to death. Criticism of the approach can appear profane because then not only are you attacking the anti-drug campaigners themselves, but you are also criticizing the constructed memory of the loved one who is unable to reply. Thus contemporary shock tactics within drug prevention have evolved into a new personalized form of prohibition. The new focus of personalized shock tactics has been on dead young women's involvement in club culture. The next section looks at the link between national and international clubbing and drug tourism.

Drug tourism and global clubbing

Drug tourism is not a new cultural activity – it can be traced back to the Renaissance. Drug tourism refers to a location which becomes popular with people because of the accessibility of drugs. Marco Polo's writings of the Assassins' drug pleasures in paradise captured the European imagination, and the fantasy of forbidden excess and desire was continued by David Urquhart, Fitz Hugh Ludlow, Gustave Flaubert and Gérard de Nerval. More recently, the Beatles went east and the intellectual Beat writers, William Burroughs and Jack Kerouac, pursued the allure of drugs, travel and the imagination. In the twenty-first century drug tourism as a commodified experience has entered a new phase of consumption as travellers move beyond Amsterdam's coffee houses to South America or Vietnam's opium dens as described in recent alternative travel guidebooks, such as Lonely Planet and Rough Guide, and novels and biographical accounts, such as Max Pam's *Going East* (1992), William Sutcliffe's *Are You Experienced* (1997), Mark Mann's *The Gringo Trail* (1999) and C. J. Stone's *Last of the Hippies* (1999). The hippie trail has now become a mass leisure travel belief where adventure is commodified and packaged by corporate holidays companies.

National and international clubbing can be seen as an extension of festival culture and bohemian hedonism (Polsky 1961: 168). Simon Reynolds (1998: xviii) places drugs at the centre of contemporary dance music, stating that 'rave culture as a whole is barely conceivable without drugs, or at least without drug metaphors'. National clubbing became so successful that the train company Great North Eastern Railway launched a specially priced ticket for clubbers to travel from London to Leeds.[17] The explosion of travel and clubbing is documented in the youth cultural dance magazines *Mixmag* and *Ministry*, which provide details of clubs across Britain, resulting in clubbers becoming a type of leisure commuter in pursuit of the most pleasurable experience. The rise of regional and international drug tourism and holidays is detailed in Harrison (1998), Turner (1999) and Pini (2001).

The twenty-first century has seen the emergence of an international clubbing scene as an organized and rationalized form of public entertainment. Aletha Sellars (1998: 614) describes how the main UK tour operators such as Club 18–30, Thomson, Escapades, First Choice and others have collaborated with the major dance music organizations to produce holiday brochures. Two examples of this are 'The Clubbers Guide to Travel', produced by the club Ministry of Sound in conjunction with Cosmos, and 'Escapades: hi-energy holidays' from MyTravel. Each travel guide is evidence of global dance entering into mainstream tourism, but carrying a hidden message of drug tourism. An examination of each brochure reveals that the written text and the visual representations affirm the connection of dance culture and drug tourism (Sellars 1998: 613). The language used reflects the argot of drug culture, which is implicitly part of dance culture, and visually the connection is reinforced through photographs of individuals or groups of people at a rave. Examples of the drug-inspired slang would include 'chilling', 'sorted', 'kickin'', 'bangin'', 'eye popping', 'you know the score', 'a hedonist's paradise'. In the travel brochures we see people in close-up with enlarged pupils, droopy half-closed eyes or visually expressing conditions of euphoria.

In literary theory Pierre Macherey (1995) develops the idea that texts are constructed so that certain things must not be spoken of. Although neither travel brochure makes an explicit reference to drug consumption, there is an evident silence about drug use which makes drugs more obvious. Through the 'unsaid' of drug consumption, we find the gap between what the brochure wants to say and what the brochure actually says. On this basis the holiday guides of Cosmos and MyTravel can be read as a narrative of evasions: it is not that the meaning is hidden or concealed, for the absence of drug consumption is addressed to an audience already in possession of the contextual meaning about ecstasy and dance culture. Applying Macherey's understanding we can see that the unspoken is thus suggested to those with insider knowledge who know what is the 'truth'. The combination of withholding information and using visual and textual metaphors of drug consumption feeds directly into the double meaning of language within dance and drug culture. The brochure hides nothing, it has no secret. Macherey (1978: 100) would describe the travel guide as 'a site of exchange': the reader is actively decoding and inserting their own experience where the gaps are presented. The link with drug tourism and club culture becomes more explicit with the holiday guide produced by the magazine *Mixmag*, which is called 'Tripping on Sunshine'. The Mixmag Club Holiday Guide is more direct in relation to drug use than the Cosmos or MyTravel brochures; it employs humorous cartoons and warnings, speaking of the 'dealer' who says 'Es straight from Amsterdam. Genuine MDMA' and the 'acid casualty'.

Global dance culture with its regular annual festivals has been quickly incorporated into the traditional holiday business. The defined social calendar makes clubbing familiar as the new drug tourist travels the neo-hippie trail where the aim is to experience the rave event rather than the local culture. Globalization has also brought massive sponsorship deals with corporate brands such as Pepsi, Sony, Silk Cut, Boddingtons and others, making dance culture a dominant force within mainstream culture and capital. At the superclub Cream 'the drug is almost seen as a part of the company's commercial image. "We accept that, not only has the culture of ecstasy become a mainstream leisure industry, but that the chemical itself has mainstreamed as well," says Jayne Casey, Cream's head of communications' (Scott 2000: 187). The new hippie trail as part of drug tourism becomes another form of branding, suggesting the values of the counterculture but affirming capital accumulation through marketing commodities sold back to affluent purchasers (Klein 2000: 21).

The Dutch coffeeshop: drug trafficking or drug tourism?

The Netherlands drug policy of decriminalization of small amounts of cannabis was the result of a revision of the Dutch Opium Act of 1976. The change in the law goes back to 1961, when the first consultations at ministerial level were held concerning cannabis.[18] The reform sought to make a separation between drug use seen as representing a low risk to individuals and communities and drug use which poses a significant risk to people's health. The drug policy of the Netherlands is not legalization of drugs; it is a strategic attempt to segregate two distinct types of drug markets and drug consumers. The coffeeshop idea represented a formal adjustment to an already existing cultural situation to enable people who like to use cannabis to do so in a risk-free environment (de Kort 1994; Williamson 1997: 123).

There are just over 60 coffeeshops in Amsterdam and approximately 800 across the country, specializing in selling cannabis, magic mushrooms, marijuana seed and different types of smoking equipment. Coffeeshops follow tough regulations to remain open: they are forbidden to sell alcohol or hard drugs, they may not sell drugs to under 18-year-olds and customers may purchase no more than five grams of hashish or cannabis weed. One of the high points in the year is the annual Cannabis Cup organized by the American magazine *High Times*, while the late 1990s saw the emergence of another Cannabis Cup, held by the Dutch magazine *High Life*, for the harvest festival awards, where over 75 varieties of hashish and cannabis will be tasted. The Cannabis Cup competitions are essentially cannabis trade fairs, held in late November, where coffeeshops, seed companies and individual growers compete for recognition. The competitions attract thousands of tourists, who participate in fun seminars and serious events focusing on drug trafficking, industrial hemp production and the regular concerns with cannabis cultivation (Matthews 1999).

The factual and fictional worlds of drug trafficking and tourism were brought together by Howard Marks (1997) in his autobiography *Mr Nice*, the story of an international drug dealer. Drug tourism is primarily understood by governments as creating social problems linked to criminality and encouraging drug consumption leading to drug trafficking (Valdez and Sifaneck 1997). Drug tourism in the Netherlands may account for as much as 25 per cent of the country's $5.3 billion tourist income (Morais 1996). The marijuana industry is a profitable sector of the economy in the Netherlands with an annual turnover of 580 million euros, while the UN Narcotics Control Board suggests that the total revenue is between $300 and $400 billion.[19] Through taxing the drug product it enables the Dutch government not only to regulate cannabis but to retain the drug money inside the country. Bob Keizer (2001) argues that the governments of Germany, France, Sweden and especially the United States, with General McCaffrey and other drug czars, have promoted ignorance at the political level about drug tourism. For him these misconceptions are ideological. Lynne Zimmer and John Morgan (1997) systematically refute the critics of the Dutch decriminalization policy and deal with each accusation in turn to demonstrate that the criticisms are a fabrication of intellectual lies promoted by professionals at the heart of the American drug prevention movement.

The context of British drug reform

Recently the British Labour government has introduced a series of changes to drug policy. These changes include:

- granting commercial trials for medical cannabis
- a pilot study of decriminalization of cannabis possession in Brixton, London

- reclassification of cannabis from class B to class C
- opening Dutch-style cannabis cafés called coffeeshops in Britain.

It is important to see British drugs reform within the wider processes of the European movement towards the normalization of drug policy, which maintains that the American abolitionists' policy is unrealistic and the military campaign of the 'war on drugs' has resulted in failure. The changes are linked not only to the government's evidence of increased drug use by young people, but also to the various pro-cannabis lobbies. There are innumerable internet sites praising and celebrating the value of cannabis. The campaign to change drug policy has come from diverse sources, including the House of Lords, the Police Federation, medical companies such as GW Pharmaceuticals, the Multiple Sclerosis Society, the *New Musical Express*, Ministry of Sound, *The Guardian*, the *Independent on Sunday*, Transform, etc. Taken together the different voices have been an influence on the changes to British drug laws because they derive from within mainstream society. Howard Parker (2001: 11) argues that this new drug policy is a courageous break with the political spin of the war on drugs.

Medical cannabis: from miracle panacea to hideous social pariah and back

In the twenty-first century there has been a growing movement in western nations in support of cannabis to be made available for therapeutic purposes, popularly described as 'cannabis medicine'. The House of Lords Select Committee on Science and Technology (1998) argued that cannabis has been in existence for over 2600 years as a means to achieve euphoria and as a medicine. In the last hundred years or so there have been several major investigations into cannabis, including: the Indian Hemp Commission in 1894, the LaGuardia Committee (New York) in 1944, the Wooton Report in 1968, the World Health Organization Report (Toronto) in 1981, and the Runciman Report in 2000. Prior to the prohibition of cannabis in the twentieth century, tinctures of cannabis were sold by major drug companies across the western world.

The House of Lords Select Committee (1998) notes that cannabis medicine was first described by the Greek pharmacologist Dioscorides, who in his *De Materia Medica* provided the first systematic herbal pharmacopoeia in AD 60. Dioscorides's drawings and descriptions of medical cannabis were influential on Paracelsus and Linnaeus in their medical advances and also on subsequent herbals produced in Britain, especially from the sixteenth century onwards, such as John Gerard's *The Herbal, or General Histories of Plants* of 1597[20] and Nicholas Culpeper's *Pharmacopoeia Londinensis, or the London*

Dispensatory of 1653.[21] The 1788 *New Edinburgh Dispensatory* and Samuel Carey's 1832 *Supplement to the Pharmacopoeia* promoted herbal remedies using cannabis. The modern era of cannabis medicine was introduced by Dr William Brooke O'Shaughnessy, professor of chemistry at the Medical College of Calcutta.[22] Within a few years doctors began to prescribe cannabis and British medical journals carried papers describing the different properties and treatment of medical cannabis. By the 1890s cannabis had been recognized as a powerful medicine for the treatment of muscle spasms, menstrual cramps, rheumatism, migraine, convulsions of tetanus, rabies, insomnia, neuralgia, asthma, epilepsy, for general pain relief and also for psychiatric purposes, depression, fatigue, insanity and delirium tremens (Carlson 1974; House of Lords 1998). Cannabis had secured its place in the United States Pharmacopoeia and the British Pharmacopoeia and major drug companies had expanded into the commercial opportunity provided by medical cannabis, making it one of the most prescribed medical agents in western medicine (Lenson 1995).

However, the position of cannabis medicine was not secure; it faced moral and medical problems. First, from the 1850s onwards cannabis was hailed as a narcotic promising mysterious, erotic and dangerous fantasies through the work of Bayard Taylor and Fitz Hugh Ludlow, who were influenced by Thomas De Quincey's opium tales. Second, the medical profession likened the condition of cannabis use to that of psychosis, it was thought that the drug offered illusions 'akin to the delusion of insanity'.[23] In the United States the connection between cannabis and madness began in 1846 with a review of Moreau de Tours's work by Dr Amariah Brigham in the *American Journal of Insanity*.[24] From the 1850s onwards a series of articles emerged from the USA, Britain, India and Egypt with a focus on cannabis and psychosis.[25] These papers suggested that cannabis was a causal factor of insanity and regular users of hashish became hospitalized for showing signs of 'weak-mindedness'.

Chopra (1940), Inglis (1975) and Berridge and Edwards (1987) demonstrate that cannabis became subject to misinformation and propaganda by British medical and colonial administrators, including the surgeon Lieutenant-Colonel Crombie, Major Willcocks, R. D. Lyall, W. C. Taylor and Dr Warnock, superintendent of the Cairo Asylum (Clouston 1896).[26] The international prohibition of cannabis began initially in 1912 at the First International Opium Conference, when delegates signed a closing protocol stating: 'It is desirable to study the question of Indian hemp from the statistical and scientific point of view, with the object of regulating its abuse.'[27] The Second International Opium Conference took place at Geneva in 1925. At the conference the Egyptian delegates Dr El Guindy and Dr A. H. Mahfooz Bey presented memoranda on hashish. El Guindy stated that 'the illicit use of hashish is the principal cause of insanity occurring in Egypt'.[28] The Egyptian delegation through its spurious scientific assertions claimed that cannabis caused insanity due to two psychotic conditions: 'acute hashishism' and 'chronic hashishism' (Willoughby 1925; Inglis 1975: 173; Mathews 1999: 192). This 'scientific' declaration provided the legitimacy for the newly emergent US Narcotic Bureau under Harry Anslinger to fantasize a link with the older myth of the delirious 'Assassins' fuelled on dope and sex. The Marihuana Tax Act 1937 and subsequent legislation effectively outlawed the drug.

The political prohibition of cannabis was accomplished with its removal from the American Pharmacopoeia in 1942 and confirmed by the World Health Organization, which claimed that 'cannabis had no therapeutic value and was obsolete in medical practice' (House of Lords 1998).[29] The British Royal College of Psychiatrists and Physicians (2000: 250) stated that the Egyptian government argued that 'smoking hashish was a frequent precursor of insanity, even though no causal relationship had been established'. But Alison Mack and Janet Joy (2001: 61) argue that cannabis use alone without additional risks is unlikely to provoke psychosis. They say: 'Drug abuse is common among people with mental illness ... while experts generally agree that heavy marijuana use can provoke schizophrenic episodes in susceptible individuals, they also concur that the drug does not cause the underlying disorder.' The medical profession established preconceived ideas in opposition to cannabis which were held to reflect the profession's own subjective evaluation of the drug. The medical account of cannabis presumed it to be the cause of insanity, when in reality it was an imaginary condition hypothesized by the medical profession.

Cannabis self-medication and commercial opportunities

Contemporary self-medication of cannabis as a popular practice in the twenty-first century could be described as a people-led initiative, not driven by corporate drug manufactures or legitimate medical authorities. A key part of the medical profession's authority is the distinction between therapeutic and non-therapeutic use of drugs; this differentiation can be identified as part of the hegemony of medical professionalism. Neil Montgomery (House of Lords 1998) questions this division and suggests considerable crossover between recreational and medical use of cannabis. He considers it is difficult to sustain these rigid boundaries, especially where pleasure and relief may merge. It is noted in House of Lords (1998) that during the 1960s and 1970s cannabis use was promoted through an ideology of healing as a force for change in society. This soulful therapeutic legacy from the 1960s gave rise to more specific drug experimentation in terms of self-medication during the 1980s and 1990s.

Throughout the twentieth century governments and the media have initiated anti-cannabis propaganda which has promoted the drug as 'evil' (Musto and Korsmeyer 2002). The position of cannabis as a schedule 1 drug in US law effectively defines the drug as being as dangerous as heroin but, crucially, restricts medical investigation. In Britain, the House of Lords (1998: 2, 2001) has accused the Medicines Control Agency (MCA), which operates drug- licensing powers, of having a negative attitude or 'stigma' towards cannabis. House of Lords (2001: 12) states that the government and relevant authorities were 'dragging their feet because they may have feared that permitting therapeutic preparations of cannabis to be prescribed would be interpreted by the public as a move towards allowing recreational use'.[30] The MCA was accused not merely of taking 'inconsistent decisions' and being 'unprepared to discuss their own decisions' but of having a 'flawed' approach to cannabis (1998: 25). In effect the House of Lords has argued that the 'MCA [has] not adopted a positive approach towards the licensing of cannabis-based medicines' (1998: 27) and has effectively caused a delay in the potential approval of such medicines. State discrimination against access to cannabis-based medicines led to the take-up of self-medication by individuals and groups, consequently leading to the prosecution of therapeutic cannabis users. Evidence from the UK Alliance for Cannabis Therapeutics, the Multiple Sclerosis Society and *Disability Now* demonstrates that many people are using cannabis for medical purposes to treat multiple sclerosis (MS), AIDS, cerebral palsy and glaucoma. In recent years the *British Medical Journal* and *New Scientist* have closely covered developments in cannabis medicine: for example Philip Robson (1994: 1035) states: 'The BMA is not alone in arguing for enhanced access to cannabinoids in clinical practice. Others include the Royal Pharmaceutical Society, the previous president of the Royal College of Physicians and many British doctors.'

Political obstructions to clinical research into cannabis have now changed with GW Pharmaceuticals granted a commercial trial of medical cannabis by the Home Secretary, David Blunkett, in October 2001. The company plans to develop prescriptive cannabis medicines for a range of treatment including MS, cancer pain and other forms of nerve pain. The media seized on the reforms: the *Observer* of 4 November 2001 proclaimed 'Cannabis medical miracle – it's official', which was followed by a BBC 1 *Panorama* documentary special entitled 'Cannabis from the Chemist' broadcast the same day. The television programme and the newspaper article asserted 'cannabis is a wonder drug'. Trevor Jackson (2001: 1136) reported that 'shares in GW Pharmaceuticals jumped from 13p to 108p'. Dr Geoffrey Guy, executive chairman of GW said in a press release on 12 March 2002: 'We are confident that this is the best way for GW to undertake science, and to investigate the future commercial opportunities.'

The introduction of corporate medical companies to investigate the commercial potential of cannabis is based on the need to identify the active compounds in cannabis for pharmaceutical standardization. This formal procedure to deliver medical cannabis can be seen as an attempt to break the historical and cultural association between recreational and medical use. Cannabis's historical association with a pre-capitalist world and its subsequent imprisonment in the twentieth century have been key features in the promotion of a pro-ideology of the drug.[31] It has an image of belonging to the people, possessing natural goodness as part of a rich tradition of folk remedies. Although the ideology of cannabis is a mass of contradictions, it promotes the drug as being a natural intoxicant which supports cultural sensitivity and collectivity. It is recognized that the illegal cannabis industry of recreational and therapeutic use is worth approximately £4 billion.[32] Both multinationals and small-time capitalist entrepreneurs see the opportunity of profits to be gained now that British law has taken a more relaxed approach towards the drug.

'Relaxation' and the British coffeeshop

Alongside the agreement permitting commercial pharmaceutical companies to undertake medical cannabis trials, the government has introduced a more relaxed approach towards recreational cannabis use. In a pilot scheme first introduced in 2001 by David Blunkett in Brixton, led by Metropolitan Police commander Brian Paddick, individuals caught in possession of cannabis are given a serious warning and have their drugs confiscated. But at the same time Keith Hellawell, the drug tsar, in his final report for the government launched an attack on supporters of the decriminalization of cannabis.[33] In March 2002 the pilot scheme gained further publicity as a result of Paddick's removal following accusations that he had used cannabis himself, but the tabloid media were more preoccupied with painting the innovator as a 'homosexual maverick'. The *Sun* labelled him a 'crackpot' for his 'softly, softly' policy on cannabis and ridiculed his homosexuality by presenting him as a member of the Village People, gay icons within 1970s and 1980s pop music.[34] Although removed from office, Paddick received overwhelming support from people living in Lambeth,[35] the south London borough of which Brixton is part, and from Sir John Stevens, the Metropolitan Police Commissioner. The pilot scheme continues and in 2002 the government reclassified cannabis as part of its new drug policy.

In Britain two Amsterdam-style coffeeshops have been opened as cannabis cafés, The Dutch Experience in Stockport Village, Manchester and The Dutch Experience II in Bournemouth. The Netherlands coffeeshop movement played a vital role in the launching of both British cafés; Nol van Schaik, a self-titled coffeeshop guru, co-founded the first café and was an adviser to the second.

The first British coffeeshop was opened on 15 September 2001 by Colin Davies, who suffers from severe spinal injuries; he is also founder of the Medical Marihuana Co-operative. The BBC's *Money Programme* screened 'Cannabis Cafés' on 24 April 2002, which followed the setting up and opening of Britain's second coffeeshop, run by James Ward. Both coffeeshop proprietors have experienced police arrest and surveillance. Further coffeeshops are planned to open across Britain including Rebel Inc in Edinburgh, Café Amsterdam in Leeds, Chillin Rooms in Liverpool, Beggars Belief in Rhyl, WHSpliff in Taunton and Herb Connection in Worthing.[36] *The Money Programme*, with its focus on the Netherlands, demonstrated the close links between recreational and medical cannabis. It specified that medical cannabis users can gain 'discounts' on their purchases and cannabis activists who want to open further coffeeshops include MS sufferers.[37]

The British newspapers' response to the Labour government changes to drug laws followed their traditional political positions. The *Sun*, the *Daily Mail*[38] and the *Daily Express*, all right-wing papers, were against the change. Their headlines claimed that Britain's children were now at risk from decriminalization of cannabis,[39] that drug use was epidemic and that cannabis caused madness.[40] The Conservative-supporting newspapers were triumphant with glee at Keith Hellawell's public announcement of his resignation. They asserted that Britain's drug policy was flawed, without foundation and expertise, using comments from Hellawell such as 'I don't know where he [the Home Secretary] got his advice from'. Hellawell's celebrity exit on BBC Radio 4's *Today* programme was a piece of theatre. Alan Travis[41] (2002) reveals that Hellawell had tendered his resignation the previous month and at his request this information was kept back from the public. By claiming not to know where the policy of reclassification came from the drug tsar made a fool of himself. Government drug advice comes from numerous official sources: the Police Federation, the House of Lords Select Committee on Science and Technology, the Advisory Council on the Misuse of Drugs, medical experts, Drugscope and lawyers.

European drug normalization

At the moment certain European governments have brought forward policy changes to drug laws. Drug prohibition remains the consistent position, but countries have moved towards different forms of drug regulation and decriminalization. Common themes can be found within the drug policies of some European countries, Canada and Australia, focusing on civil penalties and harm reduction, whereas American, Swedish and Norwegian drug policies remain based on punitive control to create a 'drug-free society' (Natarajan and Hough 2000). Historically, the Netherlands has developed the most progressive drug policies, where it has pursued a policy of 'normalization' for soft drugs, such as cannabis. This policy has been taken up in a variety of ways by Switzerland, Portugal, Italy, Spain and certain states within Germany. Furthermore, Switzerland, the Netherlands and Australia have introduced what are called heroin rooms, where drug users can register and use their drug in a safe environment – in popular language 'shooting galleries'. It would be a mistake to think that drugs are legal in these countries, however. In 2001 Portugal brought forward legislation which 'decriminalized' all drugs, but even here drugs remain illegal. At the start of the twenty-first century drugs remain within a framework of prohibition but international obligations within drug conventions have begun to show degrees of movement.

It is incorrect to argue that reform of British drug laws is now possible because it has been newly identified that United Nations drug control treaties are more flexible than previously thought (McAllister 2000). Evidence tells us that Alaska in 1975 legalized cannabis for personal use, the Netherlands began its policy of decriminalization in 1976 and 11 US states had decriminalized cannabis by 1978. These examples show that changes in national drugs policy were possible and not dependent on conformity with UN drug conventions. It could be argued that subsequent UN drug conventions were attempts to halt these changes; for example, the 1988 treaty requires countries to make possession, purchase or cultivation of illegal drugs for personal use a criminal offence (Hartnoll 1998). Drug legalization is not an option for the signatory countries to the UN agreements, but control of drugs in individual countries does hold potential flexibility. The 1988 UN convention established that drug supply and drug possession is a criminal offence, but that drug use is not criminalized. The new approach from the British Home Office towards downgrading cannabis suggests that a key element to change in British drug law is whether criminalization of drug possession is proportional to the harm thereby averted (Barton 2003). This argument is in essence the same formulation proposed by the US President Jimmy Carter in 1977 when he said: 'Penalties against possession of a drug should not be more damaging to an individual than the use of the drug itself; and where they are, they should be changed. Nowhere is this more clear than in the laws against possession of marihuana in private for personal use' (Bertram et al. 1996: 97).

Both the Police Foundation's Runciman Report (2000) and the Advisory Council on the Misuse of Drugs (2002) argue that 'the current classification of cannabis is disproportionate in relation to both its inherent toxicity and to that of other substances'.[42] The British government's reform of drug policy received support from Drugscope in their study *European Drug Laws: the Room for Manoeuvre* (Dorn and Jamieson 2001). This report confirms the development of drug normalization policies in Europe and gives legitimacy to countries wishing to work within the UN conventions on the basis of their particular experiences of drug problems. European countries are seeking to move away from custodial prison sentences for people caught in possession and for small-scale suppliers. This has taken the form of civil penalties, such as fines, warnings, confiscation of drugs, suspension of a person's driving licence, community service orders, and detoxification or health programmes for treatment and/or regular meetings. The rationale of the reform is based on the notion of a proportionate response. The logic behind this approach derives from the intervention by the Netherlands government to try and separate the market for soft and hard drugs. European drug normalization policy is based on the idea of drug differentiation, that distinctions exist between drugs. The prohibition lobby is reluctant to accept the argument of distinctions between drugs because the outcome would define certain drugs as less dangerous than others. This principle of drug distinction is based on realism: governments want to reduce the harm that drugs do within communities and to individuals. This realist policy is based on practicality, where the aim is to decrease drug use rather than promote an unrealistic idealism which seeks to eliminate drugs from society.

John Stuart Mill's responsive prohibition

John Stuart Mill worked for the East India Company from 1823 to 1855, during which time the British government conducted the first Opium War with China. British merchants with the support of the British government illegally supplied opium to China, against the wishes of the Chinese emperor. The East India Company continued to supply opium to the trading company Jardine Matheson until the company's dissolution in 1858, when it was taken over by the government, which in effect was operating a drug cartel. Mill would have been aware of opium use through two sources: as a major part of revenue for the East India Company and the British government and also through the widely acclaimed writings of Thomas De Quincey.

Arguments for the decriminalization and prohibition of drugs have consistently and selectively used the ideas of Mill's *On Liberty* (1859). Mill did not support the legalization of drugs. Zimring and Hawkins (1992) point out that he outlined four qualifications for drug controls legislation. These pertain to: children and young people; persons who are regarded as incapable of free choice; individuals who may infringe on the well-being of others; and people who attempt to sell themselves into slavery. Mill's ideas have influenced drug prevention in terms of protecting the vulnerable against antisocial drug consumption and to control drug traffickers. For prohibitionists the appeal of Mill's ethical framework, according to Vincenzo Ruggiero (1999: 127), is that 'government intrusion into personal choice is justifiable when such choice causes harm to others'. Therefore, once drugs have been intimately linked to crime, violence and moral degeneracy, it is easy for the prohibition lobby to advance their argument that the individual choice of drug consumption results in harm to others and thus demonstrates that prohibition is not only required but welcomed.

Specifically, Mill's approach to drug control is based on protective prohibition for the individual and taxation of stimulants. Writing about opium at the East India Company, he argued (1990: 106): 'The opium revenue is not derived from taxation of any class of Her Majesty's subjects, but is paid wholly by foreigners. It cannot reasonably be contended that this is an improper source of revenue.' Mill (1859/1974: 171) thought that taxation of stimulants was a form of control which was inevitable in a modern state, even though it may make drugs more difficult to obtain. He concluded: 'Taxation, therefore, of stimulants up to the point which produces the largest amount of revenue (supposing that the State needs all the revenue which it yields) is not only admissible, but to be approved of.'

Mill was writing at the time of the emergence of the temperance movement and in particular alcohol prohibition in the American state of Maine in 1851. He (1859: 156) described prohibition law in terms of its 'impracticability' and was very concerned that an organization devoted to temperance might have wider ambitions for further interference with liberty. He described prohibition as a 'gross usurpation upon the liberty of private life ... and still greater ones threatened with some expectation of success, and opinions propounded which assert an unlimited right in the public not only to prohibit by law everything which it thinks wrong, but, in order to get at what it thinks wrong, to prohibit a number of things which it admits to be innocent' (1859/1974: 156). It is clear that Mill saw the connection between the moral standards espoused by the US and British temperance movement and prohibition as a total perspective holding little flexibility for human agency, stating 'there is no violation of liberty which it would not justify' (1859/1974: 158). Mill argued that prohibition was a failure, but several states in America implemented legislation and prosecuted people with 'considerable zeal' as advocated by 'the professed philanthropists' (1859/1974: 156).

Mill saw in the temperance movement's use of religious ideology and its self-inflated moral beliefs further dangers of 'illegitimate interference with the rightful liberty of the individual'. He realized that the temperance movement had changed its political and moral ambitions, which went beyond individual abstinence to state-imposed prohibition, effectively removing any element of choice (Berkhout and Robinson 1999). He identified that drug control was being used wholesale as a collective programme for social reform of the masses by one particular faction of society. Mill was opposed to the prohibition of alcohol and saw drug control laws as a fundamental infringement on human liberty. He states that an individual's 'choice of pleasures and their mode of expending their income, after satisfying their legal and moral obligations to the State and to individuals, are their own concern and must rest with their own judgment' (Mill 1859/1974: 171).

He identified prohibition as not only a major problem for an individual's liberty, but a greater danger for society itself. 'So monstrous a principle is far more dangerous than any single interference with liberty.' (1859/1974: 158). Although Mill's ideas have been criticized over the last century as paternalistic and pompous, the value of his understanding of prohibition is its responsive flexibility. Mill showed great awareness of how powerful groups in society may seek to impose their particular vision and values of social and cultural life on the majority. Mill saw that prohibitionists want to achieve protection for the individual and society, and therefore sought to demonstrate that prohibition can be responsive, not repressive.

Conclusion

There is no such thing as a neutral drug policy. During the course of this final chapter I have sought to demonstrate that drug policy is a site of conflict, denial and contradiction. Whether legal or illegal, drugs represent a massive commercial interest; whether the application is for therapeutic or pleasurable purposes, drugs are driven by people's participation. Government commercial trials of cannabis medicine and the popularity of cannabis self-medication coexist, the attraction of cannabis remains its potential for financial reward for corporate medical companies or coffeeshop entrepreneurs.

Contemporary British drug policy has been shaped by two opposing approaches. The anti-drug crusading lobby, through private finance, sponsorship supported by government media events and policy documents, have colluded in the development of personalized shock tactics through the use of a public gallery of dead young women. New drug prohibition is invested with the anti-drug campaigner's vulnerability and loss, but messages of prohibition become blurred through the involvement of tabloid newspapers which are addicted to high-profile character assassinations of popular figures linked with drugs.[43] British drug reform has also been significantly shaped by processes of drug normalization which include the 1990s ecstasy culture, the internationalization of club culture through corporate holiday companies, drug tourism, the growth of the coffeeshop and demands for drug reform derived from mainstream society. These social and cultural changes have occurred within a European context and it is appropriate to see any revision to British drug law as influenced by the movement of European drug normalization policy.

Notes

Introduction

1   Deleuze and Guattari (1988: 286) state that 'to get high or not to get high is no longer the question'.
2   In the *Evening Standard*, 14 July 2003, Isabel Oakeshott states that cannabis 'experts estimate it is responsible for 30,000 deaths in the UK every year'.
3   The *Talk to Frank* campaign 2003.

1 Drug prohibition and the 'assassin of youth'

1   British opium importers Jardine Matheson and Dent and Co.
2   Mill (1990: 106).
3   Before Hawaii became part of the USA it had enacted various anti-drug laws against Chinese opium smoking by 1856.
4   Bewley-Taylor (1999: 36); Gordon (1994: 194).
5   Knights of Columbia, Moose and Kiwanis.
6   Becker (1963: 149).
7   Anslinger was US representative on UN drug control bodies 1930 to 1970.
8   Silver and Aldrich (1979: 62, 274), 31 January 1923 'Marihuana Makes Fiends of Boys in 30 Days: Hasheesh Goads Users to Blood-Lust' and 23 February 1928: '60% of All Violent Crimes Traced to Cocaine'.
9   Lusane (1991: 38).
10   Oxford English Dictionary defines assassin as Arab = hashish-eater.
11   (a) Anonymous (1854) The visions of hasheesh, *Putnam's Monthly Magazine*, 3, pp. 402–8. (b) Fitz Hugh Ludlow (1857) The apocalypse of hasheesh, *Putnam's Monthly Magazine*, 8, pp. 625–30. (c) Bayard Taylor (1856) The hasheesh eater, *Putnam's Monthly Magazine*, 8, pp. 233–9.
12   (1826) see II. 138–43.
13   Abel (1980).
14   Lusane (1991: 74).
15   Celebrated spy Marguerite Gertrude Zelle, alias Mata Hari, a renowned dancer, came to the attention of MI5 at Folkestone, December 1915. In 1916 MI5 passed on information about possible espionage. She was shot by a French firing squad in 1917.
16   Kohn (1992: 43).

17 Kohn (1992: 43).

18 Berridge (1984: 21–22), Parliamentary Papers, 1917 Report of the Committee on the Use of Cocaine in Dentistry, VIII, pp. 151–7.

19 For example, *World's Pictorial News*, 7 March 1926, *World's Pictorial News*, 28 March 1926.

20 *World's Pictorial News*, 7 March 1926.

21 Newspapers of Randolph Hearst regularly covered media celebrities and drug deaths, e.g. Billie Carleton, Olive Thomas, Wallace Reid and Barbara La Marr (Anger 1975).

22 Stimson and Lart (1994: 335).

23 Schur (1964), Glatt et al. (1967: 16).

24 Pullar-Strecker appears unaware that cannabis before the seventeenth century was known according to Salmon (1693) by the nickname 'Neckweed'.

25 From Herodotus, cannabis was used as an intoxicant for popular social practices. Claudius Galen (130–193 AD) was a Roman medical scholar influenced by the Greek physician Hippocrates. Galen described how cannabis acts to promote hilarity stating: 'There are some who fry and consume [cannabis] together with other desserts. I call "desserts" those food which are consumed after dinner in order to stimulate an appetite for drinking. The seeds create a feeling of warmth, and if consumed in large amounts – affect the head by sending to it a warm and toxic vapour' (Kuhn edition, 6, 550).

26 Johnson (1952: 105) states: 'The marihuana vice in the United States has spread from Mexican labourers to the young people of all classes.'

27 Peri Hyles Iatrikes, from Brunner (1977). Dioscorides argues that cannabis leaves 'when eaten in excess, diminish sexual potency'.

28 Kuhn edition, 12, 8. Galen argues 'its seed is said to make the genitals impotent'.

29 NH 20, 259 Pliny states 'if eaten in excess it quenches sexual potency'.

30 Schur did his PhD at the LSE (1959) titled Drug Addiction in Britain and America: A Sociological Study of Legal and Social Policies.

31 Glatt et al. (1967: 109), Stimson and Lart (1994: 331–3).

32 A. Linken, 'Young Drug Takers', *Sunday Times* 27 January 1963. A. Sharpley, 'Purple Hearts dearer, but still plentiful', *Evening Standard*, 1 May 1964.

33 Chapter originally based on a talk delivered to the Central Council for Health Education's Conference 1968.

34 Graham (1991) in Whynes and Bean.

2 Pleasure doomed: a history of drug control policy

1 Linklater et al. (1984: 266–84).

2 Hunt (1991: 263).

3 His papers were later published in *Narco-Analysis* (1943).

4   CIA and US military experimentation on 7000 unsuspecting soldiers in 1949 at Edgewood Chemical Arsenal in Maryland. At Lexington Hospital Dr Harris Isbell experimented on mainly black heroin addicts who were given LSD for more than 75 consecutive days. Dr Carl Pfeiffe did similar experiments on prisoners in Atlanta and New Jersey and Dr Ewen Cameron at Montreal McGill University gave frequent doses of LSD to schizophrenics (Hunt 1991).

5   See evidence of Andews (2001), Ross (2000).

6   Huggins (1987: 168) *Foreign Relations of the US, Volume VII* (I: 838, 1952–54).

7   Huggins (1998: 115).

8   Marshall (1991: 12).

9   Blaming communism for international drug smuggling was less important in the 1941 exploitation film *Devil's Harvest* that blamed the Nazi regime for corrupting American youth with narcotics.

10   Kinder (1981: 188).

11   Chiang Kai-shek's wife's Madam Chiang visited the USA to gain military support.

12   Scott (1980: 15) states: 'By 1951 the CIA was closely allied with KMT drug operations in Burma and Yunnan, through a Miami based proprietary, Sea Supply, Inc., organized by OSS veteran Paul Helliwell.' Marshall (1991: 56) states that Sea Supply was the CIAs 'opium-and-arms smuggling front'.

13   Thailand's military dictator, General Phao, in 1954 was awarded the Legion of Merit for 'exceptionally meritorious service' by the US Secretary of the Army.

14   The result of the new mission was that the armed forces avoided dramatic downsizing that occurs with the end of a war.

15   Marshall (1991: 43).

16   *The Guardian*, 19 October 1999.

17   E.P. Thompson (1985: 41) calls them 'servile parasitic elites'.

18   Drug economies employ: Peru 111,000–186,000; Bolivia 500,000; Colombia 300,000.

19   Bentham (1998) suggests worldwide cocaine income in the 1980s exceeded the gross domestic product of over 88 of the world's market economies. The Royal College of Psychiatrists and Physicians (2000: 113) argue that the income of drug barons is an annual $254 thousand million. Also J. Marks (1997) The Economic and Social Costs of Public Drug Dependence Policies, address to the European Cities' Drug Policy Forum, Paris-Montreuil, 27 October.

20   Knoester (1998); also see Jessop (1985: 237).

21   Bertram et al. (1996: 17, e.g. Jose Gonzalo).

22   As in the cases of Pablo Escobar and Roberto Suarez-Gomez: Bentham (1998, Chapters 1–2).

23   *The Guardian*, 30 October 2001.

24   Knoester (1998: 89).

25   Marshall (1991: 19, footnote 89), America's Watch, The Killings in Columbia, New York, 1989, 4–5; *Wall Street Journal*, May 18 1990.

26 Marshall (1991: 23, footnote 105), America's Watch, Human Rights in Mexico: A Policy of Impunity, June 1990, 3–4, 19–32.

27 Such as China, Korea, the Netherlands, Thailand, Pakistan, Peru, Columbia and others.

28 Marshall (1991); Makarenko (2000); MacDonald and Mansfield (2001).

29 Bewley-Taylor (1999: 213, footnote 12).

30 Marshall (1991: 20) states: 'US military aid represents far and away the bulk of Washington's anti-narcotic assistance to Columbia, even though its national police has primary responsibility for drug enforcement.'

31 Harding, (1998: 214).

32 Derrida (1993: 2–4).

3 Drugs as cultural commodities: an analysis of drugs in film, advertisements and popular music

1 For example, *The White Slave Trade* (1913), *The Drug Terror* (1914), *The Narcotic Spectre* (1914), *The Accursed Drug* (1915), *The Dividend* (1916), *The Devil's Needle* (1916), *Broken Blossoms* (1919), *The Devil Within* (1921), *The Yellow Claw* (1921), *His Pajama Girl* (1921), *Frailty* (1921), *Pawned* (1922), *While London Sleeps* (1922), *Daughters of the Rich* (1923), *Midnight Girl* (1925).

2 See also Charles Laughton in the British film *Down River* (1931).

3 For example, *Cocktails* (1928), *The Camels are Coming* (1934). *International House* (1933) contains Cab Calloway's way-out version of 'Reefer Man'.

4 The Keystone Film Company was owned by Mack Sennett; Arbuckle worked closely with Sennett's girlfriend Mabel Normand, who was also known for her use of cocaine.

5 For example, *Carmen* (1915), *To Have and to Hold* (1916), *Joan the Woman* (1917), *The Woman God Forgot* (1917), *The Roaring Road* (1919), *Too Much Speed* (1922).

6 Her film name was Dorothy Davenport.

7 Hollywood abandoned the code in 1968 and introduced the system of age-based ratings.

8 Consolidating his coolness in the 1990s, Julian Cope wrote a song about him called 'Robert Mitchum' on the 1990 album *Skellington*.

9 *NME*, 3 May 2003, 'Rap meets porn'.

10 Garland used amphetamines to remain slim and complete studio work; she committed suicide in 1969 from a drug overdose.

11 *South Park* characters have taken LSD and experienced floating through the sky.

12 'Old Hollywood' produced the first motorcycle film with Marlon Brando in *The Wild One* (1954); a major drug addiction film with Frank Sinatra in *The Man with the Golden Arm* (1955); and with James Dean in *Rebel without a Cause*

(1955) set the scene for rock 'n' roll. These films advanced Hollywood into the modern era of teenage rebels but they remained creaky and formulaic.

13 In the mid-1960s 'Old Hollywood' was still dominant. Biskind (1998: 18) states: 'Adolph Zukor at ninety-two, and the only slightly younger Barney Balaban, seventy-eight, were still on the board of Paramount; Jack Warner, seventy-three, ran Warner Bros. Darryl F. Zanuck, sixty-three, was firmly in command at 20th Century.'

14 An Oscar, a BAFTA award, a Golden Globe and a Cannes Film Festival award.

15 The phrase 'graffiti imagination' comes from Alan Stone's *Boston Review*, 1993–2000.

16 The British Board of Film Classification was established in 1913; Hollywood in the 1920s adopted the guidelines referred to as the 'Don'ts and Be Carefuls'.

17 From Olive Thomas and Wally Reid to John Belushi and River Phoenix.

18 Heroin was recognized by the British Pharmaceutical Codex in 1911 as highly addictive but Bayer did not stop production of legal heroin until 1913.

19 Channel Four (1995) 'Pot Night' booklet: 18.

20 Parke-Davis and Company's 1929–30 physicians' catalogue; see Schaffer Library of Drug Policy.

21 Claire Cockcroft in the *Guardian* 10 May 2001 points out that marijuana is not hemp: 'hemp is a distinct variety within the species'.

22 The flexibility and strength of cannabis have resulted in its use in Adidas trainers, Giorgio Armani suits, in bible paper by Kimberly Clark and by Ford and BMW in the motor industry.

23 All these drug-related terms derive from advertisements which the Advertising Standards Authority has investigated in the last few years.

24 Timothy Leary's phrase was 'Tune in, turn on and drop out'.

25 *Ministry*, July 2000.

26 *Sun*, 20 December 2000.

27 Mary Kenny, *Mail on Sunday*, 'Who wants the smell of death?', 17 December 2000.

28 Originally published in 1929, the second edition, featuring the lurid cover, dates from a later period.

29 The first picture to link fashion with drugs was introduced by photographer Corinne Day in 1995, who photographed Kate Moss.

30 The Sophie Dahl poster appeared on front page of the *Sun* again on 21 June 2001; the tabloid used it directly as a voyeuristic representation of sexual potency referring to her relationship with Mick Jagger and the Rolling Stones drug debauchery.

31 See Josie Miles's 'Pipe Dream Blues' (1924), Duke Ellington's 'Hop Head' (1927), Victoria Spivey's 'Dope Head Blues' (1927). Also 'Tea for Two', 'Tumbling Tumbleweed', 'Flying Home', 'Doctor Freeze', 'If You're a Viper', 'Viper's Drag', 'Knocking Myself Out', 'Weed Smoker's Dream', 'Here Comes the Man with the Jive', 'Jack I'm Mellow', 'Light Up' and 'Vonce' (Winick 1959: 251).

32 Paul McCartney and Wings' song 'Hi, Hi, Hi' (1972) was banned by the BBC.
33 The Fraternity of Man's song 'Don't Bogart Me', on the *Easy Rider* sound-track, is an example of drug humour in country music. The drug hero in country music, is of course, Willie Nelson, who not only ran a company called 100 Per Cent Hemp but also claimed to have smoked cannabis at the White House.
34 Cypress Hill, 'Hits from the Bong'.
35 D J Deekline had a UK underground garage hit in 1998 with 'Don't Smoke da Reefa', punning on the well-known Blue Oyster Cult song 'Don't Fear the Reaper'.
36 An earlier example is the Black Sabbath song 'Sweet Leaf' from the 1971 LP *Master of Reality*.
37 Robert Crumb did artwork for the 1968 LP *Cheap Thrills* by Big Brother and the Holding Company, featuring comic characters saying 'smack', 'acid', 'speed', 'sikaydelic', etc.
38 *Beats by Dope Demand Too!* compilations 1–5, late 1990s.
39 The poster for *Beats by Dope Demand Too!* features three smiling young women and men, dressed in cool fashions and smoking spliffs.
40 Gong members Steve Hillage and Miquette Giraudy wrote music for the debut Orb LP *UF Orb*.
41 The term 'stoner' refers to someone who deliberately displays drug con-sciousness.
42 In 1930 Haile Selassie became Emperor of Ethiopia, a black king greeted with enthusiasm throughout the Caribbean. He became a central symbol of Ras-tafarianism after his first visit to Jamaica in November 1930.
43 Rita Marley, Bob Marley's wife, also recorded a pro-marijuana song, 'One Draw' (1981).
44 Huge Mundell, Jah Mikey, Jah Hubey, Bongo Teo and Augutsus Pablo.
45 Channel 4, *Pump Up the Volume*, 27 November 2001.
46 Criminal Justice and Public Order Act 1994, section 63. London: HMSO
47 Entertainments (Increased Penalties) Act 1990, Broadcasting Act 1990, Criminal Justice and Public der Act 1994.
48 Attributed to Danny Rampling (Push and Silcott 2000: 45).
49 *Ministry*, April 1999.
50 A popular T-shirt of Sid Vicious is 'Drugs Kill', showing him injecting heroin.
51 For example 'See Emily Play', Pink Floyd's top ten hit in 1967.
52 *Ministry*, April 1999.
53 See *Q*, February 2001 for the top five heroin, cannabis, LSD, cocaine and ecstasy LPs.
54 See also the 1981 LP *Wilder* by the Teardrop Explodes, led by Cope, and 'Out of My Mind on Dope and Speed', from Cope's LP *Skellington* (1989).
55 Miles Davis's autobiography (1989: 326–31) details his real struggles, saying: 'Drugs took the place that music had occupied in my life.'

56 The 1960s countercultural phrase 'speed kills' comes from this song.

57 In reggae see Mutabaruka.

58 J. J. Cale's 'Cocaine' from the LP *Troubadour* (1976), covered by Eric Clapton, can be described as positive but does offer caution.

59 See Melly (1972: 114) on the BBC ban of the Beatles 'A Day in the Life'.

60 *NME*, 23 March 2002.

61 *NME*, 1 November 1997.

62 The group reformed in mid-1998 with the drug-ironic name E17.

63 *Evening Standard*, 30 January 1997.

64 *Evening Standard*, 30 January 1997.

65 *Sun*, 12 July 1997. Gillian Brown fed cannabis to her rabbit, which became so spaced out that it was killed by a Staffordshire bull terrier. Similarly, the *Daily Star* of 14 December 2001 ran a story headlined 'How Santa got so high', and also an article by Ian McDonald called 'Trippy Christmas', which presented drug consumption of LSD as a joke.

66 *Guardian*, 22 March 2001.

67 See Q, February 2001; *Melody Maker*, 24–30 November 1999; *Mixmag*, February 2001; *NME*, 15 February 1997 and 18 March 2000; *Ministry*, April 2000.

68 These pastoral-sounding American bands have creatively woven drug references into their material reminiscent of the Beatles. See *NME* 1998–2003 passim.

69 'We Call It Acieed' by D-Mob, with vocals by Gary Haisman.

70 The cover of Bomb the Bass's hit 'Beat Dis' (1988) used the smiley face (with blood) derived from the classic comic novel *Watchmen* (1986) by Alan Moore, with drawings by Dave Gibbons.

71 'Managing the Chemical Culture', paper presented at the Release drugs conference, June 1999, London.

72 Drugs were used as a pun for promoting material for Missy Elliott's LP *Miss E ... So Addictive* (2001).

4 Youth subcultural theory: deviance, resistance, identity and drugs

1 'Social Structure and Anomie' (1938), 'Social Continuities in the Theory of Social Structure and Anomie' (1957) in *Social Theory and Social Structure*; both papers are in this text.

2 Merton used the concept of subculture in a substantial revision of the paper for *Social Theory and Social Structure* (1957).

3 The 1938 paper has passing reference to Nels Anderson's study on *The Hobo* (1923).

4 Merton specifies that when an individual as a type disturbs the functionalist model, he or she is given a location within a typology of anomie.

5   See also Mannheim (1965).
6   Wood Report, parliamentary document.
7   David Downes and David Matza had previously suggested that deviance was only one factor of subcultural behaviour, not the determining one.
8   Private communication from Phil Cohen.
9   Hall (1980a).
10 Plant (1975: 126) states: 'It was obvious that many of those labelled "drug-takers" were, generally, very similar to non-drugtakers. ... Most of my sub-jects led relatively "normal" lives and had mundane daily routines. It would be a gross misrepresentation to suggest that in all respects, they were a race apart from non-drugtakers.'
11 He contributed a chapter to *Resistance through Ritual* but did not write the section containing the CCCS theory of subculture.
12 Blackman (1995); see theory of cultural ransacker.
13 Fyvel (1961: 18–21) talks about the Teddy Boy subculture as an international phenomenon.
14 See *The Face* magazine (1990s), on rave as an international subculture, linked to drug tourism, new age culture and hedonism.

5 'Drug normalization': a historical and contemporary critique

1   Food, materials, cloth, fishing nets, etc.
2   Book XI, 6, 15.
3   English translation by Carey (1848), Book IV, Ch. 74, 75.
4   Merlin (1972: 67); Louis Lewin (1964: 109).
5   Certain editions of the book actually remove the name of the drug nepenthe.
6   Adorno and Horkheimer (1944/1979: 63) state that in the west drugs have always been associated with the east, with the Orient, conforming to a ste-reotypical understanding of 'Orientalism'.
7   'Poppies soaked with the sleep of Lethe' and 'giving dewy honey and soporific poppy'.
8   Palaeolithic, mesolithic and neolithic.
9   Holloway (1995: 82) states: 'By 1780 the value of sales of proprietary medi-cines was estimated at £187,500 a year.'
10 Thomas Jones (1800).
11 Examples include Slowe's Infants' Preservative, Thomsons Soothing Syrup for Baby, Atkinson's Infant Preservative, Godfrey's Cordial, Mrs. Winslow's Soothing Syrup, Street's Infant Quietener, Dalby's Carminative, Kendal Black Drop, Dover's Powder, Battley's Sedative Solution, 'Mother's Friend', and others.
12 *Blackwood's Magazine* in 1830 says: 'Who can say, when eighteen hours toil

out of the four and twenty have bowed down both body and soul to the dust, a few drops of laudanum may not be, in the best terms a blessing?' (Berridge and Edwards 1987: 107).

13 For details about 'Spliffy' see Blackman (1996b).

14 Female drug users are often presented as part of society's moral decline. This is achieved by the masculinist construction of the woman as the 'mother of the nation'.

15 *Coronation Street* star Tracy Shaw features on the front page in her skimpy underwear with a giant chain woven round her body and between her legs. This story is six years old; the image is to sell her now.

16 *Daily Mirror*, 17 May 1999, front page: 'Camilla's tears: she weeps as Charles rings Tom over cocaine'.

17 On 14 January 2002 every tabloid carried headlines about Prince Harry's drug consumption, for example, *Daily Mail*: 'Harry: I'm so sorry father', *Daily Express*: 'Harry's guard facing the sack', *Sun*: 'Harry faces Eton drugs test'. On 11 November 2001 the *Mail on Sunday* had the front page headline 'Drug ordeal of Derry Irvine's son'.

18 Noel Gallagher, *NME*, 26 February 2000: 'I only know five people who haven't taken drugs and that's me mam, me gran, me father-in-law, and me new-born baby. Nothing wrong with it, all apart of growing up.'

19 Shiner and Newburn position Parker and Coffield's work as supporting grounded theory, but their respective studies are not ethnographic.

20 They also fail to incorporate the work of Nicholas Saunders (1993, 1995).

6 Schooling and substances: a critical approach to drug education

1 Actors in the film include Charles Chaplin Jr and Lyle Talbot, who played in *Wild Weed* (1949).

2 In the twenty-first century government agencies conducting research on drugs, for example, Children and Young People Unit, Drugscope and the Home Office, British Crime Survey consider that the greatest drug consumption occurs between 16 and 24, claiming that nearly half of 16- to 19-year-olds and 25- to 29-year-olds have used drugs. Earlier, Baker and Mardsen (1994: 36) stated: 'It can be said with reasonable confidence that at least seven million people between the ages of 12 and 59 have taken cannabis at some time in their lives. Perhaps a quarter of a million schoolchildren and two million young adults will have taken the drug.'

3 *Tackling Drugs Together* (1995) and *Tackling Drugs to Build a Better Britain* (1998).

4 For example, *New Musical Express, Big Daddy, Mixmag, Ministry, Arena, Front, Q, Mojo, Jockey Slut, Loaded*, etc.

5   Advisory Council on the Misuse of Drugs (ACMD) (1993) *Drug Education in Schools*; ACMD (1995) *Police, Drug Misusers and the Community*; DFE (1994) *Tackling Drugs Together* (1995); DFE Circular 4/95 *Drug Prevention and Schools*; DFE (1995) 'Drug Proof': Curriculum Guidance for Schools; DfEE (1997) *Innovations in Drug Education*; Ofsted (1997) *Drug Education in Schools*; DFE *Tackling Drugs to Build a Better Britain* (1998); DfEE (1998) *Drug Education: Getting the Message Across*; DfEE (1998) *Protecting Young People*; Standing Conference on Drug Abuse (SCODA) (1999) *Quality Standards in Drug Education*; SCODA (1999) *Guidance on Selecting Drug Education Materials for Schools*; SCODA (1999) *Managing and Making Policy for Drug-related Incidents in Schools*; Police Foundation Runciman report (2000) *Drugs and Law: An Independent Inquiry into the Misuse of Drugs Act 1971*; Health Advisory Service (2001) *The Substance of Young Needs*; ACMD (2002) *The Classification of Cannabis under the Misuse of Drugs Act.*

6   In the National Curriculum science order drug education is as follows: 5- to 7-year-olds (KS1) should learn about the role of drugs as medicines; 7- to 11-year-olds (KS2) should learn that alcohol, tobacco and other drugs can have harmful effects; 11- to 14-year-olds (KS3) should learn how the misuse of solvents, alcohol and other drugs affects health; 14- to 16-year-olds (KS4) should learn about the effects of solvents, tobacco, alcohol and other drugs on body functions. In general, this drug education conforms solely to negative information.

7   *Protecting Young People* (1998); *The Substance of Young Needs* (2001).

8   Chemical Abuse Resolution Lies in Education.

9   The positive effects have been described as improvements in the areas of peer resistance, problem solving and knowledge (Lloyd et al. 2000: 113). The early negative drug information given was, however, short term in its effect with no appreciable difference between the intervention and the control group shown three years later (Hurry and Lloyd 1997).

10   Porteous (1999: 170) for the assertion of objectivity.

11   Harm minimization advocates a non-judgemental approach towards use and information on how to use specific drugs safely with minimal personal damage.

12   Williamson (1997: 69) discusses 'Scotland against Drugs', which includes Michael Forsyth MP, a former Conservative Secretary of State for Scotland, and David Macauley, who argued that 'many of these harm reduction groups are almost promoting what they would class as safe drug use'.

13   Government 2003 *Talk to Frank* campaign trades on stereotypes and can be seen as patronizing.

14   The text does not specify which drug or drugs are being referred to, but it can be assumed to be cannabis.

15   Key performance targets for drug education and prevention, part of the new Connexions service, include reducing the proportion of 13- to 19-year-olds

using illegal drugs by 50 per cent by 2008.

16 *Behavioural Science*, 16: 98–113.

17 *The Guardian*, 8 August 2002, details how psychiatrists administered LSD to elephants, killing them.

18 *The Face*, 3 (54), 2001, report on Ozzfest.

19 According to the US federal government 76.3 million people have tried cannabis, while only 2.78 million have ever tried heroin (SAMHSA 2001).

20 Joseph Rowntree Foundation, Economic and Social Research Council.

21 Surrey Free Inns.

22 SFI's flagship 'For Your Eyes Only' site is in Park Royal, London.

23 For example, alcohol, cigarettes, sex, drugs.

7 British drug reform: towards responsive prohibition?

1 The seven were Bernard Jenkin, Francis Maude, Lord Strathclyde, Peter Ainsworth, Oliver Letwin, David Willetts and Archie Norman.

2 8 October 2000.

3 The deaths of young men from ecstasy include: Andrew Diment in 1994; Andrew Dick, John Nisbet, Andrew Stoddart, Daniel Ashton, Darren Mul-Holland, Stacey Brown, David Hampton and Robert Jeffrey in 1995; Andreas Bouzis in 1996; Andrew Woodlock and Paul Bettinson in 1997; James O'Shea in 1998; Stephen Brett and Bret Gilkes in 2001. Only Bettinson and O'Shea made the front page of the *Daily Express* – with no photograph.

4 The Rachel Whitear video is called *Rachel's Story*; it chronicles her life from cradle to grave, was funded by the Department of Health and made by Hereford LEA.

5 Leah Betts at Basildon College, Julia Dawes at Perth College, Lorna Spinks at Anglia Polytechnic University, Rachel Whitear at Bath University.

6 *Daily Mail*, 9 May 2001; the phrase 'monster' was used by Lorna Spinks's father.

7 *The Times*, 4 January 1996.

8 *Independent*, 13 January 1996.

9 Garratt (1998: 310) states: 'Leah and her friend Sarah Gargill had taken E on four previous occasions, and had also tried LSD, amphetamines and cannabis together.'

10 *Guardian*, 10 May 2001.

11 Paul Bettinson, *Daily Express*, 23 September 1997.

12 Paul Betts called for the death penalty.

13 'Drug victim's parents defend death images', Sarah Hall, *Guardian*, 2 March 2002.

14 Tabloid newspapers incorrectly report Janet Betts as the mother of Leah Betts, rather than her stepmother. This level of inaccuracy also applies to Janet Betts

herself, who in an article for the *Daily Mail* of 29 March 2000 said: 'My daughter died from a single tablet.'

15 *Daily Mail*, 29 March 2000.
16 'Drug victim's parents defend death images', Sarah Hall, *Guardian*, 2 March 2002.
17 'All aboard as London clubbers make tracks for Leeds', Helen Carter, *Guardian*, 6 February 1999.
18 The Hulsman Committee, formed in 1969, and the Baan Narcotics Working Party, formed in 1968, reported in 1972: see Wijngaart (1988).
19 Such a wide discrepancy in the figures quoted is largely due to the illegality surrounding drugs.
20 Published by J. Norton, London.
21 In 1802 one G. A. published a collective edition of Culpeper's works in four volumes. This included *The English Physician enlarged, or the Herbal*, also the *London Dispensary*.
22 O'Shaughnessy, W.B. 'On the Preparations of Indian Hemp', Bishops College Press: Calcutta 1839.
23 See Hemp Commission (1893–4); Wooton Report (1969).
24 Brigham, A. (1846) 'Review of Moreau de Tours, J. *Du Hachisch et de L'Alienation Mentale'*, *American Journal of Insanity*, 2: 275–81.
25 Woodward, S. B. (1850) Observations on the medical treatment of insanity, *American Journal of Insanity*, 7: 1–34; Gray, J. P. (1860) On the use of *Cannabis indica* in the treatment of insanity, *American Journal of Insanity*, 16: 80–9; Anon. (1878) Indian hemp the cause of 30% insanity of Bengal, *Journal of Mental Science*, 23: 612; Sandwich, F. M. (1889) The Cairo lunatic asylum, *Journal of Mental Science*, 34: 473–90; Walsh, J. H. T. (1894) Hemp drugs and insanity, *Journal of Mental Science*, 40: 21–36; Anon. (1894) Hemp drugs and insanity, *American Journal of Insanity*, 50: 571; Anon. (1898) Hasheesh, *American Journal of Insanity*, 54: 625–6; Ireland, T. (1893) Insanity from the abuse of Indian hemp, *British Medical Journal*, 2: 630.
26 Clouston, T. S. (1896) The Cairo asylum: Dr Warnock on hashish insanity, *Journal of Mental Science*, 42: 790–5.
27 Addendum and Final Protocol of the International Conference, The Hague, 1912.
28 Bonnie, Richard and Whitbread Charles, 'The Genesis of Marijuana Prohibition', <http://www.druglibrary.org/schaffer/library/studies/vlr/vlr2.htm>.
29 House of Lords Science and Technology Ninth Report 1998.
30 House of Lords, second report: 12.
31 The 'legalize cannabis' badge features a spliff looking out from behind prison bars.
32 'Cannabis Cafés', *The Money Programme*, 24 April 2002.
33 *Guardian*, 2 August 2001.
34 For an account of how Paddick was attacked by both the *Sun* and the *Daily*

Mail, see 'Paddick: My Story', front page, *Daily Mirror*, 25 March 2002.

35 Nick Hopkins in the *Guardian*, 22 March 2002, states: 'The Police Foundation reported that 83% of people living in Lambeth were in favour of the initiative.'

36 See coffeeshop websites.

37 Anthony Browne, *Observer*, 17 March 2002.

38 J. Chapman, 'Britain's rethink on cannabis "threatens health of a generation"', 26 February 2003.

39 Melanie Phillips, 'A deadly threat to all our children', *Daily Mail*, 11 July 2002.

40 Sara Nathan, 'Dope trade in the open air', *Sun*, 11 July 2002.

41 *Guardian*, 2002.

42 Opening letter by Professor Sir Michael Rawlins, Chairman, ACMD.

43 For example: Commander Paddick, Elton John, Michael Barrymore, Prince Harry, Drew Barrymore, Noel Gallagher, Naomi Campbell, Angus Deayton, Tracy Shaw.

Bibliography

Abel, E. (1980) *Marihuana: The First Twelve Thousand Years*. New York: Plenum Press.

Adkins, L. and R. (1998) *Handbook of British Archaeology*. London: Constable and Robinson.

Adorno, T. (1941/1990) On popular music, in S. Frith and A. Goodwin (eds) *On Record*. London: Routledge.

Adorno, T. (1999) *Sound Figures*. Stanford: Stanford University Press.

Adorno, T. and Horkheimer, M. (1944/1979) *Dialectic of Enlightenment*. London: Verso.

Advisory Council on the Misuse of Drugs (ACMD) (1993) *Drug Education in Schools*. London: HMSO.

Advisory Council on the Misuse of Drugs (ACMD) (1995) *Police, Drug Misusers and the Community*. London: HMSO.

Ahmad, A. (1995) The politics of literary postcolonality, *Race and Class*, 36: 1–20.

Ahmad, A. (2000) *Lineages of the Present*. London: Verso.

Aitken, D. and Mikuriya, T. (1980) The forgotten medicine, *The Ecologist*, 10(8/9): 269–79.

Akiba, O. (1997) International trade in narcotic drugs, *Futures*, 29(7): 605–16.

Allott, R., Paxton, R. and Leonard, R. (1999) Drug education: a review of British government policy and evidence on effectiveness, *Health Education Research*, 14(4): 491–505.

Anderson, B. (1991) *Imagined Communities*. London: Verso.

Anderson, N. (1923) *The Hobo*. Chicago: University of Chicago Press.

Andreas, P. (1998) The political economy of narco-corruption in Mexico, *Current History*, 97(618): 160–5.

Andrews, G. (2001) *MKULTRA: The CIA's Top Secret Program in Human Experimentation and Behaviour Modification*. Winston-Salem NC: Healthnet Press.

Andrews, G. and Vinkennoog, S. (eds) (1967) *The Book of Grass*. London: Penguin.

Anger, K. (1975) *Hollywood Babylon*. London: Arrow.

Ansell, S. (2001) Connexions and post 16 PSHE – a viable option, *Youth and Policy*, 71: 77–89.

Anslinger, H. J. with Cooper, C. R. (1937) Marijuana: assassin of youth, *American Magazine*, 18–19 July: 150–3.

Arnold, R. (1999) Heroin chic, *Fashion Theory*, 3(3): 279–96.

Arnson, C. (2000) Windows on the past: a declassified history of death squads in El Salvador, in B. Campbell and A. Brenner (eds) *Death Squads in Global*

Perspective: Murder with Deniability. New York: Palgrave.

Artamonov, M. I. (1965) Frozen tombs of the Scythians, *Scientific American*, 212: 5.

Bagot, J. H. (1941) *Juvenile Delinquency*. Liverpool: Liverpool University Press.

Bailey, J. and Elvin, A. (1999) Drugs and peer education, in A. Marlow and G. Pearson (eds) *Young People, Drugs and Community Safety*. Lyme Regis: Russell House.

Baker, O. and Mardsen, J. (1994) *Drug Misuse in Britain*. London: ISDD.

Ball, S. J. (1981) *Beachside Comprehensive*. Cambridge: Cambridge University Press.

Bangert-Drowns, R. (1998) The effects of school based substance abuse education – a meta-analysis, *Journal of Drug Issues*, 18(3): 243–64.

Barthes, R. (1977) *Image–Music–Text*. Glasgow: Fontana.

Barton, A. (2003) *Illicit Drugs: Use and Control*. London: Routledge.

Barton, N. (1997) *Stone Age Britain*. London: English Heritage.

Baudrillard, J. (1983) *Simulation*. New York: Semiotext(e).

Baudrillard, J. (1988) *The Ecstasy of Communication*. New York: Semiotext(e).

Baudrillard, J. (1998) *The Consumer Society*. London: Sage.

Baumeister, R. (1984) Acid rock, *Journal of Psychoactive Drugs*, 16: 339–45.

Bayles, M. (1994) *Hole in Our Soul*. Chicago: University of Chicago Press.

Bean, P. (1974) *The Social Control of Drugs*. London: Martin Roberston.

Beck, J. (1998) 100 years of 'just say no' versus 'just say know', *Evaluation Review*, 22: 15–45.

Beck, U. (1992) *Risk Society*. London: Sage.

Becker, H. S. (1951) The professional dance musician and his audience, *American Journal of Sociology*, 57: 136–44.

Becker, H. S. (1953) Becoming a marihuana user, *American Journal of Sociology*, 59: 235–42.

Becker, H. S. (1963) *Outsiders*. New York: Free Press.

Bennett, A. (1999) Subcultures of neo-tribes: rethinking the relationship between youth, style and musical taste, *Sociology*, 33(3): 599–617.

Bennett, A. (2000) *Popular Music and Youth Culture: Music Identity and Place*. London: Macmillan.

Bennett, A. (2001) *Cultures of Popular Music*. Buckingham: Open University Press.

Bennett, A. and Kahn-Harris, K. (2004) *After Subculture: Critical Studies In Contemporary Youth Culture*. London: Palgrave.

Bentham, M. (1998) *The Global Politics of Drug Control*. Basingstoke: Macmillan.

Berger, M. (1947) Jazz: resistance to the diffusion of a culture-pattern, *Journal of Negro History*, 23: 461–94.

Berkhout, M. and Robinson, F. (1999) *Madame Joy*. Sydney: HarperCollins.

Bernstein, B. (1977) *Class, Codes and Control*, Vol. 3. London: Routledge and Kegan Paul.

Berridge, V. (1980) The making of the Rolleston Report 1908–26, *Journal of Drug Issues*, 10: 7–28.

Berridge, V. (1984) Drugs and social policy: the establishment of drug control in

Britain in 1900–30, *British Journal of Addiction*, 79: 17–29.

Berridge, V. and Edwards, G. (1987) *Opium and the People*. New Haven: Yale University Press.

Bertram, E., Blachman, M., Sharpe, K. and Andreas, P. (1996) *Drug War Politics: The Price of Denial*. Berkeley: University of California Press.

Bewley-Taylor, D. R. (1999) *The United States and International Drug Control, 1909–97*. London: Pinter.

Bidder, S. (2001) *Pump Up the Volume*. London: Channel 4 Books.

Bishop, J. Whitear, B. A. and Brown, S. (2001) A review of substance use education in fifty secondary schools in South Wales, *Health Education Journal*, 60(2): 164–72.

Biskind, P. (1998) *Easy Riders Raging Bulls*. London: Bloomsbury.

Blackman, S. J. (1995) *Youth: Positions and Oppositions – Style, Sexuality and Schooling*. Aldershot: Avebury Press.

Blackman, S. J. (1996a) *Drug Studies and the National Curriculum*. London: Home Office, Drugs Prevention Initiative Paper 16.

Blackman, S. J. (1996b) Has drug culture become an inevitable part of youth culture? A critical assessment of drug education, *Educational Review*, 48(2): 131–42.

Blackman, S. J. (1997) 'Destructing a giro': a critical and ethnographic study of the youth 'underclass', in R. MacDonald (ed.) *Youth, the Underclass and Social Exclusion*. London: Routledge.

Blackman, S. J. (1998) 'Disposable generation?' an ethnographic study of youth homelessness in Kent, *Youth and Policy*, 59: 38–56.

Blackman, S. J. (2000) 'Decanonised knowledge' and the radical project: towards an understanding of cultural studies in british universities, *Pedagogy, Culture and Society*, 8(1): 43–67.

Blackman, S. J. and France, A. (2001) Youth marginality under post-modernism, in N. Stevenson (ed.) *Culture and Citizenship*. London: Sage.

Blum, W. (1995) *Killing Hope: US Military and CIA Intervention since World War II*. Maine: Common Courage.

Boonie, R. and Whitbread, C. H. (1974) *The Marijuana Conviction: A History of Marijuana Prohibition in the US*. Charlottesville: University Press of Virginia.

Bowden, M. (2001) *Killing Pablo*. London: Atlantic Books.

Bower, T. (1984) *Klaus Barbie*. New York: Pantheon.

Bower, T. (1987) *The Paperclip Conspiracy*. London: Michael Joseph.

Bowlby, J. (1946) *Forty-Four Juvenile Thieves*. London: Tindall and Cox.

Bowlby, J. (1953) *Childcare and the Growth of Love*. London: Penguin.

Bradley, L. (2000) *Bass Culture*. London: Penguin.

Brake, M. (1980) *The Sociology of Youth Culture and Youth Sub-Cultures*. London: Routledge Kegan Paul.

Brown, J. and Kreft, I. (1998) Zero effects of drug prevention program: issues and solutions, *Evaluation Review*, 22(1): 3–14.

Broyard, A. (1948) A portrait of a hipster, *Partisan Review*, 15(6): 727.

Brunner, T. (1977) Marijuana in Ancient Greece and Rome? The literary evidence, *Journal of Psychedelic Drugs*, 9 (3): 221–5.

Bukstein, O. G. (1995) *Adolescent Substance Abuse: Assessment, Prevention and Treatment*. New York: Wiley.

Bullington, B. and Block, A. (1990) A Trojan horse: anti-communism and the war on drugs, *Contemporary Crises*, 14: 46–56.

Bulmer, M. (1984) *The Chicago School of Sociology*. Chicago: University of Chicago Press.

Burchill, J. and Parsons, T. (1978) *The Boy Looked At Johnny*. London: Pluto.

Burgess, E. (1923) The study of the delinquent as a person, *American Journal of Sociology*, 28, 657–80.

Burt, C. (1925) *The Young Delinquent*. London: University of London Press.

Bussmann, J. (1998) *Once in a Lifetime*. London: Virgin Books.

Campbell, B. and Brenner, A. (eds) (2000) *Death Squads in Global Perspective: Murder with Deniability*. New York: Palgrave.

Campbell, R. (1977) *The Luciano Project: The Secret Wartime Collaboration between the Mafia and the US Navy*. New York: McGraw-Hill.

Carlson, E. T. (1974) Cannabis indica in nineteenth century psychiatry, *American Journal of Psychiatry*, 131: 1004–7.

Carr, I. (1982) *Miles Davis: A Biography*. New York: Morrow.

Carroll, N. (1998) *Interpreting the Moving Image*. Cambridge: Cambridge University Press.

Carson, W. G. and Wiles, P. (eds) (1971) *Crime and Delinquency in Britain*. London, Martin Robertson.

Channel 4 (1995) *Pot Night Booklet*. London: Channel 4 Publications.

Chapman, C. (1998) Reaching out to young people: informal settings and drugs, in L. O'Connor, D. O'Connor and R. Best (eds) *Drugs: Partnership for Policy, Prevention and Education*. London: Cassell.

Chatterton, P. and Holland, R. (2003) *Urban Nightscapes*. London: Routledge.

Chien, A., Connors, M. and Fox, K. (2000) The drug war in perspective, in J. Kim, J. Millen, A. Irwin and J. Gershman (eds) *Dying For Growth*. Maine: Common Courage.

Chomsky, N. (1994) *World Orders, Old and New*. New York: Columbia University Press.

Chopra, R. N. (1940) Use of hemp drugs in India, *Indian Medical Gazette*, 75(6): 356–67.

Chopra, R. N. and Chopra, G. S. (1939) The present position of hemp drug addiction, *Indian Medical Research Memorial*, 31: 1–119.

Cieslik, M. (2001) Researching youth cultures: some problems with the cultural turn in British youth studies, *Scottish Youth Issues Journal*, 2: 27–48.

Clarke, D. (ed.) (1998) *Penguin Encyclopaedia of Popular Music*. London: Penguin.

Clarke, G. (1982) *Defending Ski-Jumpers: A Critique of Theories of Youth Subcultures*.

Birmingham: stencilled paper, Centre for Contemporary Cultural Studies, University of Birmingham.

Clayson, A. (1997) *Death Disc*. London: Sanctuary.

Clayton, R. R., Catterello, A. and Johnstone, B. M. (1996) The effectiveness of drug abuse resistance education (project DARE) 5-year follow-up results, *Prevention Medicine*, 25: 307–18.

Cloonan, M. (1996) *Banned – Censorship of Popular Music in Britain: 1967–92*. Aldershot: Arena.

Cloward, R. and Ohlin, E. (1960) *Delinquency and Opportunity*. New York: Free Press.

Cockburn, L. (1989) *Out of Control: The Story of the Reagan Administration's Secret War in central America and the Contra-Drug Connection*. New York: Atlantic Monthly Press.

Cockburn, A. and St. Clair, J. (1998) *Whiteout: The CIA, Drugs and the Press*. London: Verso.

Cockcroft, C. (2001) Hemp hits its stride, *The Guardian*, 10 May.

Coffield, F. and Gofton, L. (1994) *Drugs and Young People*. London: Institute for Public Policy Research.

Coggans, N. and McKeller, S. (1994) Drug use amongst peers: peer pressure or peer preference, *Drugs: Education, Prevention and Policy*, 1(1): 15–26.

Coggans, N. and Watson, J. (1995) Drug education: approaches, effectiveness and delivery, *Drugs: Education, Prevention and Policy*, 2(3): 211–24.

Coggans, N., Sherwan, D., Henderson, M. and Davies, J. B. (1991) The impact of school-based drug education, *British Journal of Addiction*, 86: 1099–109.

Coggans, N., Haw, S. and Watson, J. (1999) Education and drug misuse: school interventions, in C. Stark, B. Kidd and R. Sykes (eds) *Illegal Drug Use in the United Kingdom*. Aldershot: Ashgate.

Coggans, N., Cheyne, B. and McKellar, S. (2002) *The Life Skills Training Drug Education Programme: A Review of Research*. Edinburgh: Effective Interventions Unit.

Cohen, A. (1956) *Delinquent Boys – The Subculture of the Gang*. London: Collier-Macmillan.

Cohen, J. (1996) Drugs education: politics, propaganda and censorship, *International Journal of Drug Policy*, 7(3): 153–7.

Cohen, P. (1972) Subcultural conflict and working class community, in *Working Papers in Cultural Studies*, CCCS, University of Birmingham, spring: 5–51.

Cohen, P. (1997) *Rethinking the Youth Question*. London: Macmillan.

Cohen, S. (1980) *Moral Panics and Folk Devils*. Oxford: Martin Robertson.

Coleridge (1808) in M. Lefebure (1974: 59) *Samuel Taylor Coleridge: A Bondage of Opium*. London: Victor Gollancz.

Colley, I. (2000) *Easy Rider*. London: York Press.

Collin, M. with Godfrey, J. (1997) *Altered States: The Story of Ecstasy Culture and Acid House*. London: Serpent's Tail.

Cope, J. (1999) *Repossessed and Head-On*. London: HarperCollins.

Courtwright, D. (1995) The rise and fall and rise of cocaine in the United States, in J. Goodman, P. Lovejoy and A. Sherratt (eds) *Consuming Habits*. London: Routledge.

Curry, A. (1968) Drugs in jazz and rock music, *Clinical Toxicology*, 1: 235–44.

Cutler, C. (1985) *File Under Popular*. London: November Books.

Dally, A. (1995) Anomalies and mysteries in the 'war on drugs', in R. Porter and M. Teich (eds) *Drugs and Narcotics in History*. Cambridge: Cambridge University Press.

Dannen, F. (1990) *Hit Men*. London: Muller.

Davies, J. B. (1996) Conversations with drug users: a functional discourse model, *Addiction Research*, 5(1): 1–18.

Davies, J. B. and Coggans, N. (1994) Media and school based approaches to drug education, in J. Strang and M. Gossip (eds) *Responding to Drug Misuse: The British System*. Oxford: Oxford University Press

Davies, L. (1984) *Pupil Power: Deviance and Gender in School*. Lewes: Falmer Press.

Davis, G. and Dawson, N. (1996) *Using Diversion to Communicate Drugs Prevention Messages to Young People*. London: Home Office, Drugs Prevention Initiative Paper 12.

Davis, M. (1989) *The Autobiography*. London: Picador.

De Grazia, E. and Newman, R. (1982) *Banned Films: Movies, Censors and the First Amendment*. New York: R. R. Bowker.

De Haes, W. and Schuurman, J. (1975) Results of an evaluation study on three drug education models, *International Journal of Health Education*, 18, supplement.

De Kort, M. (1994) The Dutch cannabis debate 1968–76, *Journal of Drug Issues*, 24: 417–27.

Decker, J. (1994) The state of rap, in A. Ross and T. Rose (eds) *Microphone Fiends*. Routledge: New York.

Deleuze, G. (1998) *Essays Critical and Clinical*. London: Verso.

Deleuze, G. and Guattari, F. (1988) *A Thousands Plateaus: Capitalism and Schizophrenia*. London: Athlone Press.

De Quincey, T. (1821) Confessions of an opium eater, *London Magazine*.

Del Olmo, R. (1998) The ecological impact of illicit drug cultivation and crop eradication programs in Latin America, *Theoretical Criminology*, 2(2): 269–78.

Denman, S., Moon, A., Parsons, C. and Stears, D. (2002) *The Health Promoting School*. London: Routledge.

DFE Circular 4/95 (1995) *Drug Prevention and Schools*. London: HMSO.

Derrida, J. (1993) The rhetoric of drugs: an interview, *Differences*, 5(1): 1–25.

Derogatis, J. (1996) *Kaleidoscope Eyes*. London: Fourth Estate.

Diamond, S. (1992) Compromised Campus: the collaboration of Universities with the intelligence community, 1945–1955. New York: Oxford University Press.

Dobkin de Rios, M. (1984) *Hallucinogens: A Cross-Cultural Perspective*. Albuquerque: University of New Mexico Press.

Dollard, J., Miller, N., Doob, L., Mowrer, D. and Sears, R. (1939) *Frustration and Aggression*. New Haven: Yale University Press.

Dorn, N. (1992) Six phases in drug prevention, in R. Evans and L. O'Connor (eds) *Drug Abuse and Misuse*. London: David Fulton.

Dorn, N. and Jamieson, A. (2001) *European Drug Laws: The Room for Manoeuvre*. London: ISDD.

Dorn, N. and Murji, K. (1992) *Drug Prevention: A Review of the English Language Literature*. London, ISDD Research Monograph 5.

Douglas, J. D. (ed.) (1971) *Understanding Everyday Life*. London: Routledge.

Downes, D. (1966) *The Delinquent Solution*. London: Routledge and Kegan Paul.

Downes, D. (1977) The drug addict as folk devil, in P. Rock (ed.) *Drugs and Politics*. New Jersey: Transaction Books.

Downes, D. and Rock, P. (1982) *Understanding Deviance*. Oxford: Clarendon Press.

Duke, S. B. and Gross, A. C. (1993) *America's Longest Running War: Rethinking Our Tragic Crusade Against Drugs*. New York: G. P. Putnam's Sons.

Durkheim, E. (1895/1966) *The Rules of Sociological Method*. London: Collier-Macmillan.

Du Toit, B. (1980) *Cannabis in Africa*. Rotterdam: A. A. Balkema.

Durlacher, J. (2000) *Agenda Heroin*. London: Carlton.

Eagleton, T. (1995) Where do postmodernists come from? *Month Review*, July–August: 59–70.

Eagleton, T. (2000) *The Idea of Culture*. Oxford: Blackwell.

Easthope, A. (1993) *Contemporary Film Theory*. London: Longman.

Eliade, M. (1951) *Shamanism: Archaic Techniques of Ecstasy*. Princeton: Princeton University Press.

Ellickson, P. L., Bell, R. M. and Harrison, E. R. (1993) Changing adolescent propensities to use drugs: results from Project ALERT, *Health Education Quarterly*, 20(2): 227–42.

Emmett, D. and Nice, G. (1998) *Understanding Drugs: A Handbook for Parents, Teachers and Other Professionals*. London: Jessica Kingsley.

Epstein, E. J. (1990) *Agency of Fear*. London: Verso.

Ettorre, E. (1992) *Women and Substance Use*. London: Macmillan.

Evans, K. (2001) Right or wrong: confusing drug education with drug treatment, *Drug Education Matters*, 11: 1–2.

Faithfull, M. (1995) *Faithfull*. London: Penguin.

Fanon, F. (1959/1965) *Studies in a Dying Colonialism*. London: Earthscan.

Felsenburg, B. (2000) 'Kids' and 'another day in paradise', in J. Stevenson. (ed.) *Addicted*. UK: Creation.

Fergusson, T. (1952) *The Young Delinquent in his Social Setting*. Oxford: Oxford University Press.

Filmer, P. (1977) Literary study as liberal education and as sociology in the work of F. R. Leavis, in C. Jenks (ed.) *Rationality, Education and the Social Organisation of Knowledge*. London: Routledge.

Flood, S. (1845) On the power, nature and evil of popular medical superstition, *Lancet*, 2: 203.

Flynn, E. (1960) *My Wicked, Wicked Ways*. London: Heinemann.

Ford, C. S. (1942) Culture and human behaviour, *Scientific Monthly*, 44: 546–57.

Fossier, A. E. (1931) The marihuana menace, *New Orleans Medical and Surgical Journal*, 84(4): 247–52.

Foucault, M. (1975) *Discipline and Punish*. London: Penguin.

Foucault, M. (1984) *The Foucault Reader*. P. Rabinow (ed.). London: Penguin.

Fountain, J., Bashford, J., Winters, M. and Patel, K. (2003) *Black and Minority Ethnic Communities in England: A Review of the Literature on Drug Use and Related Service Provision*. London: National Treatment Agency for Substance Use and the Centre for Ethnicity and Health.

France, A. (2000) *Youth Researching Youth: Triumph and Success Peer Research Project*. Leicester: National Youth Agency and Joseph Rowntree Foundation.

Freud, S. (1913) The theme of the three caskets, in The Standard Edition of the *Complete Psychological Works of Sigmund Freud*. London: Hogarth Press.

Friedlander, K. (1947) *The Psycho-Analytical Approach to Juvenile Delinquency*. London: Routledge Kegan Paul.

Frith, S and Horne, H. (1987) *Art into Pop*. London: Methuen.

Fyvel, T. R. (1961) *The Insecure Offenders*. London: Chatto and Windus.

Garratt, S. (1998) *Adventures in Wonderland*. London: Headline.

Geddes, M. and Rust, M. (2000) Catching them young: local initiatives to involve young people in local government and local democracy, *Youth and Policy*, 69: 42–61.

George, B. (1995) *Take It Like A Man*. London: HarperCollins.

Giraldo, J. (1996) *The Genocidal Democracy: Colombia*. Maine: Common Courage.

Glatt, M., Pittman, D., Gillespie, D. and Hills, D. (1967) *The Drug Scene in Great Britain*. London: Arnold.

Goddard, C. (1932) *How Science Solves Crime III: Truth Serum*. New York: Hygeia.

Gordon, D. (1994) *The Return of the Dangerous Classes: Drug Prohibition and Policy Politics*. New York: Norton.

Gordon, M. (1947) The concept of subculture and its application, *Social Forces*, October: 40–2.

Gordon, T. (1989) *Journey into Madness: The True Story of Secret CIA Mind Control and Medical Abuse*. New York: Bantam.

Gorman, D. M. (1998) The irrelevance of evidence in the development of school-based drug prevention policy 1986–96, *Evaluation Review*, 22: 118–46.

Grady, D. (1993) From reefer madness to Freddy's dead: the portrayal of marijuana use in motion pictures, in P. Loukides and L. Fuller. (eds) *Beyond the Stars III: The Material World in American Popular Film*. Bowling Green: Bowling Green University Press.

Graham, G. (1991) Criminalization and control, in D. K. Whynes and P. Bean (eds) *Policing and Prescribing: The British System of Drug Control*. London: Macmillan.

Gramsci, A. (1971) *Selections from the Prison Notebooks*. London: Lawrence and Wishart.

Graves, R. (1961) The poet's paradise, in R. Graves, *Oxford Addresses*. London: Cassell.

Grazia, E. and Newman, R. (1982) *Banned Films: Movies, Censors and the First Amendment*. New York: R. R. Bowker.

Gray, M. (ed.) (2002) *Busted: Stone Cowboys, Narco-Lords and Washington's War on Drugs*. New York: Thunder's Mouth.

Green, P. (1998) *Drugs, Trafficking and Criminal Policy*. Winchester: Waterside Press.

Griffin, C. (1993) *Representations of Youth*. Cambridge: Polity Press.

Hall, S. (1980a) Cultural studies and the centre: some problematics and problems, in S. Hall, P. Hobson, A. Lowe and P. Willis (eds) *Culture, Media and Language*. London: Hutchinson.

Hall, S. (1980b) Encoding/decoding, in S. Hall, P. Hobson, A. Lowe and P. Willis (eds) *Culture, Media and Language*. London: Hutchinson.

Hall, S. and Jefferson, T. (eds) (1975) *Resistance Through Rituals*, London: Hutchinson.

Hammersley, M. (1985) From ethnography to theory; a programme and a paradigm in the sociology of education, *Sociology*, 19(2): 244–59.

Hammersley, R., Khan, F. and Ditton, J. (2002) *Ecstasy*. London: Routledge.

Harding, G. (1998) Pathologizing the soul: the construction of a 19th century analysis of opiate addiction, in R. Coomber (ed.) *The Control of Drugs and Drug Users*. Amsterdam: Harwood.

Hargreaves, D. H. (1967) *Social Relations in a Secondary School*. London: Routledge and Kegan Paul.

Harrison, M. (1998) *High Society: Real Voices of Club Culture*. London: Piatkus.

Hartnoll, W. (1998) Informal social controls and the liberalization of drug laws and policies, in R. Coomber (ed.) *The Control of Drugs and Drug Users*. Amsterdam: Harwood.

Hastings, G. and Stead, M. (1999) *Using the Media in Drugs Prevention*. London: Home Office, Drugs Prevention Initiative Paper 19.

Hawthorne, G., Garrard, J. and Dunt, D. (1995) Does life education's drug education programme have a public health benefit, *Addiction*, 90: 205–15.

Hayter, A. (1988) *Opium and the Romantic Imagination*. Wellingborough: Crucible.

Health Advisory Service (2001) *The Substance of Young Needs*. London: Home Office.

Hebdige, D. (1979) *Subculture: The Meaning of Style*. London: Methuen.

Hebdige, D. (1987) *Cut 'n' Mix: Culture, Identity and Caribbean Music*. London: Comedia.

Helmer, J. (1975) *Drugs and Minority Oppression*. New York: Seabury Press.

Hemmelstein, J. L. (1983) *The Strange Career of Marijuana: Politics and Ideology of Drug Control in America*. Westport, CA: Greenwood.

Henderson, S. (1997) *Ecstasy: Case Unsolved*. London: HarperCollins.

Henderson, S. (1999) Drugs and culture: the question of gender, in N. South (ed.) *Drugs: Cultures, Controls and Everyday Life*. London: Sage.

Herman, E. (1987) US Sponsorship of international terrorism: an overview, *Crime and Social Justice*, 27–28: 1–31.

Hetherington, K. (2000) *New Age Travellers*. London: Cassell.

Himmelstein, J. L. (1978) Drug politics theory: analysis and critique, *Journal of Drug Issues*, 8: 37–52.

HM Government (1994) *Tackling Drugs Together*. London: HMSO.

HM Government (1998) *Tackling Drugs Together to Build a Better Britain*. London: HMSO.

Hofmann, A., Wasson, G. and Ruck, C. (1978) *The Road to Eleusis: Unveiling the Secret Mysteries*. New York: Harcourt Brace.

Hollands, R. (2002) Divisions in the dark: youth cultures, transitions and segmented consumption spaces in the night-time economy, *Journal of Youth Studies*, 5(2): 153–72.

Holloway, S. W. F. (1995) The regulation of the supply of drugs in Britain before 1868, in R. Porter and M. Teich (eds) *Drugs and Narcotics in History*. Cambridge: Cambridge University Press.

Homer (1980) *The Odyssey*. Oxford: Oxford University Press.

Hore, C. (1993) Jazz – a people's music?, *International Socialism*, 61: 91–108.

Horley, N. (1999) They're brazen, and coming to a town near you, *New Statesman*, 15 November: 32–3.

Horsley, S. (1943) *Narcoanalysis*. Oxford: Oxford University Press.

Hoskyns, B. (1996) *Waiting for the Sun*. New York: St. Martin's Press.

Hourani, A. (1991) *A History of the Arab Peoples*. London: Faber and Faber.

House of Lords Select Committee on Science and Technology (1998) *Cannabis: The Scientific and Medical Evidence*. London: HMSO.

House of Lords Select Committee on Science and Technology (2001) *Cannabis: The Scientific and Medical Evidence: Second Report*. London: HMSO.

House, R. E. (1925) Scopolamine-apomorphia amnesia in criminology, *Current Research in Anaesthesia*, 4: 162–9.

House, R. E. (1931) The use of scopolamine in criminology, *American Journal of Policy Science*, 2: 328–36.

Huggins, M. (1987) US – supported state terror: a history of police training in Latin America, *Crime and Social Justice*, 27–28: 149–71.

Huggins, M. (1998) *Political Policing: The US and Latin America*. Durham: Duke Press.

Huggins, M. (2000) Modernity and devolution: the making of police death squads in modern Brazil, in A. Brenner and B. Campbell (eds) *Death Squads in Global Perspective: Murder with Deniability*. New York: St. Martin's Press.

Humphreys, H. (2001) The real picture, *The Guardian*, 10 May.

Humphries, S. (1981) *Hooligans or Rebels?* Oxford: Blackwell.

Hunt, L. (1991) *Secret Agenda: The United States Government, Nazi Scientists and Project Paperclip 1945–90*. New York: St. Martin's Press.

Huntingdon, S. (1999) The lonely superpower, *Foreign Affairs*, 78 (2): 38–50.

Hurry, J. and Lloyd, C. (1997) *A Follow-up Evaluation of Project Charlie: A Life Skills Drug Education Programme for Primary Schools*. London: Home Office, Drugs Prevention Initiative Paper 16.

Hutnyk, J. (2000) *Critique of Exotica*. London: Pluto.

Huxley, A. (1954) *The Doors of Perception*. London: Chatto and Windus.

Ignatieff, M. (2001) Who Killed Franked Olsen, *The Guardian* April 7.

Inglis, F. (1975) *The Forbidden Game: A Social History of Drugs*. London: Hodder and Stoughton.

Irwin, D. (1999) The straight edge subculture: examining the youths' drug-free way, *Journal of Drug Issues*, 29(2): 365–80.

Ives, R. (1997) Review of understanding drugs, *Druglink*, March/April: 18.

Jackson, P. (2004) *Inside Clubbing*. Oxford: Berg.

Jackson, T. (2001) Cannabis the wonder drug? *British Medical Journal*, 323: 1136.

James, M. (1997) *State of Bass*. London: Boxtree.

Jameson, F. (2000) Globalization and political strategy, *New Left Review*, 4: 49–68.

Jaworzyn, S. (1996) *Shock*. London: Titan Books.

Jay, M. (2000) *Emperors of Dreams*. Cambridge: Dedalus.

Jephcott, P. (1954) *Some Young People*. London: Allen and Unwin.

Jessop, B. (1985) *Nicos Poultantzas: Marxist Theory and Political Strategy*. Basingstoke: Macmillan.

Jobling, P. and Crowley, D. (1995) *Graphic Design*. Manchester: Manchester University Press.

Johns, C. (1992) *Power, Ideology and the War on Drugs*. New York: Praeger.

Johnson, B. (1975) Righteousness before revenue: the forgotten moral crusade against the Indo-Chinese opium trade, *Journal of Drug Issues*, fall: 304–26.

Johnson, D. (1952) *Indian Hemp: A Social Menace*. London: Christopher Johnson.

Johnson, D. (1953) *The Hallucinogenic Drugs*. London: Christopher Johnson.

Johnson, R. (1976) Notes on the schooling of the English working class, 1780–1850, in R. Dale, G. Esland and M. MacDonald (eds) *Schooling and Capitalism*. London: Routledge.

Jones, T. (1800) English opium, *Transactions of the Society of Arts*, 18: 161–94.

Joyce, E. (1998) New drugs, new responses: lessons from Europe, *Current History*, 97(618): 183–8.

Keizer, B. (2001) The Netherlands' experiences with drug policy: practice, science and politics. Paper presented to the Joseph Rowntree Drugs Conference, Royal Society, London, January.

Kennedy, M. (1998) *The Hamlyn History of Archaeology*. London: Hamlyn.

Kent, N. (1994) *The Dark Stuff*. London: Penguin.

Kerr, M. (1958) *The People of Ship Street*. London: Routledge and Kegan Paul.

Kiger, A. (1995) *Teaching for Health*. Edinburgh: Churchill Livingstone.

Kinder, B. N., Pope, N. E. and Wallfish, S. (1980) Drug and alcohol education programmes: a review of outcome studies, *International Journal of Addiction*, 15: 1035–54.

Kinder, D. C. (1981) Bureaucratic cold war warrior: Harry J. Anslinger and illicit narcotics traffic, *Pacific Historical Review*, 50: 169–91.

Kinder, D. C. (1991) Shutting out the evil: nativism and narcotics control in the US, *Journal of Policy History*, 3(4): 472–3.

Kinder, D. C. and Walker O, III (1986) Stable force in a storm: Harry J. Anslinger and United States narcotic foreign policy, 1930–62, *Journal of American History*, 72(4): 908–27.

King, R. (1972) *The Drug Hang-Up*. New York: Norton.

Klee, H. and Reid, P. (1995) *Amphetamine Misusing Groups*. London: Home Office. Drug Prevention Initiative Paper no. 3.

Klein, M. (1965) *Samples From English Culture*. London: Routledge and Kegan Paul.

Klein, N. (2000) *No Logo*. London: Flamingo.

Knoester, M. (1998) War in Columbia, *Social Justice*, 25(2): 85–109.

Kohn, M. (1992) *Dope Girls: The Birth of the British Drug Underground*. London: Lawrence and Wishart.

Kohn, M. (1997) The chemical generation and its ancestors: dance crazies and drug panics across eight decades, *Journal of Drug Policy*, 8: 137–42.

Kristeva, J. (1982) *Powers of Horror: An Essay on Abjection*. New York: Columbia Press.

Kruger, H. (1980) *The Great Heroin Coup: Drugs, Intelligence and International Fascism*. Boston: South End Press.

Kureishi, H. and Savage, J. (eds) (1995) *Faber Book of Pop*. London: Faber and Faber.

Lacey, C. (1966) Some sociological concomitants of academic streaming in a grammar school, *British Journal of Sociology*, 17(3): 245–62.

Lacey, C. (1970) *Hightown Grammar*. Manchester: Manchester University Press.

La Guardia Report (1945) *The Marijuana Problem in the City of New York*. Catrell Press: Lancaster.

Larkin, C. (1998) *Dance Music*. London: Virgin Books.

Leary, T. (1970) *The Politics of Ecstasy*. London: MacGibbon and Kee.

Lee, A. M. (1945) Levels of culture as levels of social generation, *American Sociological Review*, August.

Lee, M. and Shlain, B. (1992) *Acid Dreams*. New York: Grove Press.

Leitner, M., Shapland, J. and Wiles, P. (1993) *Drug Usage and Drug Prevention: The Views of the General Public*. London: HMSO.

Lenson, D. (1995) *On Drugs*. Minneapolis: University of Minnesota Press.

Leonard, I. A. (1620/1942) Peyote and the Mexican Inquisition, *American Anthropologist*, 44(2): 324–6.

Levinthal, C. (1985) Milk of paradise, the history of ideas about opium, *Perspectives in Biology and Medicine*, 28(4): 561–77.

Levi-Strauss, C. (1958) *Structural Authropology*. London: Allen Lane.

Lévi-Strauss, C. (1966) *The Savage Mind*. London: Weidenfield and Nicholson.

Lewin, L. (1964) *Phantastica: Narcotics and Stimulating Drugs, their Use and Abuse*. London: Kegan Paul.

Li, L. H. (1974a) The origin and use of cannabis in eastern Asia linguistic-cultural implications, *Economic Botany*, 28: 293–301.

Li, L. H. (1974b) Archaeological and historical account of cannabis in China, *Economic Botany*, 28: 437–48.

Lindesmith, A. R. (1938) A sociological theory of drug addiction, *American Journal of Sociology*, 11(3): 593–609.

Lindesmith, A. R. (1940) Dope fiend mythology, *Journal of Criminal Law and Criminology*, 31: 199–208.

Linken, A. (1963) Young drug takers, *Sunday Times*, 27 January.

Linklater, M., Hinton, I. and Ascherson, N. (1984) *The Nazi Legacy: Klaus Barbie and the Rise of International Fascism*. New York: Holt, Rinehart and Winston.

Lipsitz, G. (1994) *Dangerous Crossroads*. London: Verso.

Lloyd, C. (1998) Risk factors for problem drug users: identifying vulnerable groups, *Drugs: Education, Prevention and Policy*, 5(3): 217–32.

Lloyd, C., Joyce, R., Hurry, J. and Ashton, M. (2000) The effectiveness of primary school drug education, *Drugs: Education, Prevention and Policy*, 7(2): 109–26.

Lombroso, C. and Ferri, E. (1901) *Criminal Sociology*. Boston: Little Brown.

Lusane, C. (1991) *Pipe Dream Blues: Racism and the War on Drugs*. Boston: South End Press.

McAllister, W. (2000) *Drug Diplomacy in the Twentieth Century*. London: Routledge.

Macan, E. (1997) *Rocking the Classics*. New York: Oxford University Press.

MacCoun, R. and Reuter, P. (2001) *Drug War Heresies*. Cambridge: Cambridge University Press.

McCoy, A. (1991) *The Politics of Heroin: CIA Complicity in the Global Drug Trade*. New York: Lawrence Hill.

McCulloch, K. (2000) Young citizens, *Youth and Policy*, 68: 34–45.

MacDonald, D. and Mansfield, D. (2001) Drugs and Afganistan, *Drugs: Education, Prevention and Policy*, 8(1): 1–6.

MacDonald, R., Mason, P., Shildrick, T., Webster, C., Johnston, L. and Ridley, L. (2001) Snakes and ladders: in defence of studies of transition, *Sociological Research On-line*, 5: 4.

MacDonald, R. and Marsh, J. (2002) Crossing the Rubicon: youth transitions, poverty, drugs and social exclusion, *International Journal of Drug Policy*, 13: 27–38.

MacGregor, S. (1998) Reluctant partners: trends in approaches to urban drug-taking in contemporary Britain, *Journal of Drug Issues*, 28(1): 185–98.

Macherey, P. (1978) *A Theory of Literary Production*. London: Routledge.

Macherey, P. (1995) *The Object of Literature*. Cambridge: Cambridge University Press.

Mack, A. and Joy, J. (2001) *Marijuana as Medicine*. Washington: National Academy Press.

McKay, G. (ed.) (1998) *DiY Culture: Party and Protest in Nineties Britain*. London: Verso.

McRobbie, A. and Garber, J. (1975) Girls and subculture, in *Working Papers in Cultural Studies*, 7/8, Centre for Contemporary Studies, University of Birmingham: 208–22.

McWilliams, J. C. (1990) *The Protectors: Harry J. Anslinger and the Federal Bureau of Narcotics (FBN) 1930–62*. Newark: University of Delaware Press.

McWilliams, J. C. (1991) Through the past darkly: the politics and policies of America's drug war, *Journal of Policy History*, 3(4): 356–92.

Maffesoli, M. (1996) *The Time of the Tribes*. London: Sage.

Makarenko, T. (2000) Terrorism and drug trafficking threaten stability in Central Asia. *Jane's Intelligence Review*, November: 28–30.

Makkai, T., Moore, R. and McAllister, I. (1991) Health education campaigns and drug use: the drug offensive in Australia, *Health Education Research*, 6(1): 65–76.

Malbon, B. (1998) Clubbing: consumption, identity and the spatial practice of every-night life, in T. Skelton and G. Valentine (eds) *Cool Places: Geographies of Youth Culture*. London: Routledge.

Malbon, B. (1999) *Clubbing: Dancing, Ecstasy and Vitality*. London: Routledge.

Mann, M. (1999) *The Gringo Trail*. Chichester: Summersdale.

Mannheim, H. (1965) *Comparative Criminology, Vols. 1–2*. London: Routledge.

Marks, A. (2001) Schooling citizens: a doomed experiment? *Forum*, 43(3): 153–5.

Marks, H. (1997) *Mr. Nice*. London: Minerva.

Marks, J. (1979) *The Search for the Manchurian Candidate*. New York: Times Books.

Marlow, A. (1999) Joined-up thinking: youth and drugs policy at the millennium, in A. Marlow and G. Pearson (eds) *Young People, Drugs and Community Safety*. Lyme Regis: Russell House.

Marsh, D. (1983) *Before I Get Old: Story of The Who*. London: Plexus.

Marshall, J. (1991) *Drug Wars: Corruption, Counter-insurgency and Covert Operation in the Third World*. Forestville: Cohan and Cohen.

Marx, K. (1843/1975) Contribution to the critique of Hegel's Philosophy of Right, in L. Colletti (ed.) *Karl Marx: Early Writings*. London: Penguin.

Marx, K. (1887/1954) *Capital Vol. 1*. London: Lawrence and Wishart.

Matthee, R. (1995) Exotic substances, in R. Porter and M. Teich (eds) *Drugs and Narcotics in History*. Cambridge: Cambridge University Press.

Matthews, P. (1999) *Cannabis Culture*. London: Bloomsbury.

Maurer, D. (1938) The argot of the underworld narcotic addict: part 11, *American Speech*, 13: 179–92.

Mays, J. B. (1954) *Growing Up in the City*. Liverpool: Liverpool University Press.

Melechi, A. (1993) The ecstasy of disappearance, in S. Redhead (ed.) *Rave Off*. Aldershot: Avebury.

Melechi, A. (1997) Drugs of liberation, in A. Melechi (ed.) *Psychedelia Britannica*, London: Turnaround.

Melly, G. (1972) *Revolt into Style*. London: Penguin.

Melrose, M. (2000) *Fixing It*. Lyme Regis: Russell House.

Merlin, D. (1972) *Man and Marijuana*. New Jersey: Associated University Press.

Merton, R. K. (1938) Social structure and anomie, *American Sociological Review*, 3: 672–82.

Merton, R. K. (1957) *Social Theory and Social Structure*. New York: Wiley.

Metcalfe, S. (1997) Ecstasy evangelists and psychedelic warriors, in A. Melechi (ed.) *Psychedelia Britannica*. London: Turnaround.

Mezzrow, M. (1946) *Really the Blues*. New York: Random House.

Middleton, R. and Muncie, J. (1981) Pop culture, pop music and post-war youth: countercultures. V203 *Popular Culture*, Block 5. Unit 20. Milton Keynes: Open University Press.

Midford, R. (2000) Does drug education work, *Drug and Alcohol Review*, 19: 441–6.

Miles, S. (1995) Towards an understanding of the relationship between youth identities and consumer culture, *Youth and Policy*, 51: 35–45.

Miles, S. (1998) *Consumerism*. London: Sage.

Miles, S. (2000) *Youth Lifestyles in a Changing World*. Buckingham: Open University Press.

Mill, J. S. (1859/1974) *On Liberty*. London: Penguin.

Mill, J. S. (1990) *Writings on India*. J. Robson, M. Moir and Z. Moir (eds). London: Routledge.

Miller, F. (1994) *Censored Hollywood*. Atlanta: Turner.

Miller, P. and Plant, M. (1996) Drinking, smoking and illicit drug use among 15 and 16 year-olds in the United Kingdom, *British Medical Journal*, 313: 394–7.

Mitchell, J. (1975) *Feminism and Psychoanalysis*. London: Penguin.

Mokhiber, R. and Weissman, R. (1999) *The Hunt for Mega-Profits and the Attack on Democracy*. Maine: Common Courage.

Monbiot, G. (2001a) Backyard terrorism, *The Guardian*, 30 October.

Monbiot, G. (2001b) Tinkering with poverty, *The Guardian*, 20 November.

Moore, A. and Gibbons, D. (1986) *Watchmen*. New York: DC Comics.

Morais, R. (1996) Just say maybe, *Forbes Magazine*, 17 June: 114–16, 118–20.

Morley, D. (1995) Theories of consumption in media studies, in D. Miller (ed.) *Acknowledging Consumption*. London: Routledge.

Morris, T. (1957) *The Criminal Area*. London: Routledge and Kegan Paul.

Muggleton, D. (1997) The post-subculturalists, in S. Redhead (ed.) *The Club Culture Reader*. Oxford: Blackwell.

Muggleton, D. (2000) *Inside Subcultures: The Postmodern Meaning of Style*. London: Berg.

Muggleton, D. and Weinzierl, R. (eds) (2003) *Post-Subculturalist Reader*. London: Berg.

Murji, K. (1999) White lines: culture, 'race' and drugs, in N. South (ed.) *Drugs: Cultures, Controls and Everyday Life*. London: Sage.

Musto, D. (1973) *The American Disease: Origins of Narcotic Policy*. New Haven: Yale University Press.

Musto, D. and Korsmeyer, P. (2002) *The Quest for Drug Control: Politics and Federal Policy in a Period of Increasing Substance Abuse 1963–81*. New Haven: Yale University Press.

Napier-Bell, S. (2002) *Black Vinyl, White Powder*. London: Ebury.

Natarajan. M. and Hough, M. (eds) (2000) *Illegal Drug Markets: From Research to Prevention Policy*. Crime Prevention Studies Vol. 11. New York: Criminal Justice Press.

Nava, M., Blake, A., MacRury, I. and Richards, B. (eds) (1997) *Buy This Book*. London: Routledge.

Naylor, R. T. (1994) *Hot Money and the Politics of Debt*. New York: Simon and Schuster.

Newsinger, J. (2002) Elgin in China, *New Left Review*, 15: 119–40.

Nuttall, J. (1968) *Bomb Culture*. London: Paladin.

Nutton, V. (1985) The drug trade in antiquity, *Journal of the Royal Society of Medicine*, 78: 138–45.

O'Connor, J. and Saunders, B. (1992) Drug education: an appraisal of a popular preventive, *International Journal of the Addictions*, 27(2): 165–85.

O'Connor, L., O'Connor, D. and Best, R. (eds) (1998) *Drugs: Partnership for Policy, Prevention and Education*. London: Cassell.

O'Sullivan, T., Dutton, B. and Rayner, P. (1998) *Studying the Media*. New York: Arnold.

Ofsted (1997) *Drug Education in Schools*. London: HMSO.

Ofsted (2000) *Follow up: Drug Education in Schools*. London: HMSO.

Ogg, A. with Upshal, D. (1999) *The Hip Hop Years*. London: Channel 4 Books.

Olmsted, K. (1996) *Challenging the Secret Government: The Post-Watergate Investigation of the CIA and the FBI*. Chapel Hill: University of Carolina Press.

Owen, D. E. (1934) *British Opium Policy in China and India*. New Haven: Yale University Press.

Owen, T. (1999) *High Art: A History of the Psychedelic Poster*. London: Sanctuary.

Paddison, M. (1996) *Adorno, Modernism, and Mass Culture: Essays on Critical Theory and Music*. London: Kahn and Averill.

Palmer, V. (1926) Field studies for introductory sociology: an experiment, *Journal of Applied Sociology*, 10: 341–8.

Palmer, V. (1928) *Field Studies in Sociology: A Student's Manual*. Chicago: University of Chicago Press.

Pam, M. (1992) *Going East*. Marval: Paris.

Panitch, L. (2000) The new imperial state, *New Left Review*, 2: 5–20.

Parker, H. (2001) Unbelievable? The UK's drugs present, in H. Parker, J. Aldridge and R. Egginton (eds) *UK Drugs Unlimited: New Research and Policy Lessons on Illicit Drugs*. Basingstoke: Palgrave.

Parker, H., Aldridge, J. and Measham, F. (1995) *Drugs Futures: Changing Patterns of Drug Use Amongst English Youth*. London: ISDD.

Parker, H., Aldridge, J. and Measham, F. (1998) *Illegal Leisure: The Normalisation of Adolescent Drug Use*. London: Routledge.

Parker, H., Aldridge, J. and Egginton, R. (eds) (2001) *UK Drugs Unlimited: New Research and Policy Lessons on Illicit Drugs*. Basingstoke: Palgrave.

Parker, H., Williams, L. and Aldridge, J. (2002) The normalization of 'sensible' recreational drug use, *Sociology* 36(4): 941–64.

Parkin, S. and McKeganey, N. (2000) The rise and rise of peer education approaches, *Drugs: Education, Prevention and Policy*, 7(3): 293–310.

Parssinen, T. (1983) *Secret Passions, Secret Remedies: Narcotic Drugs in British Society 1820–1930*. Manchester: Manchester University Press.

Payne, J. (1900) *Thomas Sydenham*. London: Fisher Unwin.

Pearce, J. (1999) Selling sex, doing drugs and keeping safe, in A. Marlow and G. Pearson (eds) *Young People, Drugs and Community Safety*. Lyme Regis: Russell House.

Pearson, G. (1991) Drug-controls in Britain, in M. Tonry (ed.) *Crime and Justice: A Review of Research*, Vol. 14. Chicago: University of Chicago Press.

Peretti, B. (1994) *The Creation of Jazz*. Chicago: University of Illinois Press.

Pike, J. (1993) *The Death of Rock 'n' Roll*. London: Faber and Faber.

Pini, M. (2001) *Club Culture and Female Sexuality*. London: Palgrave.

Plant, M. (1975) *Drugtakers in an English Town*. London: Tavistock.

Plant, M. (1987) *Drugs in Perspective*. London: Tavistock.

Plant, M. (1994) Drugs and adolescence, in J. Strang and M. Gossop (eds) *Heroin Addiction and Drug Policy: The British System*. Oxford: Oxford University Press.

Plant, E. and Plant, M. (1999) Primary prevention for young children: a comment on the UK government's 10 year drug strategy, *International Journal of Drug Policy*, 10: 385–401.

Pokorny, A. (1970) The hallucinogens in anthropology, pre-history, and the history of the plastic arts. Paper presented to at the Seventh Congress of the Collegium Internationale, Neuro-Psychopharma-Collegium, Prague.

Polan, D. (2000) *Pulp Fiction*. London: BFI.

Polo, M. (1958) *The Travels*. London: Penguin.

Polsky, N. (1961) The village beat scene: summer 1960, *Dissent*, 8(3): 339–59.

Polsky, N. (1967) *Hustlers, Beats and Others*. London: Penguin.

Porteous, D. (1999) Casing the joint: an evaluation of two drugs education projects, in A. Marlow and G. Pearson (eds) *Young People, Drugs and Community Safety*. Lyme Regis: Russell House.

Poschardt, U. (1998) *DJ Culture*. London: Quartet.

Poulantzas, N. (1974) *Fascism and Dictatorship*. London: New Left Books.

Poulantzas, N. (1975) *Classes in Contemporary Capitalism*. London: Verso.

Power, R. (1998) Contemporary issues concerning illicit drug use in the British Isles, *Journal of Drug Issues*, 28(1): 1–8.

Proctor, R. (1988) *Racial Hygiene: Medicine under the Nazis*, Cambridge: Harvard University Press.

Pullar-Strecker, H. (1952) Foreword, in D. Johnson *Indian Hemp: A Social Menace*. London: Christopher Johnson.

Purchas, S. (1626) *Purchas His Pilgrimage*. London: Henry Fetherstone.

Push and Silcott, M. (2000) *The Book of E*. London: Omnibus Press.

Randall, R. (1968) *Censorship of the Movies*. Madison: University of Wisconsin Press.

Redhead, S. (1990) *The End of the Century Party: Youth and Pop Towards 2000*. Manchester: University of Manchester Press.

Redhead, S. (ed.) (1993) *Rave Off: Politics and Deviance in Contemporary Youth Culture*. Aldershot: Avebury Press.

Redhead, S. (1995) *Unpopular Cultures*. Manchester: Manchester University Press.

Redhead, S. (ed.) (1997) *The Club Culture Reader*. Oxford: Blackwell.

Reeves, J. and Campbell, R. (1994) *Cracked Coverage: Television News, the Anti-cocaine Crusade and the Reagan Legacy*. Durham: Duke University Press.

Reinarman, C. (1998) Morele idelogies VS haaka op drugsbeleid Nederland, *Het Parool*, 30 July: 8.

Reynolds, S. (1998) *Energy Flash*. London: Picador.

Rietveld, H. (1993) Living the dream, in S. Redhead (ed.) *Rave Off: Politics and Deviance in Contemporary Youth Culture*. Aldershot: Avebury Press.

Rietveld, H. (1998a) *This is Our House*. Aldershot: Ashgate.

Rietveld, H. (1998b) Repetitive beats, in G. McKay (ed.) *DiY Culture: Party and Protest in Nineties Britain*. London: Verso.

Ringwalt, C., Ennett, S. T. and Holt, K. D. (1991) An outcome evaluation of project DARE (Drug Abuse Resistance Education), *Health Education Research*, 6(3): 327–37.

Robbins, C. (1979) *Air America*. Putnam: New York.

Robson, P. (1994) *Forbidden Drugs*. Oxford: Oxford University Press.

Rock, P. (ed.) (1977) *Drugs and Politics*. New Jersey: Transaction Books.

Rock, P. (1973) *Deviant Behaviour*. London: Hutchinson.

Rolin, J. (1955) *Police Drugs*. London: Hollis and Carter.

Rose, T. (1994) *Black Noise: Rap Music and Black Culture in Contemporary America*. London: Wesleyan University Press.

Rosenbaum, D. P., Flewelling, R. L., Bailey, S. B., Rinkwalt, C. L. and Wilkinson, D. L. (1994) Cops in the classroom: a longitudinal evaluation of drug abuse resistance education (DARE), *Journal of Research in Crime and Delinquency*, 31: 3–31.

Rosenberger, L. R. (1996) *America's Drug War Debacle*. Aldershot: Ashgate.

Rosenthal, F. (1971) *The Herb*. Leiden: Brill.

Ross, C. (2000) *Bluebird: Deliberate Creation of Multiple Personality by Psychiatrists*. Richardson, TX: Manitou Communications.

Rouget, G. (1985) *Music and Trance: A Theory of the Relation Between Music and Possession*. Chicago: University of Chicago Press.

Rowntree, J. (1905) *The Imperial Drug Trade*. London: Methuen.

Royal College of Psychiatrists and Physicians (2000) *Drugs: Dilemmas and Choices*. London: Gaskell.

Rudgley, R. (1993) *The Alchemy of Culture*. London: British Museum Press.

Rudgley, R. (1998) *The Encyclopaedia of Psychoactive Substances*. London: Little Brown.

Rudgley, R. (1999) *Lost Civilizations of the Stone Age*. London: Arrow.

Ruggiero, V. (1999) Drugs as a password and the law as a drug, in N. South (ed.) *Drugs: Cultures, Controls and Everyday Life*. London: Sage.

Rutherford, A. and Green, P. (1989) Illegal drugs and British criminal justice, in H.-J. Albrecht and A. Kalanhout (eds) *Drug Policies in Western Europe*. Frieburg: Max Planck Institute.

Said, E. (1978) *Orientalism*. London: Penguin.

Said, E. (1991) *Musical Elaborations*. London: Vintage.

Salazar, A. (1990) *Born to Die in Medellin*. London: Latin America Bureau.

Salmon, W. (1693) *Selpsium*. London: George Sawbridge.

Salt, B. (1992) *Film Style and Technology: History and Analysis*. London: Starword.

Saunders, N. (1993) *E for Ecstasy*. London: Neal's Yard Desk Top Publishing.

Saunders, N. (1995) *Ecstasy and the Dance Culture*. London: Neal's Yard Desk Top Publishing.

Savage, J. (1996) *Time. Travel*. London: Chatto and Windus.

Savage J. (1997) Psychedelic 100, in J. Henke and P. Puterburgh (eds) *I Want to Take You Higher*. San Francisco, CA: Chronicle Books.

Schroedor, M. (2000) To induce a sense of terror: Caudillo politics and political violence in Northen Nicaragua, 1926–34 and 1981–95, in B. Campbell and A. Brenner (eds) *Death Squads in Global Perspective: Murder with Deniability*. New York: Palgrave.

Schur, E. (1964) Drug addiction under British Policy, in H. S. Becker (ed.) *The Other Side*. New York: Free Press.

Scott, J. (1969) *The White Poppy*. London: Heinemann.

Scott, J. (1995) *Sociological Theory*. Aldershot: Edward Elgar.

Scott, M. (2000) Superclubs and the mainstreaming of E Culture, in Push and M. Scott (eds) *The Book of E*. London: Omnibus.

Scott, P. (1980) Foreword, in H. Kruger *The Great Heroin Coup*. Boston: South End Press.

Scruton, R. (1998) Youth culture's lament, *City Journal*, 8 (4) (City-journal.org).

Sellars, A. (1998) The influence of dance music on the UK youth tourism market, *Tourism Management*, 19(6): 611–15.

Shapiro, H. (1999) *Waiting for the Man*. London: Helter Skelter.

Shapiro, H. (2002) From Chaplin to Charlie – cocaine, Hollywood and the movies, *Drugs: Education, Prevention and Policy*, 9(2): 133–41.

Shapiro, H. (2003) *Shooting Stars: drugs, Hollywood and the movies*. London: Serpant's Tail.

Sharpley, A. (1964) Purple hearts dearer, but still plentiful, *Evening Standard*, 1 May.

Shaw, C. (1927) Case study method, *American Sociological Society*, 21: 149–57.

Shaw, C. (1930) *The Jackroller: A Delinquent Boy's Own Story*. Chicago: University of Chicago Press.

Shepherd, J., Weare, K. and Turner, G. (1997) Peer-led sexual health promotion with young gay and bisexual men – results of the HAPEER Project, *Health Education*, 6: 204–12.

Sheppard, M., Goodstadt, M. and Williamson, B. (1985) Drug education: why we have so little impact, *Journal of Drug Education*, 15(1): 1–5.

Sherman, C., Smith, A. and Tanner, E. (1999) *Highlights: An Illustrated History of Cannabis*. Berkeley, CA: Ten Speed Press.

Sherratt, A. (1991) Sacred and profane substances: the ritual use of narcotics in later neolithic Europe, in P. Garwood, D. Jennings, R. Skeates and J. Toms. (eds) *Sacred and Profane*. Oxford University Committee for Archaeology Monograph No. 32.

Shiach, M. (1991) *Helene Cixious: A Politics of Writing*. London: Routledge.

Shields, R. (1996) Foreword: masses or tribes, in M. Maffesoli *The Time of the Tribes*. London: Sage.

Shildrick, T. (2002) 'Trackers', 'spectaculars', and 'ordinary youth': youth culture, illicit drugs and social class'. Unpublished PhD thesis, University of Teesside.

Shiner, M. and Newburn, T. (1997) Definitely, maybe not? The normalisation of recreational drug use amongst young people, *Sociology*, 31(3): 511–29.

Shiner, M. and Newburn, T. (1999) Taking tea with Noel: the place and meaning of drug use in everyday life, in N. South (ed.) *Drugs: Cultures, Controls and Everyday Life*. London: Sage.

Shoemaker, P. (ed.) (1989) *Communication Campaigns About Drugs*. New Jersey: Lawrence Erlbaum Associates.

Short, J. (1960) Introduction, in C. Shaw and H. McKay *Juvenile Delinquency and Urban Areas*. Chicago: University of Chicago Press.

Silcott, M. (2000) Superclubs and the mainstreaming of E culture, in Push and M. Silcott (eds) *The Book of E*. London: Omnibus.

Silver, G. and Aldrich, M. (eds) (1979) *The Dope Chronicles 1850–1950*. San Francisco, CA: Harper and Row.

Simpson, C. (1988) *Blowback: America's Recruitment of Nazis and its Effects on the Cold War*. London: Weidenfield and Nicolson.

Simpson, C. (ed.)(1998) *Universities and Empire: money and politics in the Social Sciences during the Coldwar*. New York: The New Press.

Smart, B. (1990) On the disorder of things: sociology, postmodernity and the 'end of the social', *Sociology*, 24(3): 397–416.

Smart, C. (1984) Social policy and drug addiction: a critical study of policy development, *British Journal of Addiction*, 79: 31–40.

Sontag, S. (1979) Introduction, in W. Benjamin *One-Way Street*. London: Verso.

South, N. (1999) Debating drugs and everyday life: normalization, prohibition and 'otherness', in N. South (ed.) *Drugs: Cultures, Controls and Everyday Life*. London: Sage.

Spinley, M. (1953) *The Deprived and the Privileged*. London: Routledge and Kegan Paul.

Sprott, W. (1958) *Human Group*. London: Penguin.

Stam, R. (2000) *Film Theory: An Introduction*. Oxford: Blackwell.

Starks, M. (1982) *Cocaine Fiends and Reefer Madness*. New York: Cornwall Books.

Stevenson, J. (ed.) (2000) *Addicted*. UK: Creation.

Stimson, G. and Lart, R. (1994) The relationship between the state and local practice in the development of national policy on drugs between 1920–90, in J. Strang and M. Gossop (eds) *Heroin Addiction and Drug Policy: The British System*. Oxford: Oxford University Press.

Stone, C. J. (1999) *The Last of the Hippies*. London: Faber and Faber.

Storey, J. (1999) *Cultural Consumption and Everyday Life*. London: Arnold.

Strang, J. and Gossop, M. (1994) The British system: visionary anticipation or masterly inactivity, in J. Strang and M. Gossop (eds) *Heroin Addiction and Drug Policy: The British System*. Oxford: Oxford University Press.

Strassman, R. (1987) Book review: hallucinogens: a cross-cultural perspective, *Psychiatry*, 5: 90–3.

SAMHSA (Substance Abuse and Mental Health Services Administration) (2001) *National Household Survey on Drug Use 2000*. Washington, DC: US Department of Health and Human Services.

Sugarman, B. (1967) Involvement in youth culture, academic achievement and conformity in school, *British Journal of Sociology*, June: 151–64.

Susser, M. W. (1962) Social medicine in Britain, in A. T. Welford, M. Argyle, D. V. Glass and J. Morris (eds) *Society*. London: Routledge Kegan Paul.

Sutcliffe, W. (1997) *Are You Experienced?* London: Hamish Hamilton.

Sutherland, E. (1924) *Criminology*. Chicago: Chicago University Press.

Szasz, T. (1996) *Our Right to Drugs*. New York: Syracuse University Press.

Taqi, S. (1969) Approbation of drug usage in rock and roll music, *Bulletin on Narcotics*, 21(4): 29–35.

Taylor, A. (1998) Needlework: the lifestyle of female drug injectors, *Journal of Drug Issues*, 28(1): 77–90.

Taylor, D. (2000) The word on the street: advertising, youth culture and legitimate speech in drug education, *Journal of Youth Studies*, 3(3): 333–53.

Taylor, I., Walton, P. and Young, J. (1973) *The New Criminology*. London: Routledge Kegan Paul.

Taylor, L. (1968) *Deviance and Society*. London: Michael Joseph.

Thompson, E. P. (1985) *The Heavy Dancers*. London: Merlin Press.

Thornton, S. (1995) *Club Culture: Music, Media and Subcultural Capital*. Cambridge: Polity Press.

Thornton, S. (1997) General Introduction, in K. Gelder and S. Thornton (eds) *The Subcultures Reader*. London: Routledge.

Thrasher, F. (1927) *The Gang*. Chicago: University of Chicago Press.

Toop, D. (1995) *Ocean of Sound*. London: Serpent's Tail.

Townsend, P. (2000) *Jazz in American Culture*. Edinburgh: Edinburgh University Press.

Tracy, J. with Berkey, J. (1978) *Subcutaneously, My Dear Watson*. Bloomington: James A. Rock.

Trasler, G. (1962) *The Explanation of Criminality*. London: Routledge and Kegan Paul.

Trumpbour, J. (ed.) (1989) *Reason in the Service of Empire*. Boston: South End Press.

Turner, B. (1999) *Ibiza*. London: Ebury Press.

United National Drug Control Program (UNDCP) (1992) *The United Nations and Drug Abuse Control*. New York and Geneva: UN Dept of Public Information.

Valdez, A. and Sifaneck, S. (1997) Drug tourists and drug policy on the US–Mexican border, *Journal of Drug Issues*, 27: 879–97.

Virgil (1956) *The Aeneid*. London: Penguin.

Walker, W. III (ed.) (1992) *Drug Control Policy: Essays in Historical and Comparative Perspective*. Pennsylvania: Pennsylvania State University Press.

Walker, W. III (1996) Introduction: culture, drugs and politics in the Americas, in W. Walker (ed.) *Drugs in the Western Hemisphere*. Delaware: Scholarly Books.

Wallace, M. (1990) *Invisibility Blues*. London: Verso.

Waller, W. (1932) *The Sociology of Teaching*. New York: Russell and Russell.

Walter, N. (1996) Dead women who suit the new agenda, *The Guardian*, 18 January.

Walton, S. (2001) *Out of It: A Cultural History of Intoxication*. London: Hamish Hamilton.

Watson, S. (2000) Heroes just for one day? 'Christiane F', in J. Stevenson (ed.) *Addicted*. UK: Creation.

Webb, G. (1998) *Dark Alliance*. New York: Seven Stories Press.

Whelan, S. and Culver, J. (1997) *Don't Say 'No' Say 'DARE'?* Kirkby-in-Ashfield: North Nottinghamshire Health Promotion.

Whiteley, S. (1992) *The Space Between the Notes*. London: Routledge.

Whiteley, S. (1997) Altered sounds, in A. Melechi (ed.) *Psychedelia Britannica*, London: Turnaround.

Whyte, W. (1943/1955) *Street Corner Society*. Chicago: University of Chicago Press.

Wibberley, C. (1997) Young people's feelings about drugs, *Drugs: Education, Prevention and Policy*, 4(1): 65–78.

Wibberley, C. and Price, J. (2000) Young people's drug use: facts and feelings – implications for the normalisation debate, *Drugs: Education, Prevention and Policy*, 7(2): 147–62.

Wibberley, C. and Whitelaw, S. (1990) Health promotion, drugs and the moral high ground, *International Journal of Drug Policy*, 2(3): 11–14.

Wiener, J. (1991) *Professors, Politics and Pop*. London: Verso.

Williams, R. (1980) *Problems in Materialism and Culture*: London: Verso.

Williamson, K. (1997) *Drugs and the Party Line*. Edinburgh: Rebel Inc.

Willis, P. (1972) Pop music and youth groups. Unpublished PhD thesis, Centre for Contemporary Cultural Studies, University of Birmingham.

Willis, P. (1977) *Learning to Labour*. Farnborough: Gower.

Willoughby, W. W. (1925) *Opium as an International Problem*. Baltimore, CA: Johns Hopkins University Press.

Wijngaart, G. F. van de (1988) A social history of drug use in the Netherlands, policy outcomes and implications, *Journal of Drug Issues*, 18: 481–95.

Winick, C. (1959) The use of drugs by jazz musicians, *Social Problems* 7: 240–53.

Witkin, R. (1998) *Adorno on Music*. London: Routledge.

Witt, P. (1982) *Spider Communication: Mechanisms and Ecological Significance*. Princeton: Princeton University Press.

Witt, P., Reed, C. and Peakall, D. B. (1968) *A Spider's Web: Problems in Regulatory Biology*. Heidelberg: Springer.

Wong, J. (1998) *Deadly Dreams: Opium, Imperialism and the Arrow War in China*. Cambridge: Cambridge University Press.

Wood, R. (2003) The straightedge youth subculture: observations on the complexity of sub-cultural identity, *Journal of Youth Studies*, 6(1): 33–52.

Woodiwiss, M. (1998) Reform, racism and rackets: alcohol and drug prohibition in the United Sates, in R. Coomber (ed.) *The Control of Drugs and Drug Users*. Amsterdam: Harwood.

Worth, D. (1991) American women and polydrug abuse, in P. Roth (ed.) *Alcohol and Drugs are Women's Issues*. New Jersey: Scarecrow Press.

Wragg, J. (1992) *An Evaluation of a Model of Drug Education*. Monograph Series No. 22. Canberra: Australian Government Publishing Service.

Wyvill, B. and Ives, R. (2000) Finding out about young people's ideas on drugs and drug use-methodology, *Drugs: Education, Prevention and Policy*, 7(2): 127–37.

Yates, R. (2002) A brief history of British drug policy, 1950–2001, *Drugs: Education, Prevention and Policy*, 9(2): 113–24.

Young, J. (1971) *The Drugtakers*. London: Paladin.

Zieberg, N. (1984) *Drug, Set and Setting*. New Haven: Yale University Press.

Zimmer, L. and Morgan, J. (1997) *Marijuana Myths and Marijuana Facts: A Review of the Scientific Evidence*. New York: Lindesmith Centre.

Zimring, F. and Hawkins, G. (1992) *The Search for Rational Drug Control*. Cambridge: Cambridge University Press.

Zinrite, P. (1998) The militarization of the drug war in Latin America, *Current History*, 97(618): 166–73.

Index

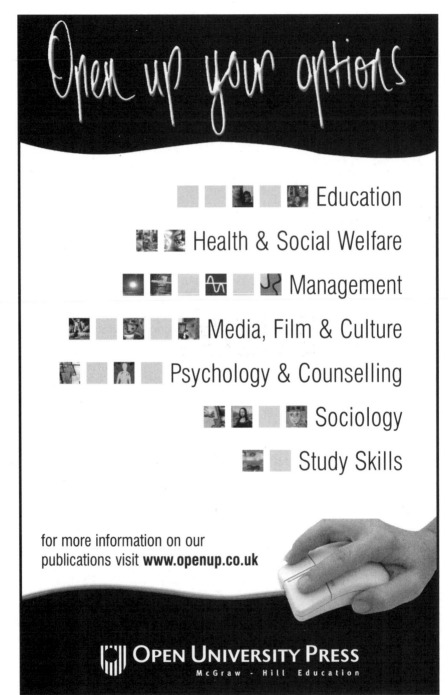